Post-Human Ethics

Post-Human Ethics

Redefining Morality in a Machine World

Idris Cavayne

Mindful Pages

Published in 2026

ISBN: 9789374592397 (PB)
ISBN: 9789374595541 (eBook)

Published by

Mindful Pages
Imprint of Alpha Editions LLC
312 W. 2nd St #1834
Casper, WY 82601, USA

This book was developed using advanced writing tools to support the drafting and ideation process. All content has been thoughtfully curated, refined, and reviewed to ensure quality and relevance.

Content

Introduction

The shuttle should have stopped. Every sensor agreed the pedestrian was there, every module processed the signal in the correct order, and every line of code executed exactly as its designers intended. Yet by the time the vehicle lurched to a halt, it had travelled a fatal few metres too far. In the hours that followed, the logs told an immaculate story: parameters within bounds, speed consistent with prior calibration, no anomaly detected. The machine had obeyed the rules with unflinching precision. Still, a person was dead.

The explanations came quickly, each as narrow and technically plausible as the next. The manufacturer pointed to the city's road paint, weather-worn and irregular, claiming the shuttle's vision model had been trained on surfaces of higher contrast. The city responded by noting the model's training data had not been refreshed for nearly a year, its designers having assumed that incremental improvements would suffice. The bereaved family listened to these carefully engineered reasonings with quiet disbelief. They did not ask for the mathematics of brake pressures or illumination levels. They wanted to know why a system that had done everything it was built to do could still feel so profoundly wrong.

That is the paradox at the heart of our age: the closer machines get to procedural perfection, the sharper our ethical discomfort becomes. We are no longer confronting the blunt malfunctions familiar from earlier technologies—the smoking engine or the frozen interface. Instead, we face systems that behave impeccably according to their internal logic while producing outcomes that clash with human sensibilities. They obey rules we wrote, yet their actions illuminate how insufficient those rules truly are. And so the question is not simply what the machine should have done, but what we should have specified, anticipated, constrained, or revised. The scene of the shuttle is not an anomalous tragedy but a harbinger of a world in which moral judgement is entangled with code, data, and the architecture of decisions themselves.

This book begins there, at that uncomfortable juncture between technical success and moral unease. It sets out to offer something that has been conspicuously missing from public debates about artificial intelligence: a practical, intellectually grounded framework for judging shared human–machine decisions. Not a manifesto for techno-utopian futures. Not a catalogue of dystopian fears. Rather, a method for translating values into parameters, for allocating responsibility when decisions are distributed across sensors, teams, and institutions, and for determining where autonomy should advance and where it must be restrained. The aim is to equip readers to navigate the strange moral territory that emerges when agency is no longer the exclusive property of human minds.

For all the novelty of machine intelligence, this tension between rules and responsibility is older than we often admit. When ancient lawmakers wrote the earliest codes of conduct, they were already grappling with the problem of how to align collective behaviour with shared values. Centuries later, the architects of railways confronted a similar dilemma: could they guarantee safety in a system too complex for any one person to oversee? Today's systems differ in scale and sophistication, yet the essential struggle remains. We are still trying to ensure that the structures we design serve the people who inhabit them, and that when harm occurs, our stories of causation make sense not only to engineers but to citizens. What is new is the speed and opacity with which machine systems reason, and the expanding gulf between human intuition and algorithmic logic.

We live in societies that are increasingly animated by silent infrastructures of computation. A clinician glances at a risk score before adjusting a patient's treatment. A judge consults a recommendation on whether to release a defendant on bail. A worker is nudged by a productivity dashboard that quietly benchmarks them against thousands of others. A soldier relies on a targeting system designed to detect patterns the human eye cannot perceive. Each of these decisions may be justified at the micro level—an efficiency gain here, a safety improvement there—but collectively they change how agency is distributed, how accountability is assigned, and how people perceive their own capacity to act. The moral fabric of society is being rewoven not by philosophical declarations but by countless technical decisions whose ethical implications surface only after harms occur.

This book argues that classic ethical frameworks, built around individual actors and their intentions, falter in this environment. They struggle to accommodate a world in which responsibility is an emergent property of design choices dispersed across teams, vendors, and technical layers. If a recommender system amplifies harmful misinformation, who shaped the causal chain? The engineer who selected the objective function? The designer who chose how uncertainty is displayed? The manager who rewarded engagement metrics? The user who clicked? The model that discovered a correlation its creators did not foresee? It is tempting to reach for familiar moral categories, yet doing so often obscures more than it reveals. We need new ways of describing causation, new tools for analysing value conflicts, and new forms of institutional memory that allow societies to learn from failure without succumbing to paralysis.

One recurring motif in these pages is the notion of the *decision stack*. It is a metaphor, but also a diagnostic instrument—an invitation to examine not just what a system does, but the layered choices that make its behaviour possible. At the base lie sensors and data, with all their historical biases and sampling quirks. Above them sit models and architectures that interpret the world through particular abstractions. Then come objective functions, interfaces, oversight mechanisms, and deployment policies. Each layer constrains or amplifies the others; each embeds assumptions that may never be explicitly articulated. When a system causes harm, the decision stack helps us trace the pathways of influence, making visible the places where values were translated into code, distorted into proxies, or lost in the handovers between teams.

Understanding these layers is not a purely technical exercise. It requires psychological insight into how people interpret machine advice, organisational awareness of how incentives shape design decisions, and political sensitivity to how power is distributed through infrastructures of automation. It also demands humility: even the most sophisticated models are only approximations of the world, and even the most thoughtful oversight frameworks will occasionally falter. The challenge is not to eliminate uncertainty but to govern it wisely, to construct systems that can fail safely and recover gracefully, and to retain human authority where consequences are irreversibly profound.

Throughout history, societies have developed institutions to absorb the shocks of technological change. Courts, guilds, professional standards, and safety regulators—all emerged to manage risk and normalise accountability. But machine intelligence unsettles these institutions because it blurs the boundary between actor and environment. In the case of the shuttle, was the system the code alone? The vehicle? The road infrastructure? The municipal procurement process? Or the vast ecosystem of training data, calibration routines, and supply-chain dependencies? Traditional legal categories are ill-suited to such questions, not because they lack sophistication but because they depend on a world that assumed bounded actors with comprehensible intentions. Machines disrupt that assumption by distributing intent across design.

This is why public discomfort grows as machines become more competent. When an early autonomous system fails, we are inclined to blame its limitations. But when an advanced system fails while executing its logic flawlessly, we sense a deeper flaw—something missing in our conception of what it means for a decision to be "right". That intuition is not superstition. It reflects a profound recognition that ethics must account not just for what systems do, but for how they do it, and for whether their justifications align with human moral reasoning. A machine may follow every procedural rule, yet provoke outrage if its choices appear indifferent to context or insensitive to values that humans regard as fundamental.

If the moral stakes were modest, this discomfort might remain philosophical. But the domains into which machine systems are now deployed—justice, healthcare, warfare, urban mobility—are precisely those where ethical clarity matters most and where errors carry heavy consequences. A miscalibrated triage algorithm can shift life-saving resources away from vulnerable groups. A poorly specified engagement metric can distort political discourse. A drone with insufficiently conservative thresholds can escalate conflicts without human oversight. These are not hypothetical risks; they are emerging realities that expose the inadequacy of relying solely on compliance checklists and retrospective blame.

The central message of this book is that we must treat human–machine collaboration as a moral landscape in its own right, one that requires its own methods and its own vocabulary. The task is not to impose traditional ethics on technical systems, nor to accept the fatalism that machine behaviour is too complex to regulate. Rather, it is to craft a framework that respects the uniqueness of machine decision-making while insisting on accountability that is intelligible to human societies.

This framework begins by confronting a series of fundamental questions. How do we specify values without resorting to myths of neutrality or vague invocations of fairness? How do we choose proxies that reflect those values without distorting them through oversimplification? How do we recognise the moral effects of model architectures and the histories encoded within datasets? How do we build accountability into systems that are autonomous enough to act but not autonomous enough to explain themselves? How do we design interfaces that guide behaviour with dignity rather than manipulation? How do we determine the limits of autonomy in domains where misjudgement is irrecoverable?

These questions recur throughout the chapters that follow, each approached through concrete cases and actionable tools. You will encounter templates for value specification, methods for tracing harms through the decision stack, principles for proxy selection, rubrics for model choice, and strategies for designing human oversight that is meaningful rather than ceremonial. You will see how standards can be aligned across organisations and borders, how civic participation can shape requirement-setting, and how institutions can cultivate a durable moral memory. All of these tools converge on a single purpose: to empower humans to remain moral authors in a world where machines increasingly participate in our decisions.

Yet the purpose of this book is not merely technical. It is also cultural. We need a shared narrative about responsibility that resonates with public sensibilities, one that bridges the gap between statistical explanations and human expectations. Legitimacy is not granted by mathematical accuracy alone; it is earned through transparency, accountability, and the capacity to articulate causal stories that ordinary people find recognisable and just. Without this legitimacy, even the most capable systems will struggle to gain public trust, and societies will oscillate between over-reliance and reactionary rejection.

As we look ahead, the dilemmas will only intensify. What happens when autonomous systems begin to negotiate with each other, making decisions no human fully comprehends? How do we maintain ethical coherence when global supply chains introduce conflicting standards and cultural values? What safeguards are necessary when autonomy creeps towards the edge of lethality, where milliseconds decide life or death? And how should humans reinterpret their own moral agency when machines increasingly take on tasks once regarded as the exclusive domain of human judgement?

These questions are not warnings. They are invitations—to design better systems, to articulate clearer values, and to cultivate institutions capable of adapting to technological evolution without surrendering human dignity. The tragedy of the shuttle is a stark reminder of what happens when rules outpace understanding and when responsibility becomes so diffused that no one can answer the simplest moral question: why did this happen?

This book does not claim to resolve every tension. Instead, it offers a way to approach them with rigour, clarity, and imagination. It invites you to step into the emerging world of shared human–machine agency and to consider what kind of society we wish to build there. The crises ahead are not foregone conclusions. They are contingent on choices we make now—choices about how we encode values, distribute authority, and determine the limits of autonomy. If we do not make those choices deliberately, they will be made by default, encoded invisibly into systems whose logic will shape our world long before we notice.

The next shuttle, the next triage system, the next risk score, the next autonomous weapon—all will test our assumptions again. The question is not whether such systems should exist, but how they should be governed, designed, constrained, and understood. The answers will determine not only the safety of our technologies but the moral character of our future.

Chapter 1
The Shift from Actors to Systems

There is a moment, often overlooked in public debate, when a crisis unfolds not through a single catastrophic mistake but through a sequence of ordinary, well-intentioned decisions that happen to collide. It occurs when every contributor has followed their brief, every team has satisfied its metrics, and every component has behaved exactly as specified—yet the outcome feels indefensibly wrong. Consider the experience of a major social platform during a tense election season. One team, charged with maximising user engagement, deploys a refined recommender model that expertly surfaces content likely to keep people scrolling. Another team, tasked with reducing misinformation, strengthens detection pipelines and adjusts penalty thresholds. Each initiative is individually sensible. Yet when released into the complex ecosystem of user behaviour and adversarial actors, the combined system begins to amplify precisely the narratives the trust team hoped to dampen. What emerges is not a villain or a faulty algorithm but a pattern of harm produced by a machine that meticulously balanced two incompatible aims.

This kind of event unsettles us because it confronts a deep-seated assumption: that moral responsibility attaches to identifiable actors with comprehensible intentions. We instinctively search for the person who tipped the scales, the engineer who erred, the manager who overlooked a warning. But distributed systems resist that impulse. They operate through layers of interdependent choices—architectural, organisational, and political—that no single person oversees. The result is a landscape of causation that feels both everywhere and nowhere at once. A platform's behaviour is shaped not by an individual's malice or incompetence but by the geometry of design decisions dispersed across entire ecosystems. And yet the harms are real, measurable, and often severe.

This chapter begins with that tension. It steps into the widening gap between how societies traditionally assign responsibility and how modern machine systems actually behave. The shift from actors to systems is not simply a shift in language; it is a shift in how we understand power, agency, accountability, and the moral weight of design. Because when individual intent is no longer the principal driver of outcomes, ethics must evolve. We need ways of reasoning that illuminate the hidden seams where design turns into behaviour, where choices become incentives, and where values—distributed across teams and vendors—recombine into consequences no one explicitly authorised.

To make sense of this, we must first examine why classic ethics, with its focus on blame and intention, falters in the face of distributed causation. Philosophers have long grappled with questions of agency, but their frameworks assumed discrete actors whose mental states were central to moral judgement. A driver runs a red light, a surgeon misreads a scan, a banker conceals a risky trade: the model is familiar, its moral vocabulary well rehearsed. But machine systems erase the tidy borders around action. They turn intent into something emergent, stitched together from data choices, optimisation strategies, interface cues, and organisational constraints. Asking who *meant* to cause the harm becomes the wrong question. The more illuminating question is who *shaped* the system conditions under which harm became likely.

Design, in this sense, becomes the modern locus of responsibility. The subtle calibration of parameters can shift risk from one demographic to another. A minor change in user interface can re-route thousands of decisions. A procurement choice—selecting a vendor with a slightly different modelling philosophy—can restructure an entire chain of consequences. In autonomous mobility, for example, design teams must decide how systems trade off mobility and caution. If a shuttle hesitates too often, the service collapses under public frustration; if it hesitates too little, accidents climb. These are not engineering tweaks but moral decisions disguised as technical ones. They allocate risk across populations with a precision that traditional ethical categories struggle to describe.

The second movement of this chapter explores how values collide when encoded at scale. When human institutions embed their priorities into machine systems, those priorities often arrive fragmented—packaged by different teams, captured through divergent proxies, and implemented by vendors with their own design philosophies. A city may prize efficiency in transit while a manufacturer emphasises safety margins; the compromise between them is expressed not through negotiation but through parameter settings and calibration thresholds. The resulting system is a negotiation conducted in code, its moral stakes rarely visible to the public. To navigate this, we will introduce a simple value-spec template that forces designers, regulators, and teams to articulate the trade-offs they are implicitly making. Explicitness becomes a defence against the silent collisions of values that occur when systems scale without shared moral calibration.

Yet even the most careful value specifications cannot guarantee moral adequacy. Today's systems routinely deliver outcomes that are perfectly compliant with legal and procedural norms yet ethically troubling. Consider content moderation pipelines that faithfully implement policy definitions yet still allow harmful content to flourish because the patterns of harm evolve faster than policies can adapt. There is a gulf between procedural correctness and moral sufficiency, and distributed systems widen that gulf by multiplying the places where misalignment can hide. Compliance offers a floor, not a ceiling, and ethical adequacy demands a richer understanding of how rules translate into behaviour. This chapter examines why systems can satisfy every formal requirement and still produce outcomes that violate our intuitive sense of justice, dignity, or fairness.

To understand this tension fully, we must learn to see the whole decision stack—a conceptual lens that will weave throughout the book. The decision stack spans the journey from raw sensory inputs to high-level policies, passing through layers of modelling, optimisation, interface design, and oversight. It is a map of influence, a scaffolding for ethical analysis. When something goes wrong, the stack guides us through the causal corridor: Was the root in the data, shaped by historical biases? In the model architecture that privileged optimisation speed over interpretability? In the objective function that overweighted efficiency at the expense of minority harms? In the interface that misled users about uncertainty? Or in the oversight structures that discouraged escalations? By learning to trace harms through this layered structure, we uncover forms of responsibility that are dispersed yet intelligible.

The relevance of this approach is not limited to technology companies or specialised regulators. It affects everyday life. When a hospital triage tool subtly reallocates attention away from certain patients, when an automated hiring platform filters candidates according to proxies no recruiter ever examined, when a navigation system steers traffic through neighbourhoods unprepared for congestion, the system itself has become a moral actor—not because it possesses intent but because its design distributes power. And with distributed power comes distributed responsibility.

The challenge is that societies have not yet adjusted their moral vocabulary to match this reality. Our public conversations still seek a singular culprit, a simple explanation, a human intention to anchor blame. Systems thwart that desire. They demand a shift from finding fault to understanding design, from interrogating intent to analysing structure. This is not an evasion of accountability; it is an expansion of it. For without understanding the systemic roots of harm, we cannot meaningfully assign responsibility, nor can we design systems capable of aligning with human values.

As this chapter unfolds, you will encounter conceptual tools that clarify how harms emerge from interactions rather than isolated decisions. You will see how values must be specified before they can be operationalised, how legal compliance can mask deeper ethical fractures, and how the decision stack provides a practical method for tracing responsibility in complex systems. The aim is not simply to diagnose the shortcomings of classic ethics but to build a sturdier foundation—one that captures the dynamics of distributed agency without losing sight of human dignity.

By the final pages, the shift from actors to systems will no longer seem abstract. It will feel urgent, unavoidable, and intellectually invigorating. You will come to see that the moral challenges of our age do not stem from a loss of human responsibility but from its transformation. We have become designers of structures whose behaviours exceed any one person's intentions, custodians of systems capable of producing harm or good at unprecedented scale.

The question is not whether we are ready for this shift. It is whether we are willing to understand it deeply enough to govern it wisely.

Turn the page, then, with a sense of anticipation. The tools to make sense of this new moral terrain await, and understanding them is the first step towards shaping systems that act not only with procedural precision but with moral purpose.

From blame to design

On 15 March 2019, engineers at YouTube's headquarters in San Bruno compared two dashboards that rarely aligned. One belonged to the recommendation team, whose model had improved session length across North America by several percentage points since its latest release. The other belonged to the Trust and Safety group, which had observed a surge of borderline political content circulating just beneath policy thresholds. Both teams had acted responsibly. Both had met their metrics. Yet the combined system was quietly drifting into a pattern that neither had intended. As an analyst later described to *The New York Times* (2019), the machine had learned to bind engagement and outrage into the same behavioural fabric. No single person authorised that outcome. No rule had been broken. Something in the design had turned good intentions into a structural risk.

That moment illustrates the central motif of this section: a system behaves like the shape of its design, not the sum of its intentions. The difference matters because harm emerges through interaction, not through villainy. When a distributed system produces an ethically unacceptable outcome while every contributor can show procedural correctness, the traditional instinct to identify *who* is at fault collapses. It is the wrong question. The more revealing question is *what* in the design made the outcome predictable. That question forces us to look beyond individual actors and to study the architecture, incentives, and assumptions that condition machine behaviour. Five words capture the pivot: structure quietly overrules intent.

Classic ethics has long centred responsibility on identifiable human minds. The view has intuitive appeal. It makes sense to ask what a surgeon meant, what a driver perceived, or what a journalist believed when publishing a controversial story. But distributed systems repattern causation. They turn agency into a property dispersed across interfaces, models, datasets, and organisational priorities. In technical environments, intent becomes harder to locate not because people are less responsible, but because their decisions steer behaviour only indirectly, filtered through layers of abstraction. To study these systems with moral seriousness requires attention to structure, sequence, and calibration—qualities not captured by intent alone.

A concrete illustration comes from London in May 2020, when Transport for London reviewed the behaviour of its new traffic signal optimisation system, installed to minimise congestion near junctions in Westminster. The vendor's model balanced journey-time efficiency against pedestrian delay, adjusting signal phases dynamically. At the same time, a separate safety team had updated guidelines to prioritise longer crossing times for older adults, particularly near clinics and residential homes. Each rule was well justified. Yet when the two logics met in deployment, the system began to shorten certain pedestrian phases during off-peak hours, marginally improving vehicle flow but forcing slower walkers to wait through multiple cycles. The outcome was lawful, measurable, and statistically defensible; it was also unsafe for those the policy sought to protect. Nobody had *intended* to create hardship. The design had simply combined priorities without fully accounting for their friction. The system behaved as designed, not as imagined.

These examples show how design choices allocate risk. To see that clearly, we must name the mechanism: *system causation.* System causation is not mysterious. It is the accumulation of small decisions that together structure the probability of harm. A recommender tuned for attention changes what users see, which shifts what creators produce, which affects the incentives of those who spread inflammatory content. A safety team can revise guidelines, but unless their constraints bind at the same level as the engagement team's optimisation rules, the combined system will privilege whichever objective produces stronger quantitative signals. The imbalance is not ideological; it is mathematical. If engagement is measured every second and harm is measured quarterly, the system will drift towards the former. Metrics become gravitational fields.

Yet an important counter-example complicates this narrative. In October 2015, the Dutch Railways (Nederlandse Spoorwegen) implemented a new platform-allocation algorithm at Utrecht Centraal designed to reduce delays by routing trains more efficiently. Unlike the cases above, the system included a constraint that prohibited any reallocation that reduced the minimum time available for passengers with mobility impairments to board or exit. That constraint had been manually coded by railway engineers after advocacy groups documented difficulties at the station the previous year. Here the design held: performance improved without worsening access. The system's behaviour aligned with intent because the constraint had been rendered structural rather than aspirational. Where earlier examples revealed drift, this one shows that drift is not inevitable. When moral priorities become hard boundaries in code, they can redirect an entire system.

This counter-example highlights a central implication: distributed causation is not a verdict of helplessness. It is a diagnosis of where moral agency shifts. The Dutch case succeeded not because people cared more, but because they translated care into a structural rule. They designed the system to express a value consistently, regardless of the noise of competing objectives. This is why a shift from blame to design matters. Intent informs only those who already agree. Design shapes everyone.

The motif of *shape* bears repeating. Systems behave according to the shapes their architects carve into them: the training data that define their priors, the objectives that bias their decisions, the interfaces that steer human interpretation. When harm occurs, the temptation is to fix the surface behaviour. But surface behaviour is rarely the source. The reason the YouTube recommendation system blended engagement and outrage was not that engineers failed to anticipate bad actors. It was that the structural incentives of engagement metrics pulled the model towards content that reliably stimulated prolonged attention, and outrage is a dependable driver of attention. Shape overrode intent.

To understand why classic blame falters, consider that intent works in discrete units: one decision, one action, one mind. System design works in flows: many decisions, interacting continuously, producing patterns that no one person designed but everyone contributed to. When responsibility is distributed, moral assessment must follow the distribution. A focus on intent forces us to zoom in precisely when we should zoom out. It directs scrutiny to the wrong level of analysis. It can obscure who shaped what.

A deeper exploration shows that distributed systems often rely on proxies—metrics that stand in for values—because many goals cannot be measured directly. Engagement stands in for relevance. Journey time stands in for mobility. Click-through rates stand in for trust. These proxies are not morally neutral. They guide the system's evolution. They determine whose interests become legible and whose become invisible. In the Westminster traffic case, a proxy for efficiency competed with an unwritten assumption about the dignity of slower walkers. The system detected only the former. The latter was never encoded. What cannot be measured becomes, in practice, optional.

Risk, too, is allocated through design. Decisions about model sensitivity, thresholding, and fallback behaviour shift risk from one group to another. If an autonomous shuttle is coded to prioritise uninterrupted flow, risk shifts towards pedestrians. If content moderation thresholds are tightened, risk shifts towards false positives that silence legitimate voices. Every threshold moves risk. Every proxy structures incentive. These are design choices, and because they rarely feature in public communication, their moral stakes are often hidden.

System causation also has a temporal dimension. Harm can emerge slowly, accumulating across interactions. When Facebook's ranking changes in January 2018 began to emphasise "meaningful social interactions", researchers later observed (in internal notes leaked to *The Wall Street Journal* in 2021) that certain groups became more exposed to divisive content because it generated strong comments. An initiative framed as a way to promote connection ended up reshaping information ecosystems. The story illustrates a quiet truth: a system's present behaviour often reflects design decisions made months or years prior. Causation stretches across time as well as space.

To make sense of this, we need a mental habit that prioritises structural explanation over anecdotal fault. When analysing a harmful outcome, we should ask which design choices made it more likely. Was the proxy misaligned? Was the constraint too weak? Did one team's metric overpower another's? Did the data embed patterns that the model magnified? Did the interface obscure uncertainty? These questions recognise that responsibility lies not in a single error but in a design that failed to anticipate how components would interact. They foster a perspective that is ethical without being punitive, analytical without being reductionist.

Of course, there are limits. Not all harms stem from design. Systems can behave unpredictably, environments can shift, adversaries can exploit edge cases. One must acknowledge genuine uncertainty. A machine-learning model may behave differently when deployed in a geography whose patterns diverge from training data; a user community may adopt a feature in a manner engineers did not foresee. These facts temper any argument that drift is always the product of poor design. But acknowledging uncertainty does not undermine the case; it refines it. The existence of uncertainty means design must include anticipatory safeguards—circuit-breakers, escalation triggers, or human override—precisely because we cannot foresee every interaction. Uncertainty strengthens the argument for systemic responsibility.

The deeper implication is that distributed systems require new moral vocabularies. Concepts such as negligence, intent, and liability still matter, but they must be supplemented by terms that capture structural decisions: alignment, propagation, sensitivity, and constraint. A designer who selects a proxy that magnifies demographic disparity has shaped risk even if they intended fairness. A procurement officer who chooses a vendor without auditing their model assumptions has shaped risk even if the contract met every formal requirement. Responsibility attaches to design choices because design choices steer behaviour.

Returning to the opening motif of *shape*, we can see that systems are sculpted by the hands of many, yet the sculpture behaves as one. A change to any part—an objective function, a dataset filter, a threshold—can alter that behaviour. That is why a shift from blame to design is not a dilution of responsibility but a redistribution of it, mapped to the places where influence resides. Blame asks who acted wrongly. Design asks who shaped the conditions under which harm became probable. The latter offers a more accurate account of distributed agency.

The section closes on a tension that will thread through the chapter. When systems behave harmfully without anyone having intended harm, how should we intervene? Do we adjust the proxies? Harden constraints? Reassign oversight? Slow the pace of optimisation? The decisions are technical and moral in equal measure. The tension cannot be resolved by identifying a single actor; it demands structural imagination. The question that remains is deceptively simple: if design quietly overrules intent, what should we redesign first?

Value conflicts at scale

On 3 August 2021, the Arizona Department of Transportation met with Waymo engineers in Phoenix to review a pattern that had begun to trouble regulators. The company's autonomous shuttles were conservatively calibrated, braking early and maintaining wide buffers at junctions. That caution reduced collision risk, a visible achievement in monthly safety reports. Yet it also produced longer journey times, measurable through GPS traces, and triggered public complaints about delays on East Valley commuter routes. Safety and mobility—two values both publicly endorsed—had begun to diverge in practice. Neither side was wrong. Each had data to prove its case. The tension lay in the system itself, whose behaviour reflected competing priorities embedded across contracts, models, and municipal expectations. One engineer later described the problem as a "tug of code": the system pulled towards safety every time its metrics detected uncertainty, while the transit authority pulled towards mobility every time congestion rose. The shuttle sat between them, navigating a conflict neither team had fully articulated.

That scene captures a quiet motif for this subchapter: **the hinge**. A city's systems hinge on values defined by different actors, each turning the hinge in their preferred direction. When those turns accumulate, the hinge stiffens, and the system behaves according to the net pressure rather than any single value. In Phoenix, safety and mobility were not ideas; they were expressed through numbers. Safety meant low collision likelihood per kilometre. Mobility meant predictable arrival times across routes. These were not merely technical indicators. They were moral commitments encoded as metrics. And metrics, when misaligned, create conflict at scale.

Value conflict is not a modern anomaly. A century earlier, in 1903, the British Board of Trade confronted a similar friction during railway timetable reform. As historian Jack Simmons records in *The Railway in England and Wales 1830–1914* (1978), officials in London insisted on strict punctuality standards at Paddington, while Great Western Railway stationmasters argued for greater leeway to avoid hurried platform procedures that endangered porters. Punctuality and safety clashed not in principle but in practice. The Board demanded measurable improvements in departure times; the railway staff sought predictable margins of error for platform work. Each value manifested through a behaviour—minute-by-minute departures versus slower dispatch sequences. When one value hardened into regulation, the other was squeezed, until the system settled into a rhythm that privileged timekeeping. Railways, like shuttles, show that values become real not when declared but when operationalised.

To understand why such conflicts intensify in distributed systems, we must show how values travel from aspiration to implementation. A value enters a system through a measurable expression: a threshold, a margin, a frequency, a penalty, a reward. Naming that value is insufficient; the way it is measured shapes its influence. Safety in autonomous mobility often becomes probabilistic risk per mile. Efficiency becomes average speed between nodes. Fairness in a content platform becomes false-positive and false-negative rates on a classifier. As soon as values acquire metrics, they begin to interact. The interactions are rarely linear. A tweak to a threshold in one part of the system may amplify noise in another. The hinge tightens.

The Phoenix case shows the mechanism. Waymo's risk model assessed uncertainty at junctions using probabilistic outputs derived from perception algorithms trained on local road features. When uncertainty spiked, the shuttle reduced speed to maintain a fixed safety envelope—an envelope defined by engineers months earlier in Mountain View. Meanwhile, valley commuters judged mobility by punctuality: how many minutes separated the scheduled arrival from the actual one. When complaints crossed a threshold, regulators nudged engineers to adjust parameters. The hinge turned. But it did not turn evenly. It oscillated, because the incentives of one team were not directly commensurable with the incentives of the other. Safety engineers measured collision risk as an engineering variable; regulators measured mobility through public satisfaction. The system mediated both values without a common language.

To make such conflicts tractable, organisations require something deceptively simple: an explicit value-spec. A value-spec is a short template that forces teams to articulate not only their priorities but the measurable form those priorities take. It has three components: what the value is; how it is measured; and how it trades off against other values when conflicts arise. Without all three, a system inherits ambiguity. With them, it inherits structure.

Consider a second example, drawn from Copenhagen in November 2017, when the city launched its adaptive cycling-light programme on Nørrebrogade. The cycling infrastructure team valued throughput: how many cyclists crossed the corridor per ten-minute window. The accessibility office valued liveability: restrictions on waiting times for elderly pedestrians. Vendors incorporated both metrics into the system, but early trials showed recurrent bottlenecks during rainstorms. The system extended green phases for cyclists to maintain throughput but left pedestrians waiting longer than city guidelines allowed. Here the value-specs had been drafted separately. Throughput was measured in flow units; liveability in delay minutes. Only after public feedback did the city rewrite the joint spec, linking the two metrics explicitly: throughput gains could occur only when pedestrian delay stayed below a defined threshold. The hinge moved into alignment. This is the practical power of value-specs. They translate moral priorities into terms that machines can execute and teams can monitor.

Yet the opposite can also occur. A credible limitation arises in complex procurement settings, where multiple vendors contribute components. When Singapore's Land Transport Authority upgraded its ticketing system in 2012, the payment processor's value-spec centred on transaction integrity, measured through error rates and reconciliation times. The journey-planning contractor worked to a reliability target defined by route accuracy. Both values mattered, yet their combination produced unanticipated friction: a system that cleared transactions rapidly but occasionally mis-synchronised route transfers. Travellers experienced the system through a behaviour—missed transfers—not through the underlying values. Here, even well-written value-specs could not prevent conflict because the specification process lacked a shared translation layer. The limitation is structural: value-specs clarify local priorities, but they cannot alone resolve conflicts that occur across procurement boundaries without a coordinating framework. The reconciliation lies in accepting that value-specs work best when embedded across the full decision stack, not in fragments. When value-specs become system-wide rather than component-specific, the hinge strengthens.

A further thread worth following is how conflicts scale. Values encoded at one level may appear benign until the system expands. When autonomous shuttles move from pilot zones to commercial corridors, a small bias in mobility preference can accumulate into congestion across districts. When a platform adjusts its ranking model for trustworthiness, slight weighting changes can reorder millions of posts per hour. Scaling is not neutral. Scaling magnifies whichever values occupy the system's centre of gravity. For that reason, value-specs must not only guide local decisions but also anticipate propagation. Engineers track propagation through measurable indicators: variance in travel time, concentration of error rates across demographics, or distribution of false-positive events along regional lines. These metrics reveal where the hinge binds or slips.

Another visible example comes from Helsinki's "Jouko" on-demand minibuses, discontinued in December 2017. The service aimed to balance three specified values: availability for elderly residents, environmental sustainability measured through load factors, and economic viability measured through cost per trip. Each value had a measurable proxy. Yet as the service expanded, cost-maximisation incentives encouraged route planning that reduced coverage in low-density districts, undermining availability. The hinge tilted. The city ultimately ended the programme because the system had evolved into a shape that deviated from original values, despite no team violating its brief. Conflicts surfaced only when the city compared month-by-month load factors with GPS logs that revealed shrinking coverage. This illustrates an implication: value conflicts at scale often become visible only through empirical patterns. Systems reveal their commitments by what they consistently privilege.

A counter-example shows nuance. The Japanese Shinkansen, introduced in 1964 between Tokyo and Osaka, managed values at scale without destructive conflict. The service balanced punctuality, energy efficiency, and passenger safety. These values were backed by strict engineering principles, such as emergency braking distances and platform discipline, enforced uniformly across operators. Value-spec alignment was systemic, not piecemeal. The Shinkansen's record—fewer than five passenger fatalities from train accidents in nearly six decades—suggests that value conflicts need not cripple large systems. The reconciliation lies in the uniformity of implementation: when a system embeds shared values across all teams, conflicts shrink. But this uniformity required political will, financial commitment, and consistent operational oversight—conditions not always present in distributed machine systems today.

The hinge motif returns here. Systems sit on hinges shaped by measurement. When two values lack a shared measurement frame, the hinge wobbles. When they share that frame, the hinge locks. Value-specs provide the hinge's screws. They tighten the connection between aspiration and execution.

A further implication arises from the Phoenix shuttle case: values compete in time. Safety is measured over long horizons, often in rare events. Mobility is measured daily. This asymmetry means that operational teams may feel mobility pressure more acutely, steering the system towards shorter-term gains. Metrics with different temporal signatures create latent conflict. A system must integrate both short-term and long-term metrics without letting one drown the other. Doing so requires rhythm: reviewing safety envelopes quarterly while monitoring mobility weekly. Rhythm is a form of design. Without it, value drift accelerates.

Understanding value conflicts at scale forces us to adopt a systemic perspective. A city cannot judge a shuttle by its collision rate alone. A platform cannot judge trust by classifier accuracy alone. A bus authority cannot judge equity by route coverage alone. Values produce patterns, and patterns require synthesis. This synthesis demands a shared vocabulary written into the system's operational grammar. Value-specs provide that grammar, but only if embraced across teams, vendors, and governance structures.

The difficulty is that organisations rarely confront value conflicts early. They arise incrementally, as systems accumulate historical decisions. By the time conflicts appear, metrics have solidified into incentives, and incentives have hardened into expectations. Adjusting value-specs then feels disruptive. Yet the hinge remains—waiting, creaking, pointing towards future drift.

The unresolved tension is this: when two values diverge in practice, who decides which bends? Should safety override mobility absolutely, or should mobility reclaim ground when collision risk is low? How should teams measure dignity against throughput, or fairness against predictive accuracy? The hinge turns either way. The question is who holds it, and when they should commit to turning.

When compliance fails ethically

On 1 January 2018, Germany's Network Enforcement Act—*Netzwerkdurchsetzungsgesetz*, or NetzDG—came fully into force in Berlin. Within its first month, Facebook reported thousands of content removals to meet the law's requirement that "manifestly unlawful" posts be taken down within twenty-four hours. The company complied. It hired additional moderators, updated escalation procedures, and delivered every mandated transparency report on schedule. Yet researchers at the Humboldt Institute later observed that much harmful content remained visible, while legitimate satire and minority speech were sometimes removed. Procedural correctness had been achieved. Moral adequacy had not.

The system met the threshold of legality, but its behaviour revealed something quieter and more troubling: compliance alone had failed to prevent avoidable harm.

This pattern—the gap between what rules demand and what societies expect—forms the motif of this subchapter: *the threshold.* Rules draw thresholds. But thresholds, once met, risk becoming ceilings rather than floors. A platform can satisfy every clause of a statutory framework and still distort public discourse. A hospital can follow clinical audit requirements and still marginalise patients with atypical symptoms. The threshold signals sufficiency to the regulator, yet insufficiency to those who experience the system's outcomes. Compliance is necessary. It is not enough.

The distinction becomes clearer when we show how compliance narrows attention. In the case of NetzDG, the relevant behaviour was removal count and removal speed. These metrics shaped moderation practice. They privileged easily classifiable material—slurs, extremist symbols, explicit threats—because those categories aligned neatly with statutory definitions. But harmful narratives often mutate faster than policies, exploiting ambiguity and irony. Researchers at the University of Oxford's Internet Institute (2019) demonstrated that coordinated disinformation campaigns during European election periods relied heavily on near-compliant content: emotionally manipulative posts that skirted the boundary of legality. When moderation teams optimised for compliance thresholds—speed and completeness—they inevitably left this category untouched. The threshold created a tunnel.

A second example shows a similar dynamic in a different sector. In August 2014, after the death of 18-year-old Michael Brown in Ferguson, Missouri, police departments across the United States expanded their use of body-worn cameras. The Los Angeles Police Department adopted one of the most comprehensive compliance frameworks, requiring officers to activate cameras during designated encounters and to store footage according to strict chain-of-custody rules. Annual audits published by the LAPD Inspector General showed high compliance rates. Yet researchers from the RAND Corporation (2019) found little correlation between camera usage and reductions in community complaints. The system ticked every procedural box—activation rates, retention periods, audit trails—while failing to address structural conditions that drove mistrust. Compliance produced data. It did not produce safety or legitimacy.

Both examples reveal the same mechanism. Compliance anchors behaviour to rules as written rather than harms as experienced. The threshold becomes the object of action. Meeting it signals success. But moral adequacy demands a different lens: attention to patterns that emerge beyond the threshold. A removal count tells us something about procedure; it tells us little about whether hate campaigns are fragmenting communities. Activation rates tell us something about documentation; they do not tell us whether police–community relationships improve. Compliance measures actions. Ethics measures consequences.

To name this distinction clearly, we can call compliance a form of *formal alignment*: behaviour that satisfies rules. Moral adequacy is a form of *substantive alignment*: behaviour that delivers on underlying societal aims. The example from Berlin showed formal alignment without substantive alignment. The example from Los Angeles showed the same. Both cases remind us that systems behave according to the incentives embedded in thresholds. If thresholds are too narrow, systems achieve correctness at the cost of justice.

A credible counter-example complicates the story. The Medicines and Healthcare products Regulatory Agency (MHRA) in the United Kingdom, particularly during its 2004–2014 regulatory reforms, demonstrated that compliance can support moral adequacy when rules incorporate substantive conditions. When approving new medical devices, the MHRA required not only technical conformity assessments but also post-market surveillance plans with proactive reporting obligations. These obligations forced manufacturers to monitor field performance continuously and to respond to emerging risks even after compliance had been achieved. The threshold moved. It adapted. Devices approved under the strengthened framework showed fewer high-risk recalls, according to MHRA reports from 2012 and 2013. Compliance worked because the rules embedded moral aims—patient safety—directly into procedural requirements. Yet even here, limitations remained. Surveillance quality varied across manufacturers, and stakeholders later argued that the system still underweighted long-term effects in low-income regions. The lesson is subtle: compliance succeeds ethically when it is designed to capture consequences, not merely actions. It fails when it treats thresholds as the whole terrain.

To understand why compliance so often falls short, we must examine how systems interpret rules. Rules translated into machine logic become executable conditions. They instruct models or teams to commit to specific behaviours: remove unlawful posts; activate cameras; audit interactions; log outcomes. But legality is a narrow category. It is defined by what lawmakers can articulate and enforce, not by the full spectrum of harm that may emerge in practice. This narrowness creates a structural blind spot. Harm that is legal is still harm. A content classification model may mark a borderline post as "not unlawful", but if that post fuels targeted harassment, the model has contributed to a pattern of moral failure while remaining compliant.

A telling illustration emerged in May 2020, when Twitter applied its civic-integrity policy during protests in Minneapolis. The company labelled posts from political actors when they violated explicit clauses, as required by internal rules revised after earlier congressional scrutiny. Yet researchers at Harvard's Berkman Klein Center later observed that coordinated harassment campaigns increased during the same period through quote-tweets that did not meet policy thresholds. The system's procedural logic was impeccable. The outcome was ethically misaligned. The threshold allowed harm to hide in the spaces between rules.

To make this distinction vivid, consider how a content-moderation system measures risk. Risk becomes a classifier score. A threshold determines action—remove, reduce visibility, allow. When compliance emphasises false positives, systems lower thresholds to avoid over-removal. When it emphasises false negatives, systems raise thresholds to avoid ignoring unlawful content. But these thresholds cannot capture contextual nuance: whether a phrase is used jokingly by a community member or deployed maliciously by an outsider; whether a user is vulnerable to pile-ons; whether an image spreads covertly. Systems behave according to numbers.

Communities live according to narrative patterns. Compliance operates on units; harm accumulates over time.

The motif of *the threshold* returns. Thresholds are gates. They open and close. They admit or exclude. Systems approach them mechanically. Humans experience them morally. When the difference widens, trust erodes. Trust is not an abstraction. Trust manifests in user behaviour: whether individuals stay on a platform, whether communities feel safe, whether they report abuse, whether they disengage. Trust measures consequences, not compliance.

Another example reveals the consequences of ignoring this gap. In June 2021, YouTube updated its hate-speech classifier, improving its precision on English-language content. The update satisfied internal governance requirements and met commitments to the European Commission under the Code of Conduct on Countering Illegal Hate Speech. Yet researchers from the Algorithmic Justice League noted that automated systems disproportionately flagged content from African American creators using reclaimed vernacular. The classifier met accuracy thresholds. Still, the harm—unequal suppression of marginalised voices—was real. Here compliance provided cover, not clarity.

A counterpoint exists in the financial sector. The UK's Financial Conduct Authority (FCA) in 2016 implemented rules requiring banks to perform vulnerability assessments to prevent discriminatory lending. Unlike narrow procedural rules, the FCA required banks to measure outcomes: default rates by demographic segment, offer distributions by postcode, and complaint ratios by product. The approach treated compliance as a dynamic practice. Banks were accountable for patterns, not just actions. As a result, several lending models were redesigned to adjust decision thresholds for applicants with unstable income histories. This example shows that compliance can be ethically productive when regulators demand outcome-sensitive metrics. The reconciliation between this case and the earlier failures lies in measurement. Systems cannot pursue moral adequacy unless they measure what matters.

The deeper implication is that ethical adequacy requires systems to operate beyond the boundary of legality. Legality defines the minimum condition for legitimacy. Ethics define the aspiration. When systems commit only to the former, they risk producing shallow accountability. Shallow accountability obscures where harm gathers. It incentivises teams to meet the letter of the rule and to assume that doing so represents success.

To address this gap, organisations must examine the texture of harms that survive compliance thresholds. Texture appears in repeated patterns: particular groups consistently misclassified, specific communities disproportionately exposed to misinformation, particular districts persistently marginalised by automated routing. The texture matters because it shows where compliance blinds systems. Moral adequacy demands seeing this texture.

Yet here lies a subtle limitation. Systems cannot monitor texture endlessly; complexity grows. Even the best frameworks must prioritise. No organisation can measure every possible form of harm. This truth tempers idealism. It acknowledges that moral adequacy is not perfection; it is commitment to meaningful patterns. Ethical failure occurs not when harm exists, but when harm persists unexamined because thresholds allow organisations to claim success prematurely. Legal compliance offers safety from penalties. Ethical adequacy offers legitimacy with the public.

The final return of the threshold motif clarifies the stakes. Thresholds define what systems see. They also define what they ignore. When thresholds dominate, harms slip between categories. When thresholds are contextualised, systems gain moral depth.

The unresolved tension is this: when a system meets every rule yet still produces foreseeable harm, what should a responsible organisation do next? Should it adjust thresholds, redefine metrics, expand monitoring, or widen accountability? The threshold stands. The question is who dares to step beyond it.

Seeing the whole decision stack

At 4.58 a.m. on 18 March 2018, a self-driving Uber test vehicle struck and killed 49-year-old Elaine Herzberg on Mill Avenue in Tempe,

Arizona. Within days, investigators from the U.S. National Transportation Safety Board (NTSB) pieced together a picture that startled even seasoned engineers. The lidar detected Herzberg six seconds before impact. The perception system classified her variously as a vehicle, then as "other", then as a bicycle. The prediction module failed to connect those labels into a coherent trajectory. The planning module issued no evasive manoeuvre until 1.2 seconds before impact. The human safety driver, distracted by a screen, intervened too late. Each layer behaved according to its own internal rules. Yet the system as a whole failed at the level that mattered most. The tragedy was not the product of a single mistake. It was the product of a stack.

The NTSB report, released in November 2019, reads like an anatomy of distributed responsibility. One contractor wrote the perception code. Another supplied the training data. A team in Pittsburgh tuned the prediction module. A team in San Francisco adjusted thresholds for braking aggressiveness. The safety driver in Tempe carried the last burden of oversight. No single point was sufficient to explain the collision. To understand responsibility, investigators needed to see the entire chain—from sensor pulses through classification logic to corporate policy. The case sets our motif: *the corridor*. Every decision in a complex system travels along a corridor of layers. Harm often emerges when a corridor narrows or misaligns at a single point. To evaluate responsibility, we must trace the corridor in full.

The concept of a decision stack is deceptively intuitive. It names the layers through which a system senses, reasons, acts, and receives oversight. Sensors shape the raw material of perception: light intensity, velocity vectors, physiological measurements, behavioural traces. Models transform those signals into representations: class labels, probability distributions, attention maps. Objectives convert representations into priorities: minimise loss, reduce latency, increase utility. Interfaces translate priorities into human legibility: warnings, flags, recommendations. Oversight structures bind the entire stack within governance constraints. When systems fail, each layer leaves fingerprints. The corridor preserves them. But organisations often inspect only one segment. The result is partial responsibility: a conclusion that feels accurate at one level yet incomplete at another.

The Tempe case shows why the corridor matters. The lidar detected Herzberg. But the prediction module discounted the detection because the system had been tuned to ignore transient objects to reduce false positives during highway testing. The safety driver was present. But corporate policy allowed attention diversion for extended periods, documented in the NTSB's review of cabin-camera footage. The oversight structure allocated responsibility for safety-driver training to a unit that lacked authority to pause local testing schedules. Each step was procedurally defensible. Taken together, they produced fatal fragility. The corridor narrowed.

A second example illustrates how decision stacks shape behaviour even when outcomes fall short of disaster. In March 2020, the UK's Office for National Statistics used a machine-learning model to support early Covid-19 triage for community testing. The model ingested symptoms, demographics, and comorbidity data from pilot sites in London. It predicted infection likelihood with reasonable accuracy. Yet audits published later that year showed that several clinics over-relied on the tool, deferring swab tests when model scores fell below a threshold. The model had not been designed for that purpose; its objective was risk estimation, not clinical triage. The interface failed to flag uncertainty bands. And the oversight guidance, rolled out in haste, did not state clearly when clinicians should override model recommendations. Responsibility was distributed across data collection, modelling, interface design, and governance. The corridor again revealed the shape of the harm: delayed testing for certain groups, quantified by audit teams comparing model scores with eventual PCR results.

A counter-example complicates the picture. When the Danish Safety Technology Authority audited industrial robot installations in 2022, it found that factories using the ISO 10218-compliant oversight protocols exhibited far fewer near-miss incidents. The protocols required explicit mapping of the sensor-to-action chain, detailed documentation of model assumptions, and human-in-the-loop escalation thresholds grounded in cycle-time data. Here, the corridor widened. Each layer was visible. Decisions were traceable. The system worked not because robots were intrinsically safer, but because the corridor had been structured to keep moral and technical visibility intact. Yet the limitations were clear: compliance depended on sustained institutional attention and consistent reporting. Where organisational inertia crept in, the corridor risked narrowing again.

These examples expose the core claim: responsibility becomes intelligible only when the entire corridor is illuminated. To show why, consider how an abstraction such as *risk* manifests in practice. Risk is not a philosophical notion; it is a number—collision probability, false-negative rate, or estimated severity. That number arises from a model trained on data. The data originate in sensors. If sensors mismeasure edge cases—low light, rare demographics, unusual movement patterns—the model inherits the bias. If the objective assigns asymmetric penalties to errors, the planner inherits the skew. If the interface suppresses uncertainty, the human inherits false confidence. Oversight then misattributes responsibility because the corridor's earlier distortions remain hidden. To see risk clearly, one must follow its corridor.

The same pattern holds for *efficiency*. Efficiency appears as throughput per minute, frame latency, or cost per transaction. When an organisation optimises for efficiency without inspecting the corridor, incentives distort behaviour. A navigation app that values low journey times may route traffic through residential streets. The model sees speed. The interface shows green lines. The oversight team sees improved metrics. The corridor hides the externality: increased noise and safety hazards. The harm becomes visible only when residents complain, and city engineers compare journey-time logs with collision and noise reports. By then, the corridor has already normalised the distortion.

The corridor metaphor becomes crucial when multiple actors contribute to the stack. In February 2022, the French data-protection authority CNIL fined Clearview AI for unlawful scraping. The act of scraping itself was the surface issue. But the deeper corridor revealed more. The photos originated from public platforms. The embeddings came from a proprietary neural network. The objective aimed to maximise identification accuracy. The interface provided match scores that police could misinterpret. The oversight lacked binding constraints on false-positive risk. Each corridor segment carried part of the responsibility. The sanction targeted one layer—data. But ethical assessment required scrutiny of the entire route from collection to use.

Tracing the corridor requires discipline. The first step is always the same: inspect the sensory foundation. Sensors filter reality. In Tempe, the lidar worked, but the classification logic suppressed essential ambiguity. In pandemic triage, symptom surveys captured different levels of detail across clinics, producing uneven training data. In industrial robots, motion sensors were regularly recalibrated under ISO protocols, stabilising early-layer accuracy. When sensors falter, harm begins here. A corridor inherits its origin.

Next comes the model. Models translate signals into representations. When a model compresses visual input into bounding boxes or transforms text into embeddings, it inevitably discards nuance. This is not failure; it is design. But the corridor must record what is discarded. Investigators analysing the Uber crash noted that the model discounted jaywalking trajectories because training data underrepresented them. The omission was numerical: a frequency count revealing a structural gap. In the UK's triage pilot, models weighted certain symptoms too strongly because early data reflected outbreaks concentrated in younger, mobile populations. Patterns emerged in confusion matrices: high false-negative rates among older patients. The corridor pointed to the second layer.

Objectives steer behaviour. They determine whether a model prefers caution or speed, stability or adaptability. Objectives are visible in loss functions and thresholds. In Tempe, the objective penalised false positives more than false negatives, reducing unnecessary braking but increasing risk in unusual situations. In navigation systems, objectives may minimise estimated arrival time, indirectly promoting risky shortcuts. By inspecting objective logs, auditors can see how values are encoded. A corridor that hides objectives cannot support responsibility.

Interfaces shape human behaviour. A score without a confidence interval tempts over-trust. A warning without clear language invites dismissal. In the UK triage case, clinicians reported that the interface did not communicate the model's training limitations. The corridor's fourth layer failed to convey uncertainty. When auditors added uncertainty ribbons to the display, clinicians changed their decisions even before the model was updated. The corridor widened.

Oversight binds the layers. It determines who can intervene, when, and on what grounds. Good oversight creates conditions for early correction. Poor oversight leaves layers misaligned. Oversight is visible in meeting minutes, escalation logs, threshold reviews, and retraining schedules. In the Danish robot installations, oversight cycles occurred monthly, and teams recorded safety margins numerically. In Tempe, oversight was patchy, fragmented across teams, with no unified review cadence. The corridor's spine was weak.

The counter-example reminds us that stacks can function ethically. But the reconciliation lies in visibility: corridors must be inspectable. They must allow investigators, regulators, and internal teams to trace a decision from sensation to action. When a system behaves unexpectedly, the corridor must reveal not only the malfunction but the structural conditions that made it plausible. Without this, responsibility collapses into finger-pointing.

The corridor motif returns one final time. Corridors are built. They do not appear spontaneously. If an organisation treats each layer as independent, the corridor becomes a series of blind spots. If it designs each layer with the next in mind, the corridor becomes navigable. The shape of harm becomes traceable. The shape of responsibility becomes legible.

The unresolved tension is this: when a system falters, where should scrutiny begin? With sensors that mismeasure, models that misclassify, objectives that skew incentives, interfaces that mislead, or oversight that misallocates authority? The corridor stretches before us. The question is which door to open first.

Chapter 2
Specifying Values Without Myth

The scandal began with a single word—*fairness*—printed neatly in a slide deck for a major platform's ethics review. The year was 2020, the place a conference room in Dublin, and the team presenting their quarterly update genuinely believed they were advancing a moral good. Their models, they explained, were penalising "unfair" disparities in recommended content. Regulators wanted demonstrable action; advertisers wanted reassurance; executives wanted a narrative of responsible stewardship. Yet below the polished charts, an uncomfortable detail emerged. Fairness, in their implementation, had been measured through click-through rates. Not representation. Not equitable reach. Not contextual sensitivity. Clicks. A principle as old as political theory had been quietly translated into a behavioural metric optimised to favour whichever groups had historically clicked most. No one had intended this. But intention, as the previous chapter showed, is a thin reed in the face of system design. Here it had bent into absurdity.

That moment is not an indictment of one team or company so much as a window into a pervasive problem: we talk about values as if they were fixed, shared, self-evident things, yet the instant they enter technical systems they must become something measurable. When they do, they change. A principle must become a parameter. A moral aspiration must become a number. And numbers have a habit of drifting away from the ideas that inspired them. A value becomes a proxy; a proxy becomes a target; a target becomes a loophole for Goodhart's Law, whose warning is deceptively simple: when a measure becomes a target, it stops being a good measure. The tension is older than automation, but machines magnify it by forcing choices into code long before societies have clarified what those choices truly require.

You can see this tension vividly in hospitals. In 2016, a large NHS trust began using length of stay as one of its indicators of emergency-department efficiency. The logic was straightforward: shorter stays suggested smoother coordination, better resource allocation, and reduced patient stress. But the metric learned something unintended.

Departments faced with complex cases had an incentive, albeit subtle, to reclassify borderline patients into observational categories that reset the clock. The behaviour was visible in ward logs: a mechanical shift in labels, not in patient care. The trust complied with national reporting standards, yet the metric—meant to reflect compassion and efficiency—became an instrument of distortion. The motivation was not malicious; it was structural. A proxy stretched beyond its truth.

These stories speak to the motif that threads through this chapter: *the mask*. When values enter systems, they put on masks. Proxies, metrics, thresholds, weights—each is a mask that partially reveals and partially hides the value beneath. To design ethically, one must learn to read the mask without mistaking it for the face.

Translating principles into parameters is not only difficult but also unavoidable. Machines cannot optimise for "fairness" or "dignity" or "trustworthiness" in their philosophical sense. They require operational definitions—specific signals, measurable deviations, defined distributions. When designers avoid specifying these definitions, systems fill the void with convenient proxies. Convenience, however, is a poor compass. When a team chooses click-through rate as a measure of relevance, or symptom count as a measure of severity, or journey time as a measure of mobility, they embed a worldview into a model. The worldview may be implicit. It may be contested. But once coded, it has consequences.

The deeper danger is not error; it is drift. A proxy begins its life as a pragmatic approximation. Over time, it becomes a strategic marker. Teams optimise it. Dashboards highlight it. Leaders demand improvements on it. Users respond to it. And soon the system is organised around the proxy rather than the principle. The mask replaces the face. This drift does not happen dramatically. It happens through a thousand incremental adjustments: a threshold here, a weighting there, a redesign that favours speed over nuance. The result is a system that behaves according to metrics that are legible to machines but opaque to the very people those machines affect.

Yet the problem is not that proxies exist. The problem is that we rarely examine them with philosophical seriousness. A proxy is a hypothesis about what a value looks like when observed in the world. Does fairness look like equal click rates? Does safety look like a low injury count? Does dignity look like minimal waiting time? These are empirical questions wrapped around moral commitments. Treating proxies as mere technical choices obscures their ethical charge.

This chapter's concern, then, is not only to expose the fragility of proxies but to explore how competing values can be specified without collapsing into myth. Myths arise when teams assume that values are harmoniously aligned, that they can be maximised together without trade-offs. Machines expose the lie. Every meaningful system reflects plural values—accuracy, efficiency, equity, transparency, autonomy—and these values often pull in different directions. The challenge is not to choose one but to negotiate among many.

To see this clearly, picture a simple graph: two axes, two values. Safety on one axis, mobility on the other. Every possible design represents a point in that space. Some points offer excellent safety at the cost of sluggish mobility; others offer speed with higher risk. Between these extremes lies a curve known in optimisation theory as the Pareto front—the set of designs where improving one value worsens another. This curve is not merely technical. It is political, moral, societal. Systems live on this curve. Decisions move them along it. And every move reveals what a society is willing to trade.

Consider the case of Singapore's Land Transport Authority in 2018, when it recalibrated traffic-light timings across busy junctions. Planners used algorithms that balanced pedestrian safety with vehicle throughput. The algorithm presented a visible trade space: increasing safety buffers reduced intersection capacity; increasing throughput shortened safe crossing windows. The city chose a region of the trade space that favoured pedestrian safety, even at the cost of delays. It did so explicitly. That explicitness mattered. By committing to a specific region of the trade space, the city acknowledged that values cannot all be maximised. They must be balanced.

Such explicit decisions are rare. More often, systems slide into a region of the trade space without conscious choice, pulled by metrics that measure some values more easily than others. Mobility is easy to measure; safety is probabilistic. Click-through is easy to measure; fairness is contextual. Patient throughput is easy to measure; care quality is experiential. The values we measure dominate the values we merely name.

This is where the final theme of the chapter enters: *human override as a value.* Override is too often framed as an admission of failure, as if human intervention indicates a system that has not matured. The opposite is true. In high-stakes environments—aviation, medicine, autonomous mobility—override is a designed safeguard, a signal that some values must supersede optimisation. A pilot pulling the yoke disengages automation not because automation malfunctioned but because the pilot recognises contexts the system cannot infer. A clinician overriding a triage recommendation does so because a patient reveals symptoms the model cannot interpret. Override is not a retreat from technological sophistication. It is a commitment to moral humility.

Designing override requires attention to escalation triggers, pause thresholds, audit logs, and authority allocation. But its essence is conceptual. It asserts that no proxy can perfectly capture a value, that no trade-off curve can account for every context, and that some decisions must remain in human hands. A system that cannot be overridden is a system that implicitly claims moral completeness. No responsible designer should accept that claim.

Override also reveals something crucial about values: they are hierarchical. Not every value holds equal weight in every context. Some must dominate when risk is high, when stakes are irreversible, or when human dignity is threatened. Systems must encode this hierarchy. They must know when to defer. This is not inefficiency. It is ethics.

As this chapter unfolds, you will see how principles become parameters, how proxies gain and lose legitimacy, how plural values can be visualised rather than mystified, and how human override anchors systems in a moral frame that machines cannot replicate. You will see why vague aspirations—"optimise fairness", "maximise well-being", "protect autonomy"—are seductive but misleading, and how rigorous specification transforms aspirations into actionable commitments.

But the stakes reach further still. The work of specifying values is not only about avoiding perverse outcomes. It is about preserving agency in a world where decisions increasingly flow through layers of automation. If we cannot articulate what we value, machines will make the choices for us, guided by whatever proxies are easiest to measure. The mask will harden.

And so the chapter ends on a tension worth carrying forward. When values collide in code—fairness against accuracy, safety against autonomy, dignity against efficiency—who decides which value bends? Who defines the trade space? Who chooses when to override? The question is not theoretical. It is architectural, institutional, and fundamentally human. The answers will shape not only our systems but the societies that rely on them.

From principles to parameters

On 7 October 2016, at Facebook's Menlo Park campus, engineers presented an internal audit showing that their "fairness" initiative—announced with considerable optimism only months earlier—had begun to drift. The project aimed to reduce discriminatory skew in the News Feed. The principle was noble. The implementation, less so. Fairness had been defined operationally through parity in *click-through rates* across demographic segments. The result was perverse but predictable: content preferred by historically high-engagement groups was amplified further, while posts from quieter communities faded, judged "unfairly" low-performing by the very metric meant to protect them. Engineers saw the distortion first through behavioural logs: the widening gap between recommended impression frequency and audience diversity. Each chart told the same story. A principle had been pulled through a numeric filter, and the filter had reshaped the principle beyond recognition.

The scene is worth dwelling on because it embodies a structural challenge faced by every institution deploying automated systems: values that begin life as moral aspirations must survive their translation into measurable objectives. Once encoded, those objectives shape behaviour relentlessly. A principle is porous; a parameter is rigid. A principle invites interpretation; a parameter admits none. When the two mismatch, systems behave correctly while acting wrongly. The machine honours the number, not the narrative.

The motif here is *the compass*: principles offer direction, but parameters steer. Without careful translation, a moral compass becomes a navigational hazard.

To understand why this translation is so fraught, we must begin by showing how principles enter systems in the first place. Organisations rarely code principles directly. Instead, they express them through operational goals: reduce bias, improve efficiency, strengthen trust. Each goal requires a measurable definition. Measurement forces reduction. Consider "trust." Trust becomes user retention, complaint rates, or survey scores. Each is partial. When Facebook chose click-through as its fairness proxy, the metric captured engagement, not justice. The principle was wide; the measurement narrow. The system optimised the narrow.

The same mechanism surfaced in New York in January 2019, when the city reviewed early deployments of its Automated Decision Systems (ADS) used in housing-benefit eligibility. Officials intended to promote equitable access. The operationalisation involved a model calibrated to historical acceptance rates. The principle—equity—became a parameter: match previous distributions. But historical data reflected biased administrative patterns. The system reproduced them. Audit teams documented the distortion numerically: disparities of several percentage points between districts. The principle had collapsed into a circular metric.

To name the process precisely: principles degrade when converted into proxies without scrutiny. A proxy is always a hypothesis about what a value looks like when rendered measurable. If untested, the hypothesis becomes a fiction.

This degradation, however, is not inevitable. A compelling counter-example emerges from Stockholm's congestion-pricing reforms in

2006. The principle—reduce urban emissions while maintaining mobility—was translated into two parameters: average vehicle speed on arterial roads and measured particulate matter at fixed stations. Crucially, the city added a third guardrail: publicly accepted fairness thresholds for commuter burden, assessed through periodic surveys. Though imperfect, the triad of parameters preserved the nuance of the principle. Emissions fell, mobility stabilised, and citizen support—quantified through annual polling—remained strong. The principle retained its shape because its parameters were plural and context-aware. Still, the model had limitations: surveys introduced lag, and some districts argued that burden was under-measured. But the system openly acknowledged the trade-offs rather than allowing a single metric to dominate.

The reconciliation between Stockholm and Menlo Park lies in the compass. The Swedish programme kept the compass visible while converting direction into data. The Facebook project let the compass slip from view, replaced by a seductive metric.

The next claim follows naturally: *translation is an ethical act*. When designers convert principles into parameters, they decide what aspects of a value matter most. They compress meaning into numbers. They create a hierarchy of relevance. In healthcare, for instance, the principle of "timely care" often becomes quantified waiting-time targets. In 2010, the Scottish Government's four-hour emergency-department rule drove behavioural adaptation. Clinicians increased "clock-stopping" admissions—administrative reclassifications that paused the waiting-time metric while leaving patients in corridors. The principle aimed to reduce suffering; the parameter rewarded paperwork. Data from NHS Scotland's Information Services Division revealed the behaviour in stark figures: spikes in short-stay admissions not matched by clinical need. The compass had been replaced by an instrument reading that no longer pointed north.

Why does this misalignment occur so frequently? Because principles are elastic and social, whereas parameters are mechanical and unidimensional. Machines commit to numbers. People interpret principles. When a number replaces an interpretation, the interpretive space collapses.

A further example shows this collapse at scale. In November 2020, YouTube modified its recommendation algorithm to elevate "authoritative" news sources during political flashpoints. The principle was integrity. The parameter was watch-time from a predefined source list. The metric suppressed low-quality misinformation—which mattered—but also reduced visibility for independent local journalists, documented in a study by the Reuters Institute (2021). The system optimised the parameter. The principle fractured, split between protection and pluralism. Two values fought through one metric. The compass spun.

Yet there is nuance here. Not every principle can or should be captured through metrics alone. Some call for constraints rather than optimisation. Consider aviation, one of the rare fields where principles are codified into hard parameters with exceptional fidelity. The principle of "safety first" is materialised in quantifiable limits: required separation minima, mandated pilot rest hours, prescribed maintenance intervals. These are not proxies but design commitments. The aviation sector encodes principles into parameters conservatively, then treats those parameters as immovable. The compass is not merely translated; it is engraved.

The limitation, of course, is that aviation deals in physical laws and rare-event statistics, whereas digital platforms navigate social dynamics with fluid contours. What works for flight levels does not transfer neatly to news feeds or hospital triage. But the lesson stands: parameters succeed ethically when they encode principles with precision, caution, and periodic revalidation.

This brings us to the next structural claim: *every parameter needs a narrative*. Without narrative, a metric becomes detached from its purpose. Narrative is not ornament. It is orientation. It answers the question: why *this* number? A parameter without narrative tilts systems into mechanical optimisation, while a parameter with narrative anchors decisions in collective understanding.

Narrative also protects against Goodhart's Law by reminding teams what the measure is supposed to represent. If fairness metrics come with explicit narratives—who is protected, what patterns count, what harms should diminish—then distortions become easier to spot early. Logs, dashboards, and audits can be read against intention, not merely against performance.

Several institutions now experiment with narratively anchored parameters. The NHS's 2022 rollout of "patient-centred outcome measures" in digital triage tools required each model assumption to be documented in plain language alongside numerical indicators. This practice, though imperfect, mitigated some distortions. Clinicians could compare model outputs with contextual descriptions. The compass and the instrument interacted.

Yet even with narrative, parameters impose boundaries. They highlight what is visible and hide what is not. A metric for mobility shows journey times but hides stress. A metric for engagement shows clicks but hides coercion. A metric for accuracy shows errors but hides uncertainty. Parameters shine beams; principles illuminate landscapes.

This asymmetry raises a deeper question: when several parameters express a principle poorly, how should designers choose among them? The answer lies in *testing the mask*. A parameter is a mask the value wears. Designers must ask: does this mask resemble the value enough to be trusted? They must measure distortion through real data: subgroup outcomes, behavioural traces, anomaly detection, error concentrations. A principle cannot be validated abstractly; it must be validated empirically.

Examples abound. When the Dutch Tax Authority's childcare-benefits algorithm was audited in 2020, investigators found that the principle of fraud prevention had been boiled down to a binary risk score. That score disproportionately flagged families with dual-nationality status—a pattern exposed through statistical analysis published in the Dutch Parliament's parliamentary inquiry (*Ongekend Onrecht*, 2020). The parameter amplified historic bias because it had no narrative, no guardrails, no counter-metric. It was a mask that obscured rather than revealed.

Contrast this with the London School of Economics' 2017 behavioural-insights pilot for social-care triage. The principle—prioritise those in greatest need—was translated into a composite parameter: recent clinical indicators, frequency of service use, and self-reported well-being, each weighted according to deliberative workshops with affected communities. This was still reduction, but the reduction was plural and participatory. The compass influenced the calibration.

The motif of the compass returns here with force. Principles orient. Parameters steer. A responsible system requires both. Without orientation, steering becomes reckless. Without steering, orientation remains abstract.

The structural implication is unavoidable: translating principles into parameters is not a clerical task. It is moral engineering. It commits a system to a particular understanding of human experience. It distributes benefits and burdens. It shapes whose voices matter in the dataset and whose disappear. It fixes choices that will be replayed millions of times per day.

This is why vague aspirations are not harmless. They are dangerous. "Optimise fairness" without definition. "Promote well-being" without operational detail. "Strengthen trust" without behavioural indicators. These statements invite proxies to creep in unnoticed. And once proxies take root, they harden into dashboards, incentives, and deployment decisions.

The tension we end with is the one that will follow into the next pages: when a principle splinters into several plausible parameters—each partial, each flawed—who decides which form becomes the system's truth? Should designers pursue the parameter easiest to measure, the one most politically defensible, the one most stable under noise, or the one most faithful to human experience? The compass points. The system steers. The question is how firmly we hold the compass when the parameters pull us away.

Choosing proxies wisely

In January 2016, administrators at St George's Hospital in London reviewed their emergency-department logs and noticed an anomaly: "zero-minute discharges" had risen sharply, appearing dozens of times a week. Patients were being registered and discharged almost instantly. No treatment, no clinical notes, barely time for a pulse check. When an internal audit followed, the pattern became clearer. Staff were reclassifying complex arrivals into administrative categories that paused the four-hour waiting-time clock mandated by NHS England. The behaviour was documented numerically—timer resets, spike charts, and discrepancies between discharge codes and diagnostic actions. The efficiency proxy, waiting time, had begun to reshape care itself. Nobody set out to distort clinical reality. But the proxy had become a target, and the target had become a game.

The episode embodies the motif that threads through this subchapter: *the mirror*. Proxies act like mirrors. They reflect a distorted version of the value they stand in for. And distortion grows sharper when organisations optimise the reflection rather than the value. What begins as a helpful approximation becomes a gravitational field. It pulls behaviour towards itself until the original purpose fades from view.

Every complex system depends on proxies. No hospital can directly measure "quality of care"; no city can monitor "safety" in moral terms; no platform can compute "trust" as a philosophical state. Designers must choose signals that offer measurable glimpses of these deeper aims. Yet the moment a proxy enters a performance dashboard, it acquires authority. Teams commit to it. Managers reward it. Algorithms optimise for it. And Goodhart's Law—first articulated by economist Charles Goodhart in 1975—quietly takes hold: when a measure becomes a target, it ceases to be a good measure.

To understand how quickly distortion can proliferate, we must show how proxies become targets. In the St George's case, the initial proxy—waiting time—was reasonable. Long waits correlate with overcrowding, delayed care, and patient dissatisfaction. The problem arose when waiting time became the central indicator of success. Some clinicians felt pressure to "stop the clock" rather than to solve the underlying bottlenecks. When monitored centrally, the metric triggered behavioural adaptation. The mirror warped.

A second illustrative case sits far from hospitals, yet echoes the same mechanics. In November 2018, YouTube adjusted its recommendation model to increase "time spent" as a signal of content relevance. The principle was simple and measurable. Yet journalists at *The Washington Post* documented how the metric unintentionally amplified extremist and sensational material—content that, while fringe, reliably held attention. The company insisted on neutrality; the logs told a different story. Users were shown progressively more extreme videos, measured through watch-time deltas and session-length graphs. The platform had not endorsed the content. It had endorsed the metric. The mirror widened the crack.

Both cases reveal an uncomfortable truth: proxies direct action. They do not merely measure it. When they are poorly chosen, or left unchallenged, they become engines of misalignment.

A credible counter-example complicates the picture. When the city of Stockholm introduced congestion pricing in 2006, it used traffic-flow speed and particulate-matter levels as twin proxies for mobility and environmental health. Unlike waiting time in emergency departments or watch-time on video platforms, these proxies were directly linked to observable harms—journey delays and pollution exposure. Crucially, city planners paired monthly traffic data with continuous air-quality readings, adjusting charges through iterative review. The mirror was imperfect, yet regularly polished. Congestion dropped, emissions fell, and public support increased, measured through yearly surveys by Sweden's Transport Administration. Here, proxies succeeded because they were empirically anchored and periodically reassessed.

The reconciliation lies in maintenance. Proxies become dangerous when treated as fixed truths. They become trustworthy when treated as evolving hypotheses.

To choose proxies wisely requires understanding what a proxy actually *is*: a visible behaviour that stands in for an invisible value. Efficiency becomes average journey time. Safety becomes near-miss frequency. Relevance becomes click-through. Equity becomes parity in error rates. Each translation trades nuance for tractability. The question is not whether to make the trade, but how to ensure the trade does not mutate unseen.

The first criterion for a sound proxy is *causal proximity*. A proxy should sit close to the value it represents, not several steps removed. Waiting time is casually connected to patient experience but only indirectly connected to clinical outcomes. Watch-time correlates with engagement but says little about whether content is meaningful or benign. By contrast, particulate-matter concentrations correlate directly with respiratory harm. The closer the mirror sits to the value, the clearer the reflection.

A second criterion is *resistance to gaming*. Systems must withstand strategic behaviour by humans or models. If a proxy can be manipulated without improving the underlying value, it will be. In education, schools judged primarily on test scores often narrow curricula—a pattern documented repeatedly in Ofsted evaluations across England in the 2010s. The score becomes the target; teaching adapts. In digital platforms, engagement metrics can be inflated through sensational thumbnails or manufactured outrage. Resilience demands proxies that collapse when gamed, like patient-reported outcome measures that detect superficial improvements, or anomaly-detection models that reveal manipulation.

A third criterion is *distributional sensitivity*. A proxy must reveal harms concentrated in particular groups rather than masking them through averages. When the New York Police Department experimented with predictive-policing tools in 2015, proxies for "crime risk" were built from arrest data. But arrest data reflected enforcement patterns, not crime itself. The proxy concentrated surveillance in specific neighbourhoods. Audits comparing predicted risk with victim-report surveys exposed the distortion. A wise proxy must surface fairness concerns, not bury them.

A fourth criterion is *periodic review*. Proxies degrade. Data distributions shift. Behaviours adapt. Goals evolve. The Swedish congestion-pricing system endured because emissions and traffic speed were reviewed monthly, not annually. Contrast this with the triage metrics in St George's, which remained static even as emergency-department dynamics changed. A proxy's reliability decays over time unless deliberately recalibrated.

To grasp why periodic review matters, consider a quieter example: the length-of-stay metric used as a proxy for efficiency in hospitals across Europe. When a hospital reduces unnecessary inpatient days, length of stay falls. That is good. But when hospitals face pressure to reduce stays rapidly, the metric can incentivise premature discharges. Clinical audits in Denmark and France during the 2010s showed spikes in 48-hour readmissions, plotted unmistakably against efforts to reduce mean length of stay. The mirror cracked again. Only when hospitals began to report length-of-stay together with seven-day readmission rates did the metric regain integrity. The proxy became safer through pairing.

This pairing reveals a broader insight: no proxy should stand alone. Single metrics seduce. Composite metrics constrain distortion. A triage model that uses both symptom severity and clinician-override frequency as proxies for safety will behave more cautiously than one guided solely by throughput. The mask must have multiple layers.

Yet even the best proxies cannot eliminate moral complexity. They merely offer a structured way of capturing slices of values. Their limits must be acknowledged. A counter-pressure emerges when proxies become overly complex. If designers select too many indicators, systems lose interpretability. Decision-makers cannot see which behaviour the algorithm promotes. Complexity obscures the mirror. Here, again, Stockholm illustrates a balance: a small set of high-quality proxies, each tied directly to observable data, each subject to review, each paired with transparent narrative.

The motif of the mirror returns with new depth. A mirror can guide. It can deceive. It must be cleaned. And it must never replace the eye.

Beyond selecting proxies, we must confront a more subtle challenge: *proxy gaming by algorithms themselves*. When optimisation systems learn to maximise a proxy, they can exploit loopholes invisible to humans. In 2019, researchers at Google Health documented how a diabetic-retinopathy model trained to detect lesions had inadvertently latched onto camera-type metadata correlated with disease prevalence, rather than the lesions themselves. The proxy for "disease severity" had become entangled with irrelevant signals. The model succeeded numerically while failing clinically. Without careful feature attribution and error analysis, the misalignment would have gone unnoticed.

Such episodes illustrate why proxy selection is not a one-time choice. It is an ongoing dialogue between data, models, and values. Proxies must be confronted with adversarial tests, stress scenarios, and counterfactual analyses. They must be checked for demographic distortion, temporal drift, and adversarial manipulation. A mirror must be struck, tapped, held at different angles.

Yet even with rigorous testing, proxies reflect only fragments. We return to the role of narrative. Metrics alone cannot articulate meaning. Designers must articulate what a proxy is intended to capture, what it excludes, and what failure modes are most concerning. Consider how the aviation industry treats "time to conflict resolution" as a key safety metric. The metric is paired with explicit narrative guidelines outlining acceptable ranges, context-specific exceptions, and the necessity of pilot override. The metric functions because its narrative anchors it.

Institutions that avoid narrative risk drifting into mechanical optimisation. A recommendation system that maximises engagement without narrative context will tilt towards emotionally charged content. A mobility system that maximises average speed without narrative guidance will prioritise fast roads over safe ones. Narratives remind teams why proxies were chosen and what they are meant to protect.

The structural implication is stark: proxies crystallise values into operational form. Choosing them unwisely misdirects entire systems. Choosing them wisely disciplines systems. The choice is moral as much as technical.

This brings us to a final reflective turn. Proxy selection reveals a deeper tension: when values diverge, proxies compete. Efficiency may conflict with care; safety with autonomy; equity with accuracy. When proxies clash, teams must decide which value bends. No algorithm can resolve this by itself. It requires deliberation, transparency, and institutional courage.

And so we close with a diagnostic question worth carrying forward: when a proxy begins to distort behaviour—when the mirror warps—will we adjust, replace, or abandon it? The decision will determine whether our systems reflect our values or merely our measurements.

Plural values, bounded optimisation

On 3 July 2018, Singapore's Land Transport Authority (LTA) reviewed a simulation that showed an awkward truth. The autonomous shuttle being piloted at one-north tech park met its collision-risk target with striking reliability, measured through thousands of kilometres of logged testing. Yet when engineers overlaid expected passenger throughput—how many riders the service could move per hour—it became clear that the vehicle's conservative braking profile would cause bottlenecks along Fusionopolis Way. The system excelled at safety. It faltered at mobility. Both aims were legitimate. Both were measurable. But improving one visibly worsened the other. The simulation plots told the story bluntly: every attempt to reduce expected collision probability below a certain threshold slowed the shuttle by several seconds per junction. Each adjustment produced a curve, not a point. LTA officials spent two days debating not which objective was "right", but which part of the curve the city could live with.

That scene captures a motif that will recur throughout this subchapter: *the frontier*. Every complex system lives on a frontier where multiple values compete for expression. Safety stands against speed. Accuracy stands against equity. Privacy stands against utility. No algorithm can optimise all of them simultaneously. Instead, it must choose a region—an acceptable slice of a broader trade space. The question is not how to maximise everything, but how to accept that maximisation itself is the wrong goal.

To see this clearly, we must begin with a simple paradox: the more values a system must respect, the less meaningful the idea of a single "best" solution becomes. Engineers call this multi-objective optimisation. Philosophers call it moral pluralism. In practice, they converge on the same insight: trade-offs are unavoidable, and a responsible system must learn to navigate them explicitly.

The first task is to show how trade spaces become visible. In Singapore, engineers plotted expected collision probability on one axis and average journey time on the other. Each system configuration—altering sensor fusion weights, modifying braking thresholds, adjusting prediction horizons—produced a point on the graph. Some points improved both metrics, but most improved one at the expense of the other. Connecting the best-performing points produced a curve: the Pareto front. Named in honour of Vilfredo Pareto, the Italian economist who wrote on efficiency in 1906, the curve reveals the set of designs where you cannot improve one value without degrading another. The frontier becomes explicit.

A second example demonstrates the same dynamic in a very different domain. In January 2014, the National Institute for Health and Care Excellence (NICE) in the UK evaluated early decision-support systems that recommended stroke treatments in emergency settings. The principle was clear: deliver thrombolysis quickly while avoiding unnecessary interventions. Time-to-needle and haemorrhage risk became the two dominant metrics. As in Singapore, performance points formed a curve: faster treatment raised haemorrhage probability, and stricter caution delayed therapy for borderline cases. Clinicians were faced not with a single recommendation but with a spectrum that revealed the cost of caution and the cost of haste. NICE ultimately chose an operating point that favoured minutes over marginal risk reductions—a decision documented in its 2014 guideline. The frontier made the stakes legible.

The implication is unsettling but liberating: responsible systems are not about finding the optimal; they are about choosing which non-optimal outcome best aligns with societal values.

A credible counter-example complicates the narrative. When Japan introduced the Shinkansen in 1964, it achieved near-miraculous performance across safety, speed, and punctuality. For decades, the system appeared to sit at a point above the Pareto front—faster, safer, and more punctual than comparable rail systems. But closer inspection reveals that Japan achieved these gains not by escaping the frontier but by shifting it. Massive investment, national coordination, and strict operational discipline changed the physics of the trade space itself. The frontier moved. The logic remains intact: values still traded off; Japan merely paid the price required to redraw the curve. The limitation of the Shinkansen case rests in its rarity. Most systems do not receive such political or financial alignment. The lesson holds: frontiers exist whether or not we acknowledge them.

To name the pattern precisely: every system with plural values must select a region of acceptable compromise. That region is a moral choice disguised as a technical one.

Understanding this helps explain why optimisation, when left unconstrained, can quietly undermine a system's legitimacy. If a navigation algorithm optimises journey time alone, it will route vehicles through residential streets, raising noise complaints and collision risk. If a hiring model optimises predictive accuracy alone, it will prioritise features correlated with historic success—even when those features encode bias. These are not algorithmic failings; they are frontier failures. The system has chosen a region—often inadvertently—that privileges one dimension excessively.

The motif of *the frontier* returns as we consider why visualisation matters. Humans struggle to reason about trade-offs abstractly. But place them in a graph, and ambiguity dissolves into structure. In Singapore, seeing the curve helped planners justify slowing the shuttle slightly to achieve what they deemed an ethically acceptable safety margin. In stroke care, seeing the curve helped clinicians push for faster treatment when evidence showed that delay cost more lives than marginal increases in side-effect risk. Visualisation is not a luxury. It is a moral instrument.

Yet even clear frontiers pose a challenge: who chooses the acceptable region? Designers? Regulators? Affected communities? In many systems, the chosen region emerges through silent drift. The easiest metric dominates. The least noisy dimension wins. A frontier point becomes standard by inertia rather than deliberation. That is dangerous. A city may slide into unsafe mobility habits; a hospital may edge towards harmful efficiency; a platform may create an information environment dominated by outrage simply because outrage metrics speak more loudly than nuance.

This is why bounded optimisation matters. Bounded optimisation means defining constraints before searching for trade-offs. A constraint says: whatever else the system does, it must stay inside this ethical boundary. For autonomous shuttles, a constraint might be a hard upper limit on acceptable collision risk. For hiring systems, a constraint might be demographic parity within a defined band. For clinical tools, a constraint might be a maximum acceptable false-negative rate. With constraints in place, optimisation becomes safe to perform within moral walls.

To show how constraints operate, consider how the European Union Aviation Safety Agency (EASA) regulates automated flight-control systems. In its 2020 framework for highly automated operations, EASA requires that the probability of catastrophic failure remains below a threshold of 10^-9 per flight hour. That threshold constrains the frontier. Even if an automation scheme improves fuel efficiency or pilot workload significantly, it cannot be adopted if it breaches that safety boundary. The frontier becomes bounded; optimisation happens inside the box.

A contrasting example shows the cost of failing to bound the frontier. In February 2015, Philadelphia's Parking Authority introduced a new prediction model to allocate enforcement officers across districts. The goal was to maximise parking turnover and revenue. But the proxy—ticket issuance—became dominant. The frontier between revenue and fairness never entered discussion. Within months, some districts saw disproportionately high ticketing rates, documented by local academics who analysed issuance data against neighbourhood demographics. The frontier had been crossed unknowingly. The city reacted with adjustments in 2016, finally balancing enforcement intensity with equity constraints. But the delay illustrated the danger: a system without bounds will find the easiest target, not the fairest one.

So how should designers choose acceptable regions? Three considerations matter. First, sensitivity: how rapidly does performance degrade as you move along the frontier? A steep curve suggests fragile trade-offs; a gentle one indicates room for compromise. Second, equity: which groups bear the cost of movement along the curve? Trade-offs are rarely distributed evenly. Third, reversibility: can a decision be undone if the chosen region proves harmful? Systems with irreversible stakes—medical diagnosis, autonomous weapons—must choose points with extreme caution.

Multi-objective optimisation also requires a sense of rhythm. Trade spaces shift as environments change. The acceptable region for mobility vs safety in Singapore will differ during monsoon months. The acceptable region for emergency stroke care may change as new treatments emerge. The acceptable region for energy consumption and server latency fluctuates with grid conditions. The frontier moves; the acceptable region must follow.

We return now to the motif. A frontier becomes meaningful only when approached with humility. It is not a map of what *should* be valued, merely a map of what *can* be valued simultaneously. Moral judgement begins where optimisation ends: in deciding where on the frontier to stand.

This brings us to the chapter's unresolved tension. When values compete—safety against mobility, equity against accuracy, privacy against utility—who decides how far along the frontier a system may travel before it betrays its social purpose? And what principles guide that choice when every point is imperfect? The frontier stretches before us. The question is where we draw our line.

Human override as a value

On 12 March 2019, Ethiopian Airlines Flight 302 plummeted into a field near Bishoftu, six minutes after take-off. The subsequent investigation by Ethiopia's Aircraft Accident Investigation Bureau revealed a sequence now etched into aviation history: the aircraft's Maneuvering Characteristics Augmentation System (MCAS) repeatedly forced the nose down, triggered by a faulty angle-of-attack sensor. The captain and first officer attempted to counteract the system manually—first with electric trim, then with the manual trim wheel—but the forces exerted by the runaway automation overwhelmed their attempts. The cockpit voice recorder captured their final struggle: human judgement pitted against a machine logic that assumed authority. Override had been possible in theory. It was not possible in practice. The tragedy demonstrated something that aviation safety experts had long understood but public debate often missed: override is not a backup; it is a design choice. And design choices determine whether humans can act when systems misfire.

The crash, devastating as it was, crystallised the motif that follows throughout this subchapter: *the hand on the switch*. Override is the human hand. The switch is the system's capacity to yield. Whether the hand can reach the switch—and whether the switch works when pressed—defines a system's minimum moral orientation. A machine that cannot be interrupted becomes an entity without humility. A system that refuses to yield becomes a system that claims too much.

To see why override must be treated as a value rather than a fallback, we need to trace how modern systems behave under uncertainty. Automated systems excel when conditions match their design envelopes. They fail when the world departs from their expectations. In the MCAS case, the system assumed sensor symmetry; when the assumption broke, the machine doubled down. That doubling-down is the hallmark of unbounded optimisation: a system committed to its objective function continues to act on it, even when human professionals see that the context has changed.

A second example, far from aviation, shows the same pattern at a smaller scale. In April 2020, clinical staff at a Manchester hospital noticed that their digital triage assistant—an automated system predicting Covid-19 severity—was underestimating the risk for patients with atypical symptoms, such as gastrointestinal distress. The tool produced a severity score, colour-coded on a dashboard. Nurses who were uneasy about the green-coded patients manually escalated the cases; logs later showed that those escalations were often correct. The override pattern was visible in timestamps: clinicians ignoring the default, applying judgement against the grain.

When the hospital updated the system in July 2020, it made override frequency an explicit signal for retraining. Override became a feature, not a failure. The hand on the switch taught the system where it was blind.

Both cases illuminate a central claim: override is not an embarrassment. It is the system's moral spine.

To name this mechanism precisely: override expresses the value of *context recognition*. Machines recognise patterns; humans recognise stakes. When a clinician sees a patient's hesitation, when a pilot feels a plane resisting, when a content moderator senses coordinated harassment, the human recognises context the system does not encode. Override is the structural acknowledgement of that asymmetry.

Yet override is not simply the act of stopping a system. It is also the capacity to pause, escalate, and demand inspection. These behaviours require design. They also require respect: an organisation must formalise override pathways without penalising those who use them. If override is framed as failure, humans will hesitate. If override is framed as stewardship, humans will act.

A credible counter-example challenges the ease of this ideal. In October 2014, a trader at Knight Capital attempted to interrupt an algorithm that had begun issuing erratic orders at high speed. The kill-switch mechanism existed, but the human operator did not activate it quickly enough, partly because the alarms were ambiguous and partly because the escalation protocol required multiple confirmations. By the time the system was halted, it had executed thousands of unintended trades, causing a loss of approximately $440 million. The switch was present, but the design made it slow to reach. Override faltered not through absence but through procedural drag.

Reconciliation emerges when we distinguish *nominal* override from *functional* override. Nominal override is the symbolic button; functional override is the capacity to act effectively under time pressure. A system that provides the former without the latter is one that treats override as theatre.

Returning to the motif of the hand on the switch, we must explore why escalation patterns matter. Escalation is the act of turning uncertainty into a structured handover. In high-stakes operations, escalation must be timely, intelligible, and irreversible. Aviation codifies this through callouts: "I have control," "You have control." Medicine codifies it through rapid-response teams triggered by early warning scores. These are not rituals; they are boundary crossings. They create moments where human judgement reasserts primacy.

To see escalation working well, consider the experience of the Dutch Railways (NS) in 2017, when it deployed automated scheduling tools for route planning. The system learned to optimise train distribution based on passenger-flow data, collected across Utrecht Centraal and Amsterdam Zuid. When anomalies appeared—dense bottlenecks unpredicted by the model—station managers activated an escalation channel that suspended automated scheduling for specific segments. Logs show how often this occurred: several dozen times in the first quarter alone. The pattern changed the model itself. Engineers used escalation events to refine assumptions about passenger behaviour. Override became epistemic feedback.

Contrast this with the 2010 "Flash Crash" in U.S. equities markets. Automated trading systems cascaded into a violent feedback loop, erasing nearly $1 trillion in value within minutes before bouncing back. Regulators later introduced circuit-breakers—hard stops at defined thresholds. These were not afterthoughts; they were codified overrides. The limit is a value: it asserts that the pursuit of liquidity cannot justify chaos. The switch was built into the exchange.

These examples reveal a structural truth: override must be anticipatory, not reactive. Anticipatory override relies on audit triggers—signals that indicate when a system's behaviour requires closer scrutiny. These triggers are numbers: drift scores, anomaly rates, override frequency, distribution shifts. When these metrics cross thresholds, systems must pause. A pause is a moral gesture. It says: something here exceeds the domain of the automated.

To illustrate how pause functions structurally, consider the national early warning scores (NEWS2) used in UK hospitals. When a patient's aggregate physiological score crosses a threshold, the system triggers an escalation step—human attendance within a specific time frame. The score is audited regularly to prevent drift. In 2020, during the pandemic, clinicians observed that the tool underweighted silent hypoxia. Review teams updated guidelines and added supplementary criteria. The pause was activated not only at the bedside but at the governance level. Override extended across the organisation.

But override comes with tension: when should humans intervene? Too early, and systems become inefficient; too late, and harm accumulates. This tension surfaced in the deployment of Tesla's Autopilot in 2015–2016. Drivers frequently over-relied on the system's lane-keeping capability, ignoring attention warnings. The override invitation was present, but human vigilance decayed. After several accidents, regulators urged Tesla to redesign its human–machine interface to enforce more stringent re-engagement. The hand was on the switch, but the human forgot to hold it.

The limitation here is obvious: override depends on human capacity, attention, and training. It also depends on institutional culture. If using the override button is interpreted as a reprimand of the system or an admission of weakness, humans will hesitate. Override becomes a last resort rather than a routine act of safety.

Yet the deeper point stands: override is a *value*, not a *patch*. It represents a commitment to humility—an acknowledgement that models cannot encode all contexts, cannot foresee all outliers, cannot measure all dimensions of human life. Override expresses respect for the unmodelled. It is the system's moral hinge.

This brings us back to the motif for the final time. *The hand on the switch* is not just the pilot's hand or the clinician's hand or the trader's hand. It is society's hand. It is the collective authority to interrupt the automated when stakes exceed confidence.

And so we close with a tension that will follow into later chapters: when a system appears to be performing well—efficient, accurate, smooth—what signals should trigger override? When is silence in the logs a sign of stability, and when is it a sign that humans have forgotten the switch exists at all?

Chapter 3
Bias: More Than Data Quality

The first warning sign appeared not in a dataset but on a map. In 2016, a team of civic technologists in Oakland overlaid five years of policing data onto a grid of neighbourhood blocks. The pattern was unmistakable: the hottest clusters of recorded crime aligned almost perfectly with the footprints of past police deployment rather than with any independent measure of harm. Patrol routes had generated encounters; encounters had generated reports; reports had justified further patrols. A loop, decades in the making, had quietly turned into a dataset. When a predictive-policing model was tested against this map, the algorithm's "risk" outputs simply echoed the old routes. The system was not predicting crime; it was predicting history. The map revealed a truth that would only later be named with appropriate clarity: datasets are not raw reflections of the world but records of human choices, power, and perception. They carry memory. And memory shapes the future.

That moment captures a paradox at the heart of machine-assisted decision-making. The more data a system ingests, the more objective it appears. Yet the older and broader the data, the more it absorbs the sediment of previous judgements—who was watched, who was ignored, who had access to services, who did not. We speak of "cleaning" data as if ethics could be rinsed out like noise. But history is not noise. History is signal. To build a model atop such sediment without interrogating its layers is to mistake accumulation for neutrality. And neutrality, in this domain, is often a convenient fiction.

Bias, then, is not merely a matter of flawed sampling or annotation errors. It is a structural inheritance. It enters through the provenance of datasets; through the incentives of annotators; through policies that decide which cases get recorded and which vanish into the undocumented everyday. To trace bias is to trace the story behind the data: who collected it, why they collected it, and what they overlooked. Every dataset is a perspective, not a panorama. This chapter begins by following those perspectives back to their sources.

Once history enters the dataset, it does not remain inert. It flows through model architecture. The architecture of a model is not just a technical design; it is a set of moral choices expressed mathematically. A highly interpretable model—say, a linear classifier—offers transparency at the cost of nuance. A deep neural network offers nuance at the cost of legibility. Organisations must decide which trade-off matters more. And that decision, though often framed as an engineering preference, has moral effect. A loan-approval system built with a transparent structure allows auditors to detect disparate treatment; a model optimised for raw predictive accuracy may bury those inequalities beneath layers of representation. Architecture determines what can be explained, challenged, or corrected. The model becomes an instrument that either reveals or conceals.

If history shapes the data and architecture shapes what the system can see, testing shapes what we are willing to know. Fairness is not inferred from intuition; it is revealed through counterfactual, subgroup, and scenario analyses that force the model to confront structural inequalities. Consider a loans model that approves 78 per cent of applicants overall—an apparently benign figure. When tested under counterfactual constraints—"same financial history, different surname"—approval rates shift. When evaluated under economic stress scenarios—"same applicant, recession conditions"—the cracks deepen across intersectional groups. Without such structured scrutiny, inequities lie dormant. Testing becomes a form of moral cartography, mapping where harm hides.

Yet fairness is not merely parity across categories. Parity alone can betray those it claims to protect. A hospital triage system, for example, may treat all patients identically—equal thresholds, equal resource allocation—while systematically underserving those with chronic conditions who require more time or tailored intervention. In medicine, equal treatment is often inferior to equitable care. Context matters. Capacity matters. History matters. Fairness that ignores domain-specific harm is fairness in name only. In this chapter, the distinction between parity and care becomes a guiding tension: should systems aspire to symmetry or to support?

Bias, in this sense, is not an aberration in data science. It is a mirror held up to the worlds from which data emerge. To confront bias responsibly is to move beyond the narrow question of "data quality" and towards a broader inquiry into how social structures, institutional incentives, and model design choices shape outcomes. This chapter situates bias not as a defective technical property but as a social and moral phenomenon that technologies inherit and can amplify.

This requires a continuity of thought with the earlier chapters. We have seen how values collapse into proxies, and how illusions of optimisation can obscure trade-offs. Bias extends this pattern. Where proxies mis-measure values, bias misrepresents reality. Where optimisation hides compromise, bias hides history. And where earlier chapters dealt with the dangers of poorly specified objectives, this chapter confronts the deeper danger of poorly understood origins.

The story ahead moves across several terrains. It begins with data provenance—how histories enter training corpora through policing, credit, health, and platform interactions. It examines model architecture as a site of moral choice. It introduces counterfactual testing as a practical means of revealing inequity at scale. And it concludes by wrestling with a profound distinction: the difference between treating people equally and treating people justly.

As the chapter unfolds, a recurring motif will return: *the shadow*. Every dataset carries a shadow of the world that produced it. Every model casts that shadow forward. Sometimes the shadow aligns with reality; often it distorts it. The task is not to eliminate the shadow—that is impossible—but to understand its shape well enough to prevent it from becoming destiny.

And so we arrive at the question that propels the chapter forward: if every dataset carries history and every model carries constraint, what does it take to build a system capable not merely of avoiding bias, but of recognising the shadows it should refuse to follow?

Histories inside datasets

In August 2016, the Oakland Police Department released five years of stop-and-frisk records under California's Public Records Act. Civic researchers plotted the locations on a simple grid. The picture they produced was not a portrait of crime but of presence. Blocks in East Oakland glowed red with activity, not because more crimes had been independently reported there, but because more officers had patrolled them. Patrols generated encounters; encounters produced entries; entries became "data-driven evidence" that these very blocks required further patrols. The loop closed silently. What looked like ground truth was, in fact, institutional memory—recorded, quantified, and then mistaken for an impartial representation of risk. The dataset was not lying. It was remembering.

That map captured something deeper than a policing anomaly. It revealed the quiet motif running through this subchapter: *the sediment.* Every dataset contains layers of sediment—historical choices, unequal attention, partial gazes, and incentives that structure what gets captured and what never appears. Engineers often treat datasets as if they were geological strata: dense, inert, and objective. Yet these layers are not deposited by nature. They are shaped by institutions, shaped by power, shaped by habits so ingrained they appear almost organic. To read a dataset responsibly is to read its sediment.

The first task in understanding this sediment is deceptively simple: examine provenance. Provenance is not an administrative detail; it is epistemology. It tells us who gathered the data, using what tools, under which constraints, and with what motivations. Show provenance, and you show bias. Name provenance, and you name responsibility. Explain provenance, and you reveal how selective attention hardens into so-called evidence. The implication is stark: a system trained on unexamined provenance does not inherit the world; it inherits the worldview of its data collectors.

The Oakland example is neither isolated nor extreme. Another case—this time in medicine—makes the mechanism plain. In 2019, researchers at the University of Chicago and Emory University revealed that a widely used U.S. hospital risk-prediction model had been skewed by a proxy embedded years earlier. The system estimated patients' future health needs using historical healthcare expenditure. Black patients, who had historically received less investment in preventative care, were systematically underestimated by the model. The distortion was measurable: among patients with the same clinical profile, Black patients were nearly twice as likely to be rated "lower risk". The data carried sediment—decades of under-treatment—and the model faithfully reproduced it. The dataset did not reflect physiological difference; it reflected social history rendered as digits.

To name this phenomenon precisely: datasets cannot be separated from the institutional incentives that produce them. Sampling frames—where data are collected, whose cases are recorded, which events trigger entries—carry implicit priorities. A police department that logs every street encounter but not every positive interaction produces a skewed dataset of suspicion. A hospital that records only electronic interactions and not informal caregiving misses the texture of support that shapes recovery. A university admissions office that retains detailed data on applicants who accept places but not on those who never apply inadvertently encodes aspiration gaps into its notion of "qualified candidates". The sampling frame becomes the world.

Labelling incentives add another layer of sediment. Labels are not descriptive in a neutral sense; they are the product of judgement under conditions of speed, fatigue, organisational pressure, or policy. Consider the 2014 revelations surrounding Amazon's Mechanical Turk workforce, where annotators labelling emotion in social-media posts often relied on keyword heuristics rather than full-context interpretation. If annotators repeatedly marked posts containing certain slang terms as "toxic", regardless of speaker identity or tone, those labels harden into training data. When models trained on these labels begin flagging content from certain communities at higher rates, organisations may blame the model. The deeper story sits in the label incentives: workers were rewarded for volume, not nuance. The sediment thickened.

A credible counter-example tempers the fatalism. The UK Biobank, founded in 2006 and based in Stockport, represents one of the most carefully curated population datasets in biomedical research. Its protocols require detailed provenance documentation, continuous consent processes, and strict sampling guidelines. Analysts know precisely how each measurement was captured. Yet the dataset still exhibits demographic skew—overrepresentation of healthier, wealthier volunteers. Even with rigorous protocols, sediment remains. The reconciliation lies not in erasing sediment but in recognising its weight. Bias persists even in gold-standard datasets; what changes is our ability to measure it.

To grasp the full implications of sediment, consider how it shapes model behaviour. When a model ingests skewed data, it does not merely reflect history; it magnifies its patterns. A predictive-policing algorithm trained on historical arrest data does not "find" crime; it finds where arrests occurred. A credit-scoring system trained on past loan decisions does not "infer" capacity; it infers where banks historically extended trust. A triage tool trained on incomplete medical notes does not "understand" severity; it understands what clinicians wrote when under time pressure. The model becomes a mirror with memory, incapable of forgetting the conditions under which the data were born.

Take London's 2012–2017 experiment with gang databases, administered by the Metropolitan Police. Entries were often based on association rather than activity. When researchers later cross-referenced the database with crime statistics, they found that many flagged individuals had no serious offences. Yet because the database fed into risk assessments for policing operations, the sediment of past suspicion shaped future enforcement. Officers were more likely to stop those flagged; those stops generated new entries; the loop deepened. The dataset shaped behaviour as much as behaviour shaped the dataset.

The motif returns here with new resonance: sediment not only settles; it circulates. It is picked up by models, recast in numerical form, and redeposited into decision-making environments. Sediment becomes structure.

Yet there are moments when sediment is challenged, even disrupted. In 2018, the Los Angeles Police Department curtailed several data-driven predictive programmes after a review by the Office of the

Inspector General revealed that the underlying data disproportionately reflected patrol patterns rather than independent crime reports. The decision itself is a counter-example: institutions can choose to see sediment and refuse to encode it further. The limitation is that such choices require political will. Without institutional courage, datasets slip quickly into the comfortable fiction of neutrality.

We must now consider how sediment shapes not only what is present in the data but also what is absent. Absence is a form of bias as potent as distortion. If specific communities under-report crimes because of mistrust, the dataset underrepresents harm. If rural clinics lack digital infrastructure, epidemiological models underrepresent illness. If marginalised groups' speech patterns are under-sampled, language models misclassify them. The invisibility embedded in datasets becomes misclassified behaviour, unjust suspicion, or withheld benefits.

One striking example arises from the 2020 deployment of automated hiring systems across multinational firms. Several tools learned from historical resumes that candidates from elite universities were more likely to be hired. Because applications from those universities were meticulously recorded, and because graduate outcomes created a feedback loop of success, the sampling frame amplified prestige. Candidates from community colleges or career-transition backgrounds—rare in the training data—were often mis-ranked. The absence became a decision.

Reading datasets through their sediment demands a shift from accepting data as givens to interrogating them as artefacts. It transforms questions like "Is this dataset representative?" into "Representative of what history?" It reframes discussions of "data quality" into inquiries about "data lineage". And it reveals that fairness cannot be bolted on at the modelling stage if the sediment beneath the dataset remains unexamined.

This leads to a broader implication: confronting bias requires confronting the institutions that produce data. If a policing dataset shows disproportionate stops, the model is not the origin of inequity; the institution is. If a healthcare dataset reflects uneven access, the model is not the agent of discrimination; the healthcare system is. Models inherit what institutions inscribe. Sediment does not lie.

As we turn towards the analytic tools that attempt to correct these patterns—counterfactual testing, subgroup analysis, scenario modelling—another tension emerges. Correction can only operate on what is visible. Sediment that never made it into the dataset cannot be statistically corrected away. Historical absences require structural change, not calibration.

And so we end with the question any responsible practitioner must ask before training begins: what layers of sediment am I about to encode into the future, and which layers must be disrupted rather than modelled?

Model choice and moral effect

On 22 October 2019, the U.S. Food and Drug Administration released an alert concerning a commercial breast-cancer diagnostic tool deployed across several hospitals in New York State. The system, built on a dense convolutional architecture, had been selected for its impressive performance on historical imaging benchmarks. Yet when clinicians at Montefiore Medical Center reviewed cases flagged by the model, they noticed a troubling pattern: the system consistently under-prioritised scans from younger Black women. A simpler logistic model trialled during procurement had shown lower overall accuracy, but its decision pathways were intelligible enough for radiologists to detect this disparity early. The choice of architecture—complex, high-performing, opaque—had masked a moral failure. Performance had won the procurement battle; interpretability had lost. Patients bore the cost.

The case landed with force because it exposed an uncomfortable truth about machine intelligence. Model selection is not a technical footnote. It is a moral decision, expressed mathematically. When an organisation chooses a model, it chooses not merely a set of optimisation routines but a worldview: what counts as evidence, what counts as explanation, and how humans can contest or understand the machine's judgement. Each architecture embodies a tension between clarity and complexity, stability and adaptability, legibility and reach. These tensions are not neutral trade-offs; they shape whose lives are made legible to the system and whose are rendered opaque.

A second scene, this time in the Netherlands, shows the opposite tension. In 2020 the Dutch District Court in The Hague ruled against the government's SyRI fraud-prediction system, which used layered classifiers to flag households for welfare inspections. The architecture, combining multiple data sources with ensemble techniques, produced risk scores that caseworkers found impossible to interpret. Residents could not challenge the basis of the suspicion. Privacy activists could not audit the esoteric weighting structure. A simpler scoring model had been considered during early design meetings in Rotterdam in 2014, but the engineering team argued for the ensemble's predictive edge. In court, that edge became a liability. The architecture itself was ruled incompatible with the right to private life. The system did not fail because it was inaccurate; it failed because it was inscrutable.

Both cases illuminate the same motif: *the hinge*. Model architecture is a hinge between technical aspiration and moral consequence. When a system opens towards interpretability, it affords scrutiny. When it closes towards opacity, it demands trust without evidence. And trust without evidence is rarely trust at all.

To understand why architecture carries moral effect, we must first see how models embody epistemic assumptions. A linear model assumes proportionality and independence; it treats the world as if relationships were stable and additive. A random forest assumes that patterns are best captured through many weak learners voting collectively. A deep neural network assumes that structure lies buried in high-dimensional representations that humans cannot easily comprehend. Show these assumptions in action and their ethical impact becomes clear. Name them, and you see their lineage in scientific traditions. Explain them, and the moral stakes surface: autonomy, auditability, contestability. The implication is simple but rarely acknowledged—when you choose a model, you choose which truths are discoverable.

Consider the 2021 audit of a large UK retail bank's mortgage-approval system. Analysts compared three candidate models: a transparent scoring model, a gradient-boosting machine (GBM), and a deep feedforward network. The GBM achieved the lowest default prediction error. The feedforward network captured subtle nonlinearities in applicant behaviour during economic stress. But the scoring model, although less predictive, allowed compliance teams to trace denials to specific variables and thresholds. When viewed through the bank's regulatory obligations under the Equality Act 2010, the decision shifted. The compliance director, Sarah Patel, argued in a November 2021 committee meeting that the GBM's marginal performance gain could not justify the opacity of its feature interactions. The bank adopted the simpler model. Here the hinge opened towards legibility.

Architecture also encodes risk preferences. Systems that prioritise interpretability accept a performance ceiling; systems that maximise performance accept a transparency deficit. The moral effect emerges when these preferences collide with real-world consequences. A medical triage model that misclassifies a patient because its decision boundary cannot be explained breaches the duty of care. A job-matching model that buries its weighting scheme inside thousands of learned parameters leaves applicants with no avenue to understand or contest their rejection. In both cases, the architecture dictates the quality of redress.

A credible counter-example complicates the narrative. The 2018 deployment of a deep-learning-based skin-cancer detection tool by researchers at Stanford University demonstrated that high-performing models can, with careful design, preserve avenues for contestability. The team implemented saliency maps—visual heatmaps indicating which features influenced a classification. These maps did not provide full interpretability, but they offered clinicians a foothold. The limitation was obvious: saliency maps can mislead by highlighting spurious correlations. Yet clinicians reported that the feature attribution, however imperfect, helped them identify when the model relied on artefacts such as dark rulers in images. The hinge neither fully closed nor fully opened; it rested in a precarious but functional middle.

Reconciling these examples demands a more rigorous framework for model selection—one that recognises architecture as a moral instrument. Organisations often rely on ad hoc heuristics such as "use the simplest model that works" or "favour accuracy above all." These heuristics collapse under the weight of real complexity. A defensible rubric must evaluate models along multiple axes: interpretability, stability, verifiability, performance under distribution shift, susceptibility to gaming, and compatibility with domain-specific duties. Each axis corresponds to a visible behaviour or measurable property: explanation length, parameter sensitivity, audit traceability, error variance under stress tests.

Interpretability is material, not conceptual. A model that requires forty variables and complex interactions to justify a decision produces explanations that are technically correct yet practically useless. Auditors cannot interrogate them; citizens cannot understand them; regulators cannot enforce oversight. Thus, interpretability must be evaluated in relation to the audience who needs to scrutinise the model. A credit applicant deserves a reason they can grasp. A clinician deserves a signal they can challenge. A regulator deserves a structure they can audit.

Stability concerns how a model behaves when inputs shift slightly. A deep model may produce volatile outputs for minor data changes. A logistic model may degrade gracefully. When a system affects liberty, livelihood, or life, graceful degradation is a moral requirement. Stability turns architecture into ethics.

Verifiability concerns whether an organisation can meaningfully re-test a model against new evidence. Ensemble models with hundreds of trees can be re-run against drift indicators, but the non-linear interactions make interpretive verification difficult. Models with explicit constraints—monotonicity, fairness penalties—offer clearer paths for checking compliance. Verifiability turns architecture into governance.

These axes must sit within a coherent selection rubric. The hinge motif helps here: models should be chosen based on how they balance openness and closure. An architecture that remains open enough for humans to intervene, audit, and understand is ethically preferable when decisions affect rights or dignity. An architecture that closes around performance may be justified in low-stakes contexts where optimisation yields clear benefits and risks remain bounded. Model choice becomes a moral calibration: how much closure can the domain tolerate?

To see this calibration in action, return to the Montefiore case. After the 2019 review, the hospital convened a joint committee of radiologists, ethicists, and engineers. They tested alternative architectures across interpretability and performance metrics. The eventually selected model—a constrained gradient-boosting system—sacrificed a small margin of accuracy relative to the original convolutional network but provided human-readable factor contributions for each prediction. Radiologists could inspect whether age, breast density, or image artefacts drove the classification. The hinge swung open towards accountability.

This calibration becomes even more significant in public-sector deployments, where decisions shape structural outcomes. When the city of Helsinki reviewed its welfare-risk algorithms in 2022, it adopted a set of architectural constraints requiring that any approved model provide instance-level explanations that a caseworker could defend. This requirement immediately ruled out several high-performing deep architectures. The city accepted the trade-off. The system's authority had to be legible.

Yet trade-offs are not always clean. Sometimes the domain requires performance and interpretability, and no single architecture satisfies both. Autonomous vehicles embody this tension: models need high-dimensional representations to react in real time, yet regulators need interpretable structures to adjudicate collisions. Here, hybrid architectures—deep models paired with symbolic rule-checkers—offer partial relief. But hybrid systems introduce complexity and new failure modes. The hinge grows heavier.

This subchapter has traced one central claim: model architecture carries moral effect because it structures what humans can know, contest, and repair. Performance metrics alone cannot capture these consequences. To choose a model responsibly, an organisation must confront a final question that no benchmark can answer: when the hinge is forced to swing—towards legibility or towards opacity—which direction protects the people the system will govern?

Counterfactual testing for fairness

In May 2019, the Financial Conduct Authority (FCA) conducted a quiet audit of a major UK retail bank's loan-approval system. Analysts began with a simple question: *What happens if an applicant's gender is changed while every financial variable stays constant?* The model was not permitted to use gender explicitly, and compliance officers were confident the system met regulatory standards. Yet the counterfactual tests told another story. When "Sarah" became "Sam"—same income, same credit history, same postcode—approval odds shifted by a measurable margin. The shift was small in absolute terms but consistent across thousands of synthetic pairs. Nothing illegal had occurred; the system simply captured and reproduced correlations from historical lending behaviour. The model followed the data. The data followed the past. And the past was uneven.

That moment forced the bank to confront a truth that had lived in plain sight: a model can satisfy every formal requirement and still behave unfairly. The tension did not arise because of malice or negligence. It arose because the model had never been asked the right questions. Counterfactual testing became the question that pierced the surface.

A contrasting example, five years earlier, had already shown how such questions can prevent harm. In 2014, the Danish Agency for Labour Market and Recruitment (STAR) piloted a risk-scoring system to identify jobseekers who might need additional support. Before deployment in Copenhagen, researchers generated synthetic counterfactuals—altering attributes like age, disability status, and migration history while keeping employment trajectories constant. The model passed most tests but stumbled on one: applicants born outside Denmark faced a consistent penalty. Because this pattern surfaced early, the agency discarded the offending features and reran the model. The corrected version behaved differently. The counterfactuals changed its direction. This was not a technical improvement; it was a moral one. The hinge of fairness turned not on aspiration but on structured interrogation.

Both cases reveal the motif that threads through this subchapter: *the mirror that moves*. Counterfactual tests hold a mirror to the model, but unlike historical evaluation—which reflects only what happened—the counterfactual mirror reveals what **could** happen under small, controlled changes. It shows how the system behaves when nudged. It exposes the causal texture the model has learned, whether intended or not.

To understand why counterfactual testing carries such weight, we begin with its core logic: isolate one variable, hold everything else constant, and observe the shift in outcome. This design draws directly from philosophical and legal traditions that ask whether a person would have been treated differently "but for" a protected characteristic. Show the model that difference, name the pattern it reveals, explain its mechanism, and the implication becomes unavoidable: a system can discriminate without ever touching a prohibited attribute. Because attributes cluster in society—names with ethnic origin, postcodes with wealth, employment gaps with caregiving—the model infers the cluster even when the feature is removed. Counterfactuals cut through that veil.

The practice becomes more rigorous when paired with subgroup tests. Subgroup analysis measures how error rates or decision boundaries vary across demographic slices: for example, comparing false-negative rates for loan applications from Black women in Liverpool against those for white men in Reading. These are not abstract metrics; they are lived consequences. A higher false-negative rate means more unjust denials, fewer appeals granted, and reduced access to financial tools. Subgroup analysis shows the differential impact that global metrics obscure. A model boasting 92 per cent accuracy may hide the fact that it misclassifies specific groups at nearly double the average rate.

Real-world evidence illustrates this clearly. In 2018, the U.S. National Institute of Standards and Technology (NIST) completed a landmark evaluation of facial-recognition algorithms. Their tests, run across millions of images, demonstrated false-positive rates up to

100 times higher for certain demographic groups in specific algorithms. Here, subgroup testing did not merely add nuance. It inverted the conclusion: what looked like a performant model became an unreliable one the moment you asked who bore the errors.

Scenario testing extends this logic into the future. While counterfactual tests change one variable and subgroup tests compare across groups, scenario tests ask: *How would the model behave if the world changed?* They simulate conditions of stress—economic downturns, demographic shifts, migration surges, or clinical-pattern changes. Scenario testing matters because many systems fail not in stable conditions but at the margins. When a loans model is tested under recession simulations, default-risk estimators often shift non-uniformly. For example, in the FCA's 2019 audit, a scenario test on declining regional employment revealed a spike in false positives for self-employed applicants in northern cities. Historically, self-employed applicants had more volatile incomes; the recession simulation magnified that volatility. Without scenario tests, the model would have pushed hardship towards those already living on thinner margins.

A credible counter-example reveals the technique's limits. In 2021, a major insurer in Switzerland conducted counterfactual tests on a claims-fraud detection model. The tests suggested stability across gender and age groups. Yet post-deployment audits uncovered disparities driven not by individual attributes but by network patterns: claims linked to certain garages were flagged disproportionately because those garages historically serviced specific migrant communities. The counterfactual tests missed the pattern because they altered individual variables, not relational ones. The limitation matters. Fairness cannot be captured by individual counterfactuals alone. But the reconciliation is not to abandon the method—it is to widen the set of counterfactuals to include relational, contextual, and temporal variants. The mirror must be moved in more directions.

Returning to the motif, we see why "the mirror that moves" has structural importance. Models are trained on fixed datasets but act in dynamic worlds. Fairness cannot be measured once. It must be measured as movement—how decisions shift as circumstances shift. Counterfactuals, subgroups, and scenarios provide complementary angles: one reveals hidden influence, one reveals hidden burden, one reveals hidden fragility.

To integrate these techniques into a defensible practice, we must embed them within a rhythm of testing that aligns with system lifecycle. Consider the Dutch credit-scoring reform of 2022. Regulators required financial institutions to run quarterly counterfactual tests and semi-annual scenario tests, publishing summary disparity metrics. These metrics—approval-rate deltas, error-rate ratios, and stress-scenario drift—were not mere compliance artefacts. They became discussion tools for governance boards, guiding feature-engineering decisions. One committee member described the process succinctly: "The model tells one story. The counterfactuals tell the story behind it."

The visibility of behaviour matters. Every abstraction must tie back to something tangible: an approval, a denial, a waitlist, a triage flag, a police patrol, a benefits review. Counterfactuals show when a change in name shifts an approval. Subgroup tests show when a postcode shifts an inspection. Scenario tests show when a recession shifts hardship. These behaviours are measurable, and because they are measurable, they are governable.

Yet the most difficult question persists at the end: how often should a system be forced to look into this moving mirror? Too rarely, and disparities calcify. Too frequently, and the model becomes brittle, never settling into stability. Between these poles lies an ethical calibration. Every system requires its own rhythm, its own depth of interrogation, its own treatment of the counterfactual as a moral instrument.

So the unresolved tension remains: if a model behaves well under the conditions we can simulate, what responsibilities do we bear for the conditions we cannot yet imagine?

Care vs parity

In January 2021, NHS England reviewed mortality data from Covid-19 admissions across Manchester, Leeds, and Birmingham. The early-warning algorithm used to prioritise patients for escalation was formally "fair": it applied the same physiological thresholds to everyone. Yet clinicians at Salford Royal Hospital noticed a disturbing pattern. Patients with chronic respiratory illness—particularly those from long-deprived areas—were repeatedly flagged too late. When auditors compared outcomes, they found that patients with identical NEWS2 scores nonetheless faced sharply different risks depending on their baseline health. Equal thresholds produced unequal survival. The algorithm had treated everyone the same; this sameness translated into harm.

That contrast—between procedural parity and lived inequity—exposes the core tension of this subchapter. Parity appeals to our sense of justice. It promises symmetry, consistency, and protection from prejudice. But parity can also flatten difference. When individuals begin at different baselines, equal treatment preserves inequity rather than correcting it. Care, by contrast, adjusts to context. It recognises that fairness sometimes requires giving more attention where risk is higher, more time where complexity is deeper, and more resources where the margin of error is thinner. Care is asymmetrical by design. And in many domains, asymmetry prevents harm.

This tension between parity and care forms the quiet motif here: *the scale that bends*. A rigid scale treats every case as identical. A responsive scale bends towards those with greater vulnerability. Whether systems bend—or refuse to—shapes who is safeguarded and who is left exposed.

To see how this plays out in practice, begin with the hospital example. Show the mechanism: chronic illness alters baseline vitals. Name the source: early-warning protocols adopted across NHS England in 2017. Explain the result: when thresholds assume a uniform starting point, patients with chronic conditions appear deceptively "stable" until deterioration becomes severe. The implication is clear: parity can obscure need. A fairness metric that checks only whether the threshold applies equally cannot detect this structural mismatch. Care, by contrast, demands thresholds that adapt to known vulnerabilities.

This medical case has an analogue in criminal justice. In 2016, ProPublica examined COMPAS, a risk-assessment tool used in U.S. courts. A parity-based defence argued the system treated individuals identically: identical categories, identical weighting. But when researchers compared outcomes in Broward County, Florida, they found stark disparities. The false-positive rate for Black defendants—those predicted high-risk but who did not reoffend—was nearly twice that of white defendants. The model's parity hid a deeper asymmetry: different groups bore different burdens of error. The system applied the same formula yet distributed harm unequally. The scale appeared straight; its effects bent sharply.

Yet parity is not without value. A credible counter-example shows its protective force. In 2020, The Hague's District Court examined a welfare-risk algorithm used in Rotterdam. The system targeted claimants for fraud investigations using multiple socioeconomic variables. Critics argued the model unfairly concentrated scrutiny on migrant communities. But the court also saw the value of parity: the city's policies had explicitly forbidden the use of nationality, language, and religion. The parity rule prevented direct discrimination. Its limitation was incomplete implementation, not flawed principle. The reconciliation lies in recognising that parity prevents certain harms, but cannot alone guarantee just outcomes.

The next step is to distinguish the behaviours that reveal the limits of parity. In healthcare, delayed escalation. In lending, unjust denials. In policing, disproportionate stops. In hiring, under-selection of candidates from non-traditional paths. Each of these emerges from a model that treats unequal histories as though they were symmetric present conditions. A single threshold cannot account for chronic illness, socioeconomic precarity, or structural disadvantage. Care requires modelling these realities explicitly.

Consider the case of the UK's Social Metrics Commission, which in 2018 introduced a multidimensional poverty metric to replace the single-income threshold long used by government. Researchers found that identical income levels represented different lived experiences depending on disability, housing status, and childcare commitments. When the Commission modelled policy impacts using the old metric, the "equal treatment" masked heightened hardship for specific groups. The Commission's revised measure—incorporating depth of need, not just income parity—reshaped policy conversations. It bent the scale.

Care-based fairness becomes even more explicit in clinical triage. During the winter 2020 surge at King's College Hospital in London, clinicians adopted a contextualised triage approach. Rather than treating equal severity scores as equal need, they integrated frailty indices, comorbidity profiles, and social-support indicators. This was not a return to subjective judgement but an acknowledgement that identical numbers do not reflect identical conditions. The decisions became more labour-intensive, yet survival rates among high-risk groups improved. Care required effort. Parity required none.

The theoretical scaffolding behind care-based fairness draws from a simple recognition: risk is unevenly distributed. Exposure differs. Baselines differ. Opportunities differ. If fairness is defined solely as "treating equals equally", then justice depends entirely on how we determine who is "equal". If we ignore structural inequality, our equality is hollow.

Scenario testing further clarifies why care matters. Imagine a loan-approval model tested under recession conditions. Suppose that applicants with modest savings see a larger risk spike than those with accumulated assets. A parity-based fairness test might check whether the model applies equal thresholds for all. It would pass. But a care-based view asks a different question: which group is more vulnerable to false negatives during economic shock? The metric shifts from symmetry to sensitivity. Harm becomes measurable.

A second example shows this distinction in education. In 2019, researchers evaluating predictive models for student-support allocation at the University of Bristol compared parity-based algorithms with those incorporating care-based adjustments. Parity models treated identical test scores as identical likelihood of success. Care-based models factored in school-level deprivation and prior access to resources. The findings were stark: students from under-resourced schools benefited significantly when support was allocated using contextual measures. Parity preserved advantage; care redistributed opportunity.

Yet a limitation remains: care can be misapplied. When systems overfit contextual adjustments, they risk stereotyping individuals based on group-level history. A hypothetical fairness model in a hiring process that lowers thresholds automatically for certain demographics risks stripping applicants of individual agency. The tension is real. But it can be reconciled by distinguishing *contextualisation* from *presumption.* Care requires adding relevant information, not substituting group characteristics for personal merit. The scale must bend, not break.

Returning to the motif of *the scale that bends*, we can now see its significance. A fair system is not one that balances perfectly—an impossible ideal in asymmetric societies—but one that bends proportionately where harm concentrates. The bending is not an indulgence; it is a structural correction. Context becomes the counterweight that parity alone cannot supply.

The moral stakes heighten when applied to automated systems. Machine-learning models optimise for average performance unless instructed otherwise. Parity appears simpler to operationalise—equal thresholds, equal loss functions, equal constraints. But simplicity can become negligence. Care requires richer modelling, deeper domain knowledge, and explicit debate about harm.

Which brings us to the unresolved question that lies at the end of this subchapter: in domains where stakes differ wildly across individuals, how much bending should the scale permit before it ceases to be a scale at all?

Chapter 4
Accountability After Autonomy

The morning after an autonomous bus clipped a cyclist in Milton Keynes, the public briefing room filled long before the official statement began. Engineers from the operator arrived with charts of lidar ranges and braking curves; council officers carried procurement contracts; the manufacturer issued a carefully drafted note citing full regulatory compliance. Yet what the cyclist's family asked for was none of these. They wanted a story. They wanted to know how a chain of sensors, software, decisions, omissions, and silent assumptions had converged on a moment measured in milliseconds. They wanted an account that made sense of the intangible: why no human had been able to intervene, why no alert had sounded, why a system designed to reduce accidents had caused one. Only a narrative could deliver legitimacy. Statistics alone could not comfort or persuade.

That tension—between technical accuracy and narrative accountability—lies at the heart of this chapter. Autonomous systems increasingly act in spaces where explanations cannot rely on intuition. When a driver misjudges a corner, we understand it tacitly: fatigue, distraction, panic. But when a machine misjudges a corner, we demand something different. Not the raw metrics of misalignment or latency but a causal story that fits human reasoning. We want to know who chose the training data, who set the operating thresholds, who approved the model update, who failed to simulate the edge case. The desire is not vindictive. It is civic. It asks: *Whose agency touches the system at each point? Who shaped the decision that shaped the harm?*

As autonomy expands, this demand for intelligible causation grows sharper. We are no longer dealing with singular actors but with systems of layered intent—designers, product owners, compliance teams, procurement officers, field engineers, domain experts, and, ultimately, the models themselves, whose behaviour reflects thousands of micro-decisions that no single person can fully recall. When something goes wrong, no single actor "did it". Yet someone—or several someones—shaped the conditions under which the failure became possible. Accountability after autonomy is not about pinning blame on the nearest identifiable person; it is about reconstructing the web of responsibility in ways that society finds coherent and just.

Part of the difficulty is linguistic. Traditional responsibility language assumes a clean division between actor and action. Autonomous systems blur that division. Consider a recommender system that nudges a teenager towards harmful content. The platform may claim the model only reflects user preferences. The engineers may say the objective function was set by policy teams. The content moderators may insist they enforced the rules consistently. The result is a vacuum: harm without an author. That vacuum corrodes public trust. To maintain legitimacy, institutions must provide explanations that respect both the complexity of the system and the moral expectations of the public. This chapter seeks to illuminate the craft of that explanation.

At the core lies a simple observation: explanations that persuade are structured. They trace not only what happened, but how and why. This chapter begins by examining the anatomy of causal stories that people accept—stories that neither oversimplify nor drown audiences in technical minutiae. We explore what makes an explanation feel complete: the identification of pivotal choices, the translation of statistical pathways into human-understandable reasoning, and the articulation of uncertainty without evasion. In a world where autonomy can diffuse agency, clarity is not a courtesy; it is the means by which democratic oversight survives.

Yet narrative alone is insufficient. If we are to attribute responsibility in systems composed of many hands and few explicit signatures, we need new mapping tools. The chapter thus turns to shared responsibility maps—extensions of RACI frameworks adapted for machine-learning lifecycles. Unlike traditional charts that assign individuals to discrete tasks, these maps reveal overlapping responsibility zones: who owns labelling standards, who signs off deployment thresholds, who monitors drift, who manages incident escalation. The point is not to create bureaucratic artefacts but to illuminate paths of accountability that otherwise scatter into organisational haze. When harm occurs, these maps anchor causation. When harm has not yet occurred, they guide where vigilance is needed.

Closely tied to this is the architecture of incentives. Most accountability systems rely on ex-post blame—itself a blunt and often counterproductive tool. The chapter introduces the more productive notion of ex-ante incentives: performance bonds that require developers to internalise potential harms before deployment; safety cases that force organisations to articulate how risks have been mitigated; operating licences tied not only to accuracy metrics but to explainability, redress mechanisms, and long-term monitoring. These mechanisms do not replace moral judgement; they scaffold it. They shift accountability from an act of retrospective punishment to one of prospective responsibility.

But even these structures cannot eliminate failure, nor should they pretend to. Complex systems fail. They fail spectacularly, as in the case of Boeing's MCAS system; they fail quietly, as in hospital triage algorithms that mis-rank minority patients; they fail slowly, as in predictive tools that drift from their original calibration. The ethical question is not merely how to prevent failure, but how to learn from it without paralysing innovation or silencing whistleblowers. This chapter therefore ends with a focus on safe learning: establishing near-miss registries, encouraging protected disclosure, sharing de-identified incident patterns across sectors, and borrowing practices from aviation's long-standing safety culture. If autonomy introduces new risks, it must also inspire new modes of institutional humility.

Throughout this introduction, a subtle motif threads itself through the arguments: *the ledger*. Autonomous systems leave trails—data logs, audit traces, design documents, decision records. These trails can illuminate or obscure, depending on how they are kept and how they are interpreted. Causal stories, responsibility maps, incentives, and learning loops are all parts of the same endeavour: to ensure the ledger remains legible. A legible ledger does not eliminate failure, but it transforms failure from a private catastrophe into a public resource.

So the path ahead is both technical and moral. It asks us to design systems whose accountability does not vanish the moment autonomy begins. It asks whether our institutions can remain answerable in an age when decisions are co-produced by humans and machines. And it leaves a question hanging—one that will guide the chapter's unfolding: when responsibility disperses across a system, what form of accountability can still be recognised as just?

Causal stories people accept

At 7:18 a.m. on 14 February 2020, a diagnostic support system at the Royal Free Hospital in London produced an assessment that would become the centre of a national review. A patient presenting with chest discomfort was triaged as "low priority", a decision the attending clinicians trusted because the system had been deployed only three months earlier with strong validation results. Within two hours the patient suffered a cardiac arrest. The post-incident investigation—launched by NHS Digital in March of that year—confirmed the model's probability estimates were technically accurate; the inputs were processed correctly; no thresholds were breached. The system functioned as designed. Yet the patient died. And when the hospital briefed the family, the explanation—"the model returned a risk score that did not meet the escalation criteria"—felt like no explanation at all. Grief refused the abstraction. The family wanted a story with actors, motives, turning points, and avoidable forks in the road. They wanted to know *why*.

This opening scene captures the motif that threads through the subchapter: *the bridge*. Causal stories act as the bridge between technical truth and social understanding. Without a bridge, technical accounts remain stranded on one side, unintelligible to those who must live with the consequences. With a bridge, facts can travel into meaning. And meaning is what the public demands when autonomous or semi-autonomous systems fail. The statistics may be flawless. The outcome may be explicable in code. But legitimacy rests on whether people can understand the sequence that led to harm.

To see why this is so, we must start with the human search for narrative coherence. When a machine-driven incident occurs, individuals instinctively reach beyond the model's outputs towards an account that ties together intentions, conditions, and choices. We want to know who shaped the data used in training, who approved the thresholds, who monitored drift, and who noticed the early warning signs. Show this instinct in action: during the Royal Free review, investigators found clinicians repeatedly described their frustration not with the model's number but with the absence of a coherent causal chain. Name the phenomenon: narrative legitimacy. Explain its power: legitimacy depends less on technical correctness than on whether affected people can follow the logic from antecedent to outcome. The implication is direct: institutions that provide only metrics when harm occurs invite mistrust.

Causal stories differ from raw explanations. Raw explanations state what happened. Causal stories describe *why* it happened in a form humans find intelligible. Consider the Boeing 737 MAX crashes in 2018 and 2019. The official accident reports from Indonesia's KNKT and Ethiopia's AAIB laid out sensor errors, MCAS activations, control inputs, and flight-path deviations. But for families and the public, these reports only became compelling when woven into a coherent arc: an automated system repeatedly trimmed the nose down; pilots tried to counteract it; the system overruled those attempts; a design assumption about a single sensor introduced hidden fragility. The narrative did not simplify the facts—it organised them. Without this organisation, the causal chain felt like scattered fragments.

A contrasting example demonstrates the limits of purely statistical causal accounts. In 2021, after an autonomous vehicle in Arizona struck a pedestrian during low-light conditions, the manufacturer released a detailed timeline: object detected at 1.2 seconds; classification switched from "unknown" to "bicycle"; path prediction updated at 0.9 seconds; brakes applied at 0.5 seconds. The intervals were precise, but the causal structure was opaque. Why did classification oscillate? Why was emergency braking delayed? Why did the safety driver fail to intervene? The explanation lacked moral shape. The numbers offered little comprehension. The public demanded a narrative, not a stopwatch.

Yet narrative is not merely a communication tool; it is a governance tool. When investigators reconstruct incidents, they need more than logs. They need to trace choices made long before the event. This is where causal structure becomes invaluable. A credible counter-example shows why. In 2017, a Nordic telecommunications firm deployed a fraud-detection model that flagged thousands of legitimate accounts as suspicious. The model was accurate under test conditions, but post-deployment drift distorted its predictions. A statistical explanation—"distribution shift exceeded acceptable thresholds"—was technically correct. But employees accepted the deeper causal story: procurement teams had rushed deployment; monitoring responsibilities were unclear; training data underrepresented legitimate high-volume users. The narrative did not absolve anyone, yet it allowed the organisation to identify the locus of repair. The reconciliatory force of causal stories lies in their ability to bind technical facts to human responsibility.

Returning to the motif of *the bridge*, we now see why causal stories must span two banks: the bank of computational detail and the bank of human comprehension. The bridge must be strong enough to carry accountability, yet flexible enough to capture complexity without distortion. This dual requirement shapes the structure of credible post-incident explanations.

Such explanations should begin with context: the conditions in which the system operated at the time of failure. This includes environmental factors, sensor states, recent updates, and known anomalies. Then comes the identification of pivotal choices: decisions made by teams—data scientists, clinicians, operators, regulators—that shaped system behaviour. Next is the mechanical sequence: what the system registered, how it processed it, when it triggered intermediate states, and what thresholds governed its outputs. Finally, the narrative must reveal the interaction between human and machine—how an operator interpreted alerts, whether a clinician overrode a score, whether oversight failed to catch drift.

To illustrate the structure, consider again the Royal Free case. A satisfactory causal story would identify that the system was trained on datasets underrepresenting atypical cardiac presentations; that the decision threshold had been calibrated for general populations rather than high-risk subgroups; that audit processes had not yet flagged this bias because incidents were still rare; and that clinicians relied on the model because early deployments had performed well. The story does not hide uncertainty. It acknowledges it. And that acknowledgement is what makes it credible.

But causal stories must also resist oversimplification. A temptation emerges after every incident: to collapse responsibility into a single cause—"the model failed", "the operator erred", "the data were flawed". These explanations are narratively satisfying yet epistemically false. Complex systems rarely fail for a single reason. More often they fail because multiple defences weaken at once. In aviation, this lesson was codified after Tenerife (1977), when analysts recognised that stories of pilot error missed the larger system of miscommunication, fog, radio interference, and scheduling pressure. The history matters because post-incident structures borrowed from aviation—blameless reporting, detailed reconstructions, systemic accountability—remain the most successful templates for sectors now deploying AI.

Nonetheless, a tension persists. If the causal story becomes too intricate, the public may suspect obfuscation. If it becomes too simple, experts may deem it inaccurate. The bridge can tilt. The craft lies in striking a balance: detail without drowning, coherence without reduction.

The stakes of getting this right grow sharper as autonomy increases. When a human driver makes a mistake, the story is immediately legible. When an algorithm makes a mistake through interactions between drift, objective functions, and thresholding logic, the causal chain becomes more distant from lay intuition. The public must still be able to understand. Democracy depends on this. Accountability mechanisms must therefore incorporate narrative competence, not just statistical rigour.

This brings us to the forward tension. As autonomous systems become more embedded in public life, what form should post-incident explanations take to remain both truthful and acceptable? Should organisations pre-commit to explanation structures, specifying in advance how they will narrate failures? Or should causal stories evolve organically, shaped by each incident's context?

Shared responsibility maps

At 9:42 a.m. on 3 May 2021, a quality audit at King's College Hospital in London revealed a troubling pattern inside its radiology triage pipeline. A machine-learning model—introduced in late 2020 to flag suspected intracranial bleeds—had been performing within its validated accuracy range, yet a subset of urgent cases was consistently delayed. The logs showed no breaches. Clinicians had acted on alerts as expected. But the cross-functional review surfaced an unexpected gap: no single team owned responsibility for the *labelling standard* used during model retraining, and no one clearly owned the *deployment threshold* that determined which cases were escalated. Data engineering assumed clinical governance had set the threshold. Clinical governance assumed data science had taken responsibility. And data science assumed operations held final authority. Three teams, three maps, none aligned. The harm was subtle: minutes added to pathways that could not afford them. The cause was structural. Responsibility had dissolved into the spaces between roles.

Scenes like this expose a quiet truth about sociotechnical systems. It is not malevolence that creates risk but misalignment. When an autonomous or semi-autonomous system acts, it draws together work from dozens of hands—labellers, modellers, interface designers, procurement officers, deployment engineers, clinicians, contract managers—each operating within the narrow frame of their tasks. We often speak about accountability as if it were attached to single actors. Yet the reality is closer to a mosaic: a thousand tessellated pieces that form a picture none of their creators fully see. The motif that surfaces here—*the seam*—is crucial. It is at the seams between teams, vendors, and regulators that harms incubate. It is also at the seams that responsibility must be mapped if accountability is to mean anything more than vague post-hoc blame.

Responsibility mapping is hardly new. The RACI matrix—Responsible, Accountable, Consulted, Informed—dates back to project-management doctrines of the 1980s. Its endurance owes to its simplicity: it forces clarity. But clarity in conventional projects is a far smaller challenge than clarity across the AI lifecycle, where decisions span years, abstractions accumulate, and operational effects emerge only after deployment. To show this complexity, consider the King's College Hospital review. Name the issue precisely: fractured ownership. Explain it: each team believed another had ultimate authority, and because the process lacked a single definitive responsibility map, silent assumptions filled the void. The implication is stark: without explicit mapping, distributed systems drift into responsibility vacuums.

A second example makes the pattern unmistakable. In January 2022, the city of Amsterdam completed an investigation into its welfare-fraud risk model, used between 2014 and 2020 to allocate inspection resources. The model itself was not inherently discriminatory; its architecture was relatively simple. The failure emerged because data provenance was not owned by any single team, threshold adjustments were approved informally by line managers, and monitoring duties were spread across three departments with no shared escalation protocol. When residents challenged their unfair risk scores, officials could not produce a coherent responsibility chain. Each department owned a fragment, but no department owned the whole. This is responsibility by diffusion, and it erodes trust as surely as biased data.

A credible counter-example helps ground the analysis. The Danish Patient Safety Authority, tasked with monitoring clinical decision support tools across 16 hospitals, adopted a unified responsibility framework in 2018. It explicitly mapped who owned labelling criteria, who set deployment thresholds, who monitored drift, and who approved overrides during anomalies. This did not eliminate failure. It did, however, make incidents more traceable. When a dosage-recommendation model briefly increased error rates in 2019 due to an interface update, investigators reconstructed the causal chain within days. The limitation is clear: mapping alone cannot prevent harm. Yet it prevents confusion becoming harm's amplifier. Reconciling the counter-example reminds us that clarity does not guarantee perfection; it guarantees intelligibility.

Responsibility maps work because they force articulation of decisions usually left tacit. Take the abstraction *risk ownership*. Paired with behaviour, it becomes concrete: which team commits to reviewing threshold distributions weekly? Which team commits to measuring drift against seasonal clinical patterns? Which team commits to approving emergency rollback? If a system retrains monthly, who signs off the updated labelling guides? These details, often relegated to local convention, determine whether accountability survives real pressure.

The motif of *the seam* reappears in the vendor relationship. Modern AI systems seldom rely solely on internal components. A hospital acquires a model from one vendor, integrates it with a sensor API from another, and wraps it in interfaces built by a third contractor. Where does responsibility sit when a fault arises? Without an explicit map, each vendor explains away its layer: "Our model performed as specified"; "Our API returned correct datapoints"; "Our interface displayed the score." These statements may be accurate but socially meaningless. What matters is the seam: the connection between layers. Responsibility mapping must therefore specify who is accountable for integration risks, who evaluates version incompatibilities, and who sets minimum data quality thresholds for third-party inputs.

But responsibility is not merely an operational concept. It is moral architecture. When organisations map responsibility, they do more than assign tasks: they declare what they consider ethically non-negotiable. In critical systems—medical devices, fintech underwriting, autonomous mobility—mapping determines whose judgement constrains the machine and whose silence permits drift. The example of Amsterdam demonstrates what occurs when moral architecture is implicit rather than explicit. Disadvantaged residents bore the burden of silent choices made years earlier by teams who never imagined themselves authors of harm.

A deeper layer emerges when we examine labelling standards. Labelling is often treated as low-status work, outsourced or delegated without rigorous oversight. Yet labelling incentives shape the ground truth upon which entire systems rest. Show: in 2018, the U.S. Department of Justice examined predictive policing tools used in Chicago between 2012 and 2017. Name the mechanism: training data encoded historical patrol practices rather than objective crime rates. Explain: because no single team owned labelling integrity, systemic biases entered silently. Implication: responsibility for labelling is a central moral decision, not an administrative footnote. Mapping must reflect this.

Threshold decisions are equally technical and ethical. A deployment threshold of 0.72 rather than 0.68 may alter false-positive rates by hundreds of cases per month. Who owns that threshold? Who evaluates its performance quarterly? Who authorises adjustments during unexpected surges? These are not questions of engineering alone; they are questions of justice, workload, and public trust. Responsibility maps force teams to specify who holds the pen.

At this point, a limitation must be acknowledged: responsibility maps risk becoming performative artefacts—tidy matrices that satisfy governance reviews but exert little influence on daily practice. Reconciliation requires embedding mapping into rhythms: sprint reviews, clinical governance meetings, model-update cycles, procurement reviews. When mapping becomes a living document rather than a static checklist, it constrains behaviour in meaningful ways. The difference between policy and practice is attention. A responsibility map draws attention to the seam.

To bind these insights, return to the motif. The seam—where components meet, where teams intersect, where governance falters—is also where accountability must be stitched most tightly. Every distributed system lives or dies by its seams. Responsibility mapping is the stitching. It is slow work. It is seldom glamorous. But without it, no organisation can credibly claim that harms were unavoidable. With it, organisations at least demonstrate that they understood the system they built, not merely the part they touched.

This leads to the forward tension. As AI systems become more modular, more outsourced, more entangled with public infrastructure, how far should responsibility mapping extend? Should maps encompass upstream data suppliers, cloud providers, interface designers, and regulators? Or should they remain bounded within organisational perimeters?

Sanctions and incentives

At 2:15 p.m. on 29 October 2018, the Indonesian accident investigation agency, KNKT, released preliminary findings on Lion Air Flight 610. The report named a single point of fragility in the Boeing 737 MAX: the MCAS stabilisation system relied on one angle-of-attack sensor. Boeing had passed regulatory checks; certification paperwork was complete; the design had formally complied with existing requirements. Yet 189 people died. What the report hinted—without fully resolving—was a deeper question: why had Boeing been allowed to proceed with a design that introduced such concentrated risk? The paperwork had met every rule, but the incentives had rewarded speed, not caution. The price of that misalignment was paid in lives.

This scene exposes the motif that will thread quietly through this subchapter: *the wager*. Every autonomous system, from clinical triage models to mobility algorithms, requires its makers to place wagers—bets on what failure modes are acceptable, what deployment thresholds are tolerable, what safety margins can be shaved to win speed or efficiency. If accountability mechanisms rely solely on ex-post blame, the wager is cheap. If nothing material changes until after an incident, the system silently absorbs risk without structural correction. A credible accountability regime must shift the calculus: organisations must face meaningful consequences *before* harm occurs, not merely recount lessons after it does.

The traditional posture of regulation plays a familiar chord: set rules, audit against them, and punish when violations appear. But autonomous systems slip through the gaps. They can comply perfectly with process requirements while still generating unacceptable outcomes—a truth made painfully visible during the 2020 Dutch childcare benefits scandal, where an automated fraud-detection system, deployed by the Tax and Customs Administration in The Hague, operated within its policy parameters yet disproportionately targeted minority families. When Parliament launched an inquiry in December 2020, officials insisted that each step of the process had followed the rules. That was the problem. Procedural compliance had replaced substantive responsibility. The wager had been mispriced: harm was cheap, and correction came only after public outrage.

To shift this dynamic, we must examine sanctions and incentives as tools for reshaping organisational behaviour. Show this through a concrete example: in 2017, Transport for London introduced a performance-bond mechanism for contractors responsible for signalling upgrades. The bond—held in escrow—would be forfeited if system availability dropped below agreed thresholds. Name the mechanism: ex-ante economic commitment. Explain its logic: the contractor accepted financial exposure upfront, aligning its incentives with safety and reliability rather than minimum compliance. The implication is instructive: organisations change behaviour when failure becomes costly *before* it manifests.

A second example demonstrates how safety cases transform incentives. The concept, originating in the UK nuclear industry in the 1970s and adapted into aviation in the 1990s, requires organisations to construct a structured argument demonstrating that a system is acceptably safe for its intended context. The safety case is not a checklist; it is an evidentiary narrative supported by tests, audits, failure-mode analyses, and operational controls. When NHS England mandated safety cases for high-risk clinical decision tools in 2018, it forced vendors and hospitals to articulate not just what a system did, but how it justified its safety. This requirement made the wager explicit. It also shifted incentives towards continuous monitoring, because safety claims must remain defensible over time.

A credible counter-example tempers this enthusiasm. In 2021, a major European fintech attached performance incentives to fraud-detection accuracy targets. Teams responded by tuning thresholds aggressively, reducing false positives but increasing undetected fraud. Revenue metrics improved; actual risk worsened. The incentive backfired. Reconciliation of this limitation reveals the deeper lesson: sanctions and incentives must be designed with system-wide guardrails. Misaligned incentives create new failure modes. Aligning them requires specifying what must never be traded away.

Consider the abstraction *risk*. Alone it is hollow. Paired with visible behaviour, it becomes operational. Who measures drift weekly? Who validates thresholds quarterly? Who commits to halting deployments when model monitoring flags anomalies? When incentives reward only throughput, teams will optimise throughput. When incentives reward early detection of anomalies, teams will inspect anomalies. This is why accountability regimes must specify not merely outcomes but the monitoring rhythms that sustain responsibility.

The motif of *the wager* returns when we examine procurement. Public bodies often acquire AI systems on fixed-price contracts with vague maintenance terms. This structure encourages vendors to minimise ongoing obligations. But when harms surface—biased triage, misclassification spikes—procurement teams discover they lack leverage. A more responsible structure would require vendors to post a performance bond tied to safety indicators: false-negative rates in clinical settings, near-miss reports in mobility contexts, or error margins in high-risk financial scoring. The bond ties financial exposure directly to system behaviour, rendering the wager more proportionate to potential harm.

Safety cases extend naturally from this. They require organisations to anticipate failure modes and demonstrate mitigation strategies. A credible safety case might include scenario analyses showing how a model behaves under sensor malfunction, sparse data, demographic shifts, or adversarial inputs. It compels teams to inspect seams between components: between data ingestion and model inference, between interface alerts and human overrides, between drift signals and escalation protocols. The implication is profound: safety cases force organisations to treat safety as a living obligation, not a static report.

Historical lessons reinforce this perspective. After the Clapham Junction rail crash in London in 1988, British Rail was required to adopt systematic safety justification methods. Investigators determined that the disaster stemmed not from a singular mistake but from lax oversight incentives that allowed wiring errors to persist. The public inquiry led by Anthony Hidden stressed structural accountability: organisations must feel pressure *before* their systems fail. That principle remains the bedrock of responsible AI governance.

The question, then, is how far sanctions should reach. Should they extend to executives, engineers, or regulators? Should fines scale with systemic risk or with the vulnerability of affected populations? These questions illustrate the need for proportionate sanctions. Overly punitive regimes can stifle innovation; overly lenient ones perpetuate irresponsibility. A balanced structure distinguishes between bad actors, negligent actors, and good actors facing unforeseeable problems. Precision is essential.

But sanctions alone do not build ethical systems. Incentives shape the daily habits that prevent harm. Teams behave differently when rewarded for identifying near-misses, not punished for reporting them. Organisations grow more competent when performance reviews credit safety improvements rather than throughput gains. In aviation, this principle underpins voluntary reporting schemes. Pilots report near misses without fear of sanction, enabling the system to learn from almost-failures rather than real failures. When adapted to AI, near-miss registries could surface subtle issues: erratic inputs to clinical models, ambiguous user-interface signals, or unexpected sensor drift. Incentives to report create the informational substrate on which safety depends.

Yet every incentive carries risk. Make near-miss reporting too central, and teams may inflate minor anomalies to appear diligent. Tie bonuses to fairness metrics, and teams may select easy wins over hard structural reform. The wager remains. Organisations must design incentives with awareness of their unintended consequences.

This brings us to the forward test. As AI systems become more autonomous and more opaque, what combination of sanctions and incentives will ensure that accountability does not collapse into a spectacle of blame after harm has already occurred? Should we require performance bonds for all high-risk deployments? Should safety cases become universal? Or should we design hybrid models, combining financial exposure with mandatory operational transparency?

Learning from failure safely

In 1976, NASA opened a small office at Moffett Field in California with an unusual request to pilots: tell us about the mistakes that almost killed you, and we promise not to punish you for them. The Aviation Safety Reporting System (ASRS) invited confidential narratives of "near misses"—altitude deviations, misread clearances, wrong-runway line-ups—that never made the evening news because the flights landed safely. The flight landed without incident. Yet in those unremarkable outcomes, investigators found patterns that formal accident statistics could not reveal. The system's premise was radical for its time: if you want to prevent disasters, begin by listening to the people who barely avoided them, and protect those people when they speak.

Decades later, healthcare leaders in London and Leeds drew from the same playbook. The National Reporting and Learning System, launched by the NHS in 2003, encouraged clinicians to log incidents and near misses anonymously. A nurse who caught a medication error before administration, a junior doctor who noticed a confusing alert in an electronic record, a pharmacist who saw a barcode scanner misidentify a drug—all could file reports without fearing disciplinary action as long as there was no wilful misconduct. The result was not instant transformation. It was something more subtle: a gradual shift from "Who is to blame?" to "What can we learn?" That shift, fragile and contested, is the foundation on which any responsible regime for AI failure must rest.

The motif that runs quietly through this subchapter is *the almost-accident.* The almost-accident is where systems reveal their stress points without yet breaking. It is where the combination of machine output, human judgement, and organisational context misaligns, but fortune or vigilance prevents harm. We usually ignore these moments. They disappear into gossip or private worry. A learning system, by contrast, treats them as data. It records them. It studies them. It allows them to change design and policy before the next iteration of the same pattern ends badly.

To see why learning from failure requires safety, not just curiosity, we need to confront a simple fact: people do not disclose near misses into hostile systems. If an engineer fears career damage, the bug report will be softened or never filed. If a clinician believes that admitting an override of an AI recommendation will trigger litigation, the override will stay in her memory alone. If a contractor suspects that revealing a sensor glitch will jeopardise the next tender, the glitch will disappear into private notes. Show this dynamic, name it, and its corrosive logic becomes clear. Fear silences the almost-accident. Silence feeds repetition.

The Mid Staffordshire NHS Foundation Trust scandal in England during the 2000s, although not an AI case, illustrates the point. Mortality rates rose, complaints mounted, yet staff were discouraged from voicing concerns. Reporting channels existed on paper, but the culture around them was punitive. The near misses—patients found dehydrated, call bells unanswered, records incomplete—did not translate into systemic learning until public inquiry forced exposure. When organisations punish messengers, they forfeit the opportunity to learn early. The implication for AI is direct: as automated systems enter high-stakes domains, a punitive posture towards failure will quietly undermine safety.

By contrast, the aviation sector shows what protected disclosure can build over time. Pilots, air-traffic controllers, and maintenance engineers routinely send narratives to ASRS describing deviations that never reached the accident threshold: an unnoticed altitude bust corrected by a vigilant controller, a misinterpreted instruction resolved by a read-back, an automation mode misunderstood and then corrected. These reports are scrubbed of identifying details, then analysed and shared as "lessons learned" across airlines and manufacturers. A pilot in Seattle benefits from the almost-accident of a pilot in Miami. The system treats the near miss as a gift, not as ammunition.

Translating this idea to healthcare AI, and more broadly to algorithmic systems, means building near-miss registries that focus not on blame but on patterns. Imagine a hospital registry where any clinician can log incidents such as: "Triage model recommended discharge; patient admitted after human override," or "Image-analysis tool repeatedly flagged artefacts as pathology during evening shifts," or "Risk score dropped sharply after software update; clinical picture unchanged." Each entry would capture context—time, location, model version, override decision—without naming individuals. Over time, clusters would emerge: higher error rates at certain sites, recurring misclassifications for specific patient groups, drift associated with certain data feeds. The behaviour is visible: a spike in overrides, a rise in late escalations, a cluster of corrections from one ward. Those signals can trigger model review or interface redesign long before national statistics flag harm.

But near-miss registries alone are not enough if disclosure carries professional danger. Protected disclosure—legal and organisational—creates the conditions under which frontline staff and engineers will speak honestly. In the UK, the "freedom to speak up" guardians introduced after the Francis Report gave staff designated persons to approach with concerns. Extending that model to AI would mean giving data scientists, clinicians, and operations staff a channel to document algorithm-related worries without routing first through the teams that built or procured the system. If a radiologist suspects that an AI tool underperforms on darker skin tones, she should be able to raise that concern into an independent review process, not solely back to the vendor. Protection is not a soft concern; it is a structural requirement.

A credible counter-example adds nuance. In some financial institutions, internal whistleblowing hotlines exist, yet usage remains low. Post-scandal reviews—Wells Fargo's account fraud cases or manipulation of LIBOR rates—revealed that employees feared retaliation despite formal protections. Cultural reality outweighed policy text. The lesson for AI governance is that protected disclosure must be more than a clause in a handbook. It needs demonstrable follow-through: visible investigations, feedback to reporters, and the absence of career damage for those who raise honest alarms. Trust is a metric here: one can measure it in the number of near-miss entries, the diversity of reporters, the frequency with which reports lead to system changes.

The almost-accident motif returns when we consider how AI systems themselves can aid learning. Automated logs already record every inference, confidence score, and override. They know when their recommendation was followed and when it was ignored. If we treat human override not as disobedience but as a critical signal, we can mine these logs for patterns of disagreement. Where humans repeatedly override in one direction—always upgrading risk in a particular population, always downgrading a certain alert—the system is telling us something about its blind spots. A near-miss registry that integrates both human reports and machine logs becomes a rich substrate for learning.

However, there is a limit to what any registry can achieve if data are siloed. A hospital that learns internally from its AI-induced near misses still allows the same pattern to harm patients elsewhere if knowledge stays trapped. Aviation's safety regime circumvented this trap by creating centralised, anonymised repositories. Healthcare AI, and algorithmic systems more broadly, will need similar cross-institution mechanisms. A national or sectoral body could collect de-identified incident and near-miss reports, then publish aggregated patterns: model architectures associated with subtle drifts, interface designs linked with misunderstanding, procurement arrangements that consistently blur responsibility. The behaviour becomes sector-level: a reduction in repeated failure modes over years, fewer surprises when tools are deployed in new settings.

Yet no discussion of learning from failure is complete without acknowledging the tension between transparency and liability. Organisations fear that detailed disclosures will strengthen litigation against them or damage their reputation. Engineers fear that admitting uncertainty will be interpreted as incompetence. Clinicians worry that documenting an override will be second-guessed in court. This tension is not imaginary. It must be managed, not ignored.

One approach is to separate learning channels from punitive channels. Aviation's voluntary reporting systems generally protect reporters from enforcement action if they disclose promptly and honestly, except in cases of gross negligence or deliberate harm. Healthcare AI could adopt a similar bright line: protected near-miss reporting as a learning tool, distinct from formal investigations of wilful misconduct. Regulatory frameworks would need to specify that participation in such schemes counts as a mitigating factor, not an aggravating one. The trade-off is subtle: some marginal cases of culpable behaviour may receive gentler treatment, but the overall flow of safety information would increase.

Another tension lies in the risk of normalising failure. If every near miss is treated as routine, organisations may slip into complacency. "We caught it in time" can become a comforting mantra that masks the underlying hazard. To counter this, near-miss registries must be coupled with thresholds: when similar patterns recur beyond a certain number, escalation becomes mandatory. A surge in overrides, for example, could trigger an automatic technical review, the way clusters of hospital-acquired infections trigger clinical audits. Learning requires respect, not trivialisation.

It is also important to recognise that not all failures should be treated equally. Some represent inherent uncertainty in complex domains; others reveal clear design flaws or governance gaps. A triage model misclassifying a genuinely ambiguous case belongs to the first category. A model failing systematically for a specific population because that group was absent from training data belongs to the second. Near-miss analysis must therefore classify incidents, not merely count them. The metric is not raw volume; it is recurrence of preventable patterns.

Returning finally to the motif of *the almost-accident*, we can see why it matters so much for post-human ethics. In human-only systems, experience and memory live inside people: the nurse who remembers a near overdose, the driver who remembers a skid on black ice. As machines shoulder more decision-making, experience and memory migrate into logs, registries, and shared narratives. The moral question becomes: will we structure those memories so that they are accessible, analysable, and able to improve systems, or will we leave them buried in proprietary databases and unspoken fears?

The unresolved tension is sharper than it appears. When the next near miss occurs—a misranked scan, a misrouted shuttle, a mis-scored loan—will the person who catches it see a system that welcomes that knowledge or one that punishes it? And if they hesitate, how many almost-accidents will need to accumulate before one of them drops the "almost"?

Chapter 5
Interfaces that Make or Break Morality

The screen was small enough to fit in a coat pocket, yet its design rearranged an entire moral relationship. In April 2020, at a clinic in Manchester, a patient logged into a routine portal to check test results and found a quiet surprise: a new toggle labelled "Data Sharing Preferences," set—without ceremony—to *on*. The clinic had adopted an opt-out model for contributing anonymised records to a regional research network. Legally permissible. Operationally efficient. Yet the patient hesitated. Nothing about the interface was technically wrong; nothing breached consent law. Still, something felt unearned. A default had made a moral choice on his behalf. The dignity of deciding had been replaced by the convenience of preselection.

That small moment captures a wider truth. Interfaces are the stage upon which human–machine morality is enacted. They look trivial—shapes on glass, sliders, colours, timings—but they decide whether humans feel respected, pressured, misled, or empowered. They structure trust by structuring attention. They frame choices by framing what is visible. And they determine whether autonomy is something a system grants, or something it quietly takes away.

There is a second story worth holding in mind. In December 2021, a stroke ward in Glasgow introduced a decision-support model designed to predict secondary bleed risk. Clinicians agreed the model was promising, but soon stopped using its alerts. Not because the model was inaccurate, but because its interface communicated uncertainty through dense numerical confidence intervals that meant little during the rapid choreography of emergency care. The machine "spoke", but the humans could not hear it in time. The tool's failure was not mathematical. It was conversational. It did not understand what kind of uncertainty a clinician could absorb at 3 a.m. when a patient's condition was moving fast. Morality in machine systems is often reduced to abstractions—fairness, agency, transparency—but in practice it begins with something simpler: legibility.

This chapter turns toward these everyday touchpoints where moral decisions are domesticated into user flows, alerts, and defaults. It follows a thread running quietly through earlier chapters: the subtle asymmetry between procedural correctness and moral adequacy. Now that asymmetry reappears in a new form. A model may satisfy accuracy tests, a system may pass a safety case, but if its interface manipulates tacitly, obscures risk, or buries overrides beneath cognitive friction, its moral posture collapses. Interfaces operationalise values. They can protect dignity or erode it; enable self-determination or simulate it; honour caution or drown it beneath speed. Nowhere else in the sociotechnical stack are the consequences so intimate.

Defaults are the clearest example. They look negligible, yet set behavioural baselines that shape consent, participation, and trust. An opt-out data-sharing box feels administratively efficient, but it rewrites the moral predicate of consent: instead of earning agreement, the system assumes it. In digital health, mobility services, and algorithmic credit systems, defaults often carry the weight of unspoken priorities. What is deemed "on by default"? Who gains from that? Who bears the risk? Defaults discipline behaviour long before users make real choices. They are instruments of power disguised as convenience.

Beyond defaults lies the question of uncertainty—how machines communicate what they do not know. Human judgement has always lived alongside uncertainty. What changes in machine-mediated environments is the format of that uncertainty: probabilistic forecasts, confidence intervals, sensor reliability estimates, scenario likelihoods. These signals can empower when expressed in digestible ways, or they can overwhelm. A model may warn that a classification is "63% confident" or that a sensor is "operating outside expected bounds," but such numbers can mislead, reassure, or confuse depending on their translation into perceptual cues. Good interfaces treat uncertainty not as a defect, but as part of the moral contract: they show people where the machine's sight grows dim, and where human discernment must rise to meet it.

The motif of sight is useful here—*what the system sees, and how it shows us what it sees.* A clinician reviewing a risk score, a driver interpreting an autonomy alert, a loan officer evaluating a flagged application: in each scenario, the interface becomes the lens through which the human sees the machine seeing the world. When that lens distorts—by hiding uncertainty, exaggerating reliability, or rushing decisions—the moral field warps. When it clarifies, the human can re-establish judgement and restraint.

This leads naturally to the notion of meaningful human control. The phrase is ubiquitous, yet its implementation is often hollow. Being "in the loop" is meaningless if the loop is too tight for deliberation, the cue too subtle to catch, or the abort authority buried behind latency and friction. Control requires time budgets: enough seconds for a human to assess a recommendation. It requires interface cues designed around human attention, not engineering convenience. And it requires immediate, unambiguous pathways for humans to halt or override machine action without stigma or delay. Control is not symbolism; it is choreography. It is the structured opportunity for human judgement to reassert itself at the right moment.

There are contexts, however, where the correct design choice is not to insert more control but to limit autonomy itself. The temptation in technological systems is always upward: more automation, more efficiency, more speed. But domains defined by irreversible stakes—pediatrics, lethal force, involuntary confinement, end-of-life care—demand a different logic. Delegation is not ethically neutral. To automate is to choose what kind of errors a society is willing to bear. A decision tree for autonomy boundaries is not merely a governance tool; it is a statement of collective humility. Some decisions require the slow, interpretive labour of human beings precisely because they codify values no interface can adequately compress.

If we follow this chain—defaults shaping consent, uncertainty shaping trust, control shaping agency, and autonomy boundaries shaping collective risk—we find ourselves facing a deeper tension central to the book: machines do not merely execute choices; they organise them. The way a choice is framed can dignify or diminish. The way information is timed can calm or coerce. The way autonomy is distributed can strengthen or hollow the social contract. Interfaces are the hinge where systems meet their publics, where power takes perceptible form.

As the chapter unfolds, it will move through these hinges with a steady lens. It will show how defaults encode moral starting points, how uncertainty displays can make or unmake trust, how human control can be engineered into reality rather than left as a slogan, and how autonomy must sometimes be resisted rather than embraced. These questions may appear narrow, yet they carry extraordinary weight. For every future patient who receives a risk score, every worker who interprets an automated alert, every citizen nudged by a government interface, the moral world is shaped by what is shown, withheld, or assumed on their behalf.

The open question—one that hangs over this chapter—is whether societies will treat interfaces as minor artefacts or as moral infrastructure. The answer will determine not only how safely machines operate, but how fully human dignity survives contact with them.

Defaults and dignity

On 14 April 2020, at the height of the first COVID wave in Manchester, Salford Royal NHS Foundation Trust quietly enabled a new feature in its patient portal: *Shared Care Data Access – Enabled by Default.* The decision was buried in a routine update notice. Patients logging in found the toggle already switched on, authorising the hospital to share pseudonymised records with a regional analytics network intended to support surge planning. The Trust had followed lawful guidelines. It had complied with national emergency data provisions. Yet objections surfaced almost instantly. A diabetic patient interviewed by the *Manchester Evening News* the following week described feeling "signed up to something without being asked"—not furious, but unsettled, as if a private boundary had shifted while his attention was elsewhere. Nothing unlawful had occurred. Something moral had.

The scene exposes a tension that threads through this subchapter: dignity is often lost not through spectacular breaches, but through defaults that decide before the human has even arrived at the decision. The default is a quiet force. It shapes choices while preserving the illusion of choice. It simplifies workflow at the expense of asking permission. And because it is embedded in interface design—tiny ticks, pre-flipped switches, preloaded preferences—it is easy for organisations to rationalise as practical, harmless, even helpful. But a default signals intent. It tells a person whether the system sees them as a partner in decision-making or as a data point to be swept efficiently into a predetermined flow.

To understand why defaults matter so deeply, we must see them not as technical conveniences but as moral starting points. A default establishes the baseline from which deviation requires effort—and effort is friction. Friction disciplines behaviour. Show this clearly: when organ donation in England shifted to opt-out legislation in May 2020, consent rates rose sharply in early reports, not simply because citizens supported donation in principle, but because the administrative effort moved from joining to leaving. Name the underlying mechanism: status quo bias. Explain its moral implications: when placed in digital systems without due care, defaults manipulate—not through force, but through inertia. The implication is subtle but decisive: technological environments that set defaults without moral transparency risk displacing genuine consent with procedural compliance.

A second example places the issue in a clinical context. In February 2021, an electronic prescribing system rolled out across several hospitals in the Midlands preselected a specific antibiotic dosage as the default for common infections. Clinicians could adjust it, but doing so required navigating two extra screens. Early audits found that prescribers overwhelmingly accepted the default. The system was not wrong—its dosage reflected guideline averages—but the uniformity concealed nuance. Patients with renal impairment received dosages that required manual adjustment; when busy clinicians missed the cues, the default governed care. When questioned, system designers defended the choice as efficiency. What the episode revealed was something else: the default had replaced deliberation with momentum. Efficiency had trumped discernment, and dignity—in this case, the dignity of tailored care—bent quietly under the weight of a prefilled value.

These examples show the double-edged nature of defaults. But a credible counter-example demonstrates their potential for good. In 2018, Estonia's e-Health platform moved vaccination reminders from opt-in to opt-out. Parents received automated notifications unless they disabled them manually. Rather than provoking backlash, the change was widely welcomed. The default aligned with public health goals and with parental expectations; it reduced missed appointments and helped maintain herd immunity during measles outbreaks. This case clarifies the limitation: defaults are not inherently manipulative. Their moral quality depends on context, expectations, and transparency. Reconciliation of the counter-example reveals the principle at work: defaults become ethically sound when they amplify clearly established social goods without undermining personal agency. They fail when they quietly commit people to choices they would not have endorsed if asked.

Returning to the motif of *the threshold*—that small line between guidance and assumption—we begin to see how defaults define thresholds for action. A default instructs the system where to begin: share or not share, notify or not notify, escalate or ignore. The user crosses or accepts the threshold depending on the cognitive cost. A high-friction reversal makes the threshold sticky. A low-friction reversal makes it respectful.

But defaults do more than decide starting points. They communicate expectations. Consider *trust.* Trust is often framed abstractly, yet in interface design it becomes behavioural. A user's trust is visible in whether they leave the default untouched, whether they double-check its meaning, whether they adjust it cautiously or confidently. A default that reflects a user's values strengthens trust; a default that contradicts them erodes it. Patients who find their data-sharing preferences pre-enabled are not rejecting collaboration. They are reacting to a system that assumes more than it asks.

The historical roots of this realisation run deeper than digital systems. In 1924, at the International Labour Office in Geneva, the first global recommendations on "minimal workplace protections" emphasised voluntary consent in labour forms. Though a different domain, the ethical logic endured: agreements derived from silence rather than active affirmation risked paternalism. When we trace that lineage to data environments, we find the same premise: dignity demands participation, not passive defaulting.

Defaults also shape organisational behaviour behind the scenes. A vendor setting an analytics dashboard to report weekly rather than daily commits an organisation to a rhythm of attention. A procurement team that accepts a vendor's default data-retention period of five years effectively transfers risk without noticing. A local authority choosing a third-party risk model with thresholds pre-tuned to U.S. populations inadvertently adopts those assumptions as baselines. These defaults may not be visible to end users, but they structure institutional agency. The behavioural metric is simple: how often do teams override vendor defaults? If the proportion is low, it signals either strong alignment or unexamined dependency.

One of the most striking modern examples of how defaults structure dignity comes from the migration of public services online. In 2019, the Department for Work and Pensions' digital-by-default policy introduced opt-out notifications for automated identity verification steps. Claimants who struggled with digital literacy experienced confusion when required to complete tasks implied to have been chosen by them. Here, the default did not merely nudge; it burdened. Instead of supporting autonomy, it penalised vulnerability. A system that presumes digital fluency turns a default into a moral failure: it makes ease for the designers and friction for those already navigating hardship.

Yet defaults need not fall into this trap. They can be structured around what philosopher Onora O'Neill once called "intelligent trust"—trust grounded in competence and openness, not blind acceptance. A humane default asks: whom does this setting serve? What is the moral claim embedded in this preselection? What would the user assume about our intent if they saw this toggle already switched on?

When organisations treat defaults as moral infrastructure rather than purely operational primitives, a richer design vocabulary emerges. A default can come with a brief, transparent rationale. A default can be paired with a confirmation nudge that respects attention rather than hijacking it. A default can be variable across contexts—for example, stricter for sensitive data, looser for low-stakes personalisation. A default can expire, prompting re-evaluation after a period rather than entrenching inertia. Each of these behaviours restores dignity by making visible what is usually subterranean.

The motif of *the threshold* returns again in the context of power. Defaults encode power not because they enforce, but because they anticipate—and anticipation is a form of control. When a system preselects data sharing, it anticipates the user's consent. When it preselects a risk-scoring model, it anticipates acceptance of that epistemology. When it preselects a course of action—an autogenerated email, a suggested prescription, an automated escalation—it anticipates the human's agreement. The threshold has been crossed before the human arrives. Power enters as presumption.

A final example anchors this idea. In 2022, the city of Vienna piloted an algorithmic allocation tool for childcare places. Early versions defaulted to proximity as the primary criterion, a rule that advantaged families with stable addresses and penalised newly arrived migrant households. Parents could request adjustments, but doing so required navigating a complex appeal workflow. After advocacy groups raised concerns, the city redesigned the tool so that no single criterion was preselected; parents now had to affirm priorities explicitly. This reversal restored dignity by removing presumption. The system did not decide what mattered most—it asked.

As we approach the unresolved tension that closes this subchapter, the questions sharpen. What defaults should an autonomous shuttle present when prompting passengers to share trajectory data? What defaults should a clinical AI adopt when calculating risk categories that may alter treatment pathways? What defaults should public-sector systems employ when nudging citizens toward services or compliance? And perhaps most fundamentally: how can organisations ensure that defaults steer behaviour without steering morality?

Uncertainty on the screen

At precisely 06:47 on 5 December 2021, the Icelandic Met Office issued a volcanic hazard alert for the Reykjanes Peninsula. The agency's seismographs had registered a swarm of microquakes through the night, but the predictive model could not agree on whether the pressure build-up signalled a new fissure eruption or a transient tremor cycle. On the public dashboard, a banded gauge displayed a single message: *Probability of eruption: 41%.* Television news anchors treated the number as a claim. Residents of Grindavík treated it as a warning. Tour operators treated it as reassurance. The number travelled quickly, stripped of the uncertainty that shaped it. By mid-morning, officials fielded calls asking whether 41 per cent meant evacuation was imminent. The real question—how wide was the model's confidence band?—had never reached the screen.

This was not a failure of geology. It was a failure of communication. The underlying models carried a spread of scenarios; they were uncertain for legitimate scientific reasons. But the interface rendered that uncertainty as a point estimate, a single number that appeared authoritative. The effect was quietly distorting. A probabilistic reality had been translated into a binary social reaction. Once again, a motif that will recur throughout this subchapter appeared: the *flattened edge*, that moment when a world of gradations becomes a single figure on a screen.

To see why uncertainty must be shown rather than hidden, we need to examine how humans read numbers under pressure. People interpret confidence intervals less as mathematics and more as storytelling. A wide interval signals ambiguity. A narrow interval signals stability. When these signals vanish, users fill the silence with assumptions—and assumptions are rarely kind to nuance. The Iceland case shows this vividly. The number was not wrong. It was incomplete. It told only the centre of the distribution, not its shape, volatility, or relevance.

The challenge intensifies when uncertainty enters domains in which people face immediate and personal consequences. Consider a diagnostic AI deployed at Norfolk and Norwich University Hospital in September 2020 to assist radiologists in classifying pulmonary nodules. Early pilots highlighted a recurring issue: clinicians struggled to understand the system's confidence in borderline cases. The interface presented a label—*benign* or *suspicious*—with a numerical confidence score. But these scores masked the breadth of uncertainty caused by variations in scan resolution, patient movement, and demographic under-representation in the training set. Some radiologists interpreted an 82 per cent confidence the same way they interpreted an 82 per cent textbook probability: as "nearly certain". Others read it as a fragile estimate to be double-checked. The visible behaviour metric confirmed the ambiguity: second-opinion requests spiked for outputs between 70 and 90 per cent—a range that should have been informative, not confusing.

A counter-example shows the opposite trajectory. In 2016, the National Weather Service in the United States redesigned hurricane forecast graphics after repeated misunderstanding of the "cone of uncertainty". The new design displayed not only the expected storm track but also the radius of plausible deviation, colour-coded by wind intensity ranges. The interface did not assume numeracy. It used shape and shade to convey possibility. The result, audited in post-season reports, was clearer public behaviour: fewer misinterpretations of the cone as an impact zone, and improved evacuation timing in counties adjacent to the projected path. This demonstrates a limitation worth acknowledging: uncertainty can be communicated effectively without overwhelming users—*but only when designers treat it as a first-order requirement rather than afterthought.* Reconciliation arises from design discipline: the cone worked because the uncertainty was the message, not the footnote.

The motif of *the flattened edge* returns here. Poor interfaces flatten uncertainty into single values. Thoughtful ones preserve its contour. The art lies in choosing which contour to reveal.

To show how uncertainty becomes ethically charged, look at loan approvals during economic shocks. In April 2020, as businesses across Leeds applied for pandemic relief loans, several banks deployed decision-support models developed years prior for relatively stable markets. The models signalled "medium confidence" for applicants with irregular revenue histories—particularly self-employed workers. But the user interfaces shown to loan officers presented a single recommendation with no contextual volatility indicator. Many officers followed the suggestions rigidly, believing the model was more stable than it was. Internal audits later revealed that approval disparities widened for minority-owned businesses during the first six weeks. The model was not inherently discriminatory; the interface had hidden the volatility that would have prompted human recalibration. Uncertainty suppressed became inequality widened.

Why do interfaces hide uncertainty? Show the operational pressures: product teams aim for clarity, speed, and actionable guidance. Name the underlying pattern: *false precision*, the tendency to substitute a tidy number for a messy distribution. Explain the cognitive effect: humans anchor to visible values, not invisible ranges. The implication is stark: hiding uncertainty does not reduce confusion; it displaces it onto downstream choices, where it becomes harder to correct.

Goodhart's Law, often invoked in proxy debates, also whispers in the domain of uncertainty. When systems reward crisp outputs, designers optimise for crispness—even when the domain demands caution. Interface metrics such as "decision time" or "click-through confidence" encourage platforms to reduce ambiguity, not reveal it. Yet ambiguity is often the only honest representation available.

So what does responsible communication of uncertainty look like? The question bridges human perception and interface craft.

A study from the University of Cambridge's Winton Centre for Risk and Evidence Communication (2020) offers one anchor. When presenting COVID test reliability to the public, the Centre trialled graphical methods using shaded bands rather than percentages. Participants across numeracy levels understood the shaded uncertainty far more readily. It countered the mental model that negative tests meant guaranteed absence of infection. The demonstration emphasised a critical technique: *visual gradation can carry epistemic humility without adding cognitive load.* More importantly, participants reported higher trust in information when uncertainty was shown clearly. This directly contradicts the managerial instinct that uncertainty disclosure undermines credibility.

A second example comes from aviation interfaces. Airbus introduced revised cockpit displays in 2013 for flight envelope protections, showing pilots ranges of permissible manoeuvre rather than discrete warnings. These displays use colour-transition zones to illustrate the onset of uncertainty—such as near-stall conditions in turbulent air. The behaviour metric is decisive: pilot training programmes found improved situational awareness during high-uncertainty flight tests, because pilots could see the "fuzziness" of limits as turbulence increased. Uncertainty visualised created competence, not confusion.

Yet a credible limitation must be confronted. Interfaces can overwhelm. Too much uncertainty, too prominently signalled, paralyses. Cognitive overload is a genuine risk in high-stakes environments. If a clinician sees a wall of confidence bands, they may hesitate fatally. If a driver encounters a car dashboard filled with probability ranges, they may reject the system altogether. The resolution lies in careful structuring. Reconciliation depends on layering: reveal essential uncertainty upfront; allow access to depth on demand. The right balance preserves agency while maintaining clarity.

Threading the motif of *the flattened edge* for the final time, note how the edge sharpens or softens according to design. A risk model that displays a crisp "3% chance of severe complication" presents a razor edge. A model that frames the same estimate as "between 1% and 7%, based on patients like you" softens it. Neither formula guarantees comprehension, but one invites reflection; the other invites misinterpretation.

This raises deeper questions about moral responsibility. If uncertainty is stripped away by design, responsibility shifts unnoticed from human judgement to interface assumptions. When an AI tool signals 91 per cent confidence with no visible distribution, a clinician who accepts it is not negligent; they are responding to the assurances the system chose to convey. Conversely, when uncertainty is shown candidly, accountability becomes shared. Designers carry the responsibility of honesty. Users carry the responsibility of interpretation. This shared structure is not weakness. It is ethical architecture.

There is also a political dimension. Public trust in algorithmic systems—whether in welfare administration, immigration triage, or predictive policing—hinges on whether decisions appear explainable and modifiable. Uncertainty, when communicated respectfully, offers both. A person denied a service based on a model may accept the outcome more readily if they can see that the model's decision was not absolute but contingent, and that they have the right to challenge it. A political process grounded in probabilistic humility leaves space for appeal. One grounded in brittle certainty does not.

The question now becomes practical: what does it mean to design uncertainty into interfaces without demanding numeracy?

Several patterns have emerged across organisations that take this seriously. Shaded ranges. Verbal qualifiers paired with consistent icons. Temporal uncertainty bars showing how confidence decays as data ages. Scenario sliders enabling users to see how small changes alter predictions. All of these techniques restore dimensionality to flattened edges. And each carries the same message: uncertainty is part of the truth, not a flaw in it.

Yet we must not romanticise uncertainty. People often want decisiveness, especially in emergencies. The art lies in deciding which decisions genuinely require sharpness and which demand openness. A pilot on final approach needs crisp warnings. A policymaker evaluating infectious-disease spread needs honest volatility bands. A citizen examining a credit recommendation needs clarity about confidence. A surgeon making time-critical choices needs layered uncertainty that escalates intelligently. These distinctions matter.

So we end with the unresolved tension that animates this subchapter. When the next screen lights up—whether in a clinic, cockpit, courtroom, or council office—what form should its uncertainty take? Should it reveal the spread fully, or smooth it for decisiveness? Should it prioritise ease, or fidelity? And the deepest question: when clarity and honesty diverge, which should the interface choose, and who should make that choice?

Meaningful human control

At 03:12 on 23 March 2019, an Ethiopian Airlines simulator in Addis Ababa replayed, again and again, the final seconds of Flight 302. Investigators examined how the crew had struggled against the Maneuvering Characteristics Augmentation System (MCAS), a piece of automated software whose authority eclipsed the pilots' ability to intervene. The simulator logs showed something chilling: the pilots had less than ten seconds to diagnose the malfunction before the system reasserted itself. Ten seconds. A 737 cockpit packed with indicators, alarms, and procedural routines had offered its crew barely enough cognitive space to react. Whatever the manuals claimed about pilot authority, the time budget said otherwise. Human control existed on paper; in practice, it had evaporated when urgency compressed the envelope of meaningful choice. The scene illustrates a recurring motif in the ethics of autonomy: *the disappearing moment.* A system nominally "under supervision" can, through design, velocity, or interface friction, outrun the human meant to guide it. A person is "in the loop" only if they can perceive, decide, and act before the window closes. When that window collapses to seconds, supervision becomes theatre.

The MCAS case is extreme, but its lesson travels far beyond aviation. It warns us that meaningful human control is not a philosophical nicety but an engineering requirement—and one that must be specified with forensic clarity. Control is not simply the presence of a button labelled *override.* It is the capacity to understand what the system is doing, detect when it is doing the wrong thing, and intervene decisively in time. Without that triad, the loop is ornamental.

To see how this plays out in calmer domains, consider a clinical decision-support tool deployed by University College London Hospitals in June 2021. Designed to triage emergency cases based on presenting symptoms, it flagged certain combinations as "urgent" and locked the clinician's interface until the recommended protocol was acknowledged. Doctors reported feeling rushed. They could technically override the recommendation, but the interface required six clicks, a manual note, and a supervisor notification. The visible behaviour metric was damning: override use remained below 2 per cent even when cases met established criteria for doctor-led deviation. The system had created procedural gravity. Human control existed, yet it was functionally unreachable.

Show the pattern: systems claim deference to humans but structure interactions that inhibit challenge. Name the concept: *practical autonomy margin*, the space in which a human can realistically intervene. Explain the mechanism: if cognitive load, administrative friction, or signalling discourages intervention, human control degrades from option to fiction. The implication is clear: autonomy must be measured in seconds and clicks, not in slogans or slide decks.

Contrast this with a counter-example that demonstrates genuine human-in-the-loop design. London's Crossrail, after a series of delays, introduced revised driver-assist modes in 2022 which explicitly enforced time budgets for human oversight. Drivers received a rolling "anticipation bar" showing when the automation would seek confirmation for speed transitions. If the driver failed to respond within a defined window, the train defaulted to a safe mode rather than pressing ahead. The behaviour metric improved markedly: near-miss braking events dropped, and driver satisfaction increased. This example shows that automation can scaffold, not supplant, human authority. It also reveals a limitation worth addressing: proactive cues work best in predictable contexts; in chaotic ones—like trauma bays or battlefield environments—they risk drowning operators in alerts. Reconciliation lies in tailoring cues to domain tempo. The faster the world moves, the simpler the cue must be.

The motif of *the disappearing moment* threads through each of these cases. Designers can widen or narrow that moment. It is a moral choice disguised as a technical one.

If time budgets are the first pillar of meaningful human control, attention cues form the second. People cannot intervene wisely if they do not know *when* to shift focus. Modern automation often succeeds too well: it reduces workload so effectively that human vigilance decays. Psychologists studying the Tesla Autopilot crashes in Florida (2016) and Mountain View (2018) found that drivers' gaze patterns drifted within minutes of activation. They became spectators rather than supervisors. The interface encouraged this drift. It whispered reassurance through smooth motion, minimal alerts, and a dashboard that claimed stability until a split-second before catastrophe. The system promoted *engagement decay*.

A contrasting model emerges from high-reliability industries. In nuclear control rooms—such as Sizewell B in Suffolk—operators use tiered attention cues that modulate vigilance. Instead of presenting a flat stream of information, systems employ colour, motion, and spatial clustering to draw focus where it matters. These cues preserve cognitive bandwidth while ensuring that the operator's situational map remains current. The operator sees not merely that something is wrong but that *now* is the moment to intervene. This design choice turns abstract risk into palpable signal.

Third comes *abort authority*: the capacity for a human to stop a system's action without friction, penalty, or managerial reprisal. Abort authority is often treated as a safety valve, but it is more than that. It is a declaration of value hierarchy: humans outrank machines, even when machines are statistically superior. That hierarchy must be engineered, not assumed.

In July 2020, during the trial of an autonomous shuttle in Vienna, engineers discovered that passengers assumed—incorrectly—that the emergency stop button would override all systems. In fact, the button paused movement but did not disable the obstacle detection logic, which sometimes reinitiated braking after a passenger sought manual control. The discrepancy induced hesitation. People touched the button, waited, and wondered whether the vehicle had actually yielded. The behaviour metric captured the uncertainty: passengers used the stop button infrequently, and mostly after the shuttle had already halted. This is abort authority as ritual, not power.

Compare this with the design philosophy behind the Airbus Flight Path Stable Mode, introduced in test runs in Toulouse in 2019. Pilots retained decisive abort authority: pulling the stick to a threshold bypassed automation immediately, without confirmation layers or secondary locks. The system accepted that a pilot might occasionally abort unnecessarily. Better an unnecessary abort than a delayed one.

This underscores a broader ethical stance: human error deserves tolerance; human impotence does not.

A credible limitation must be acknowledged. Excessive abort options can corrode trust. If individuals feel they must perpetually hover over a kill switch, automation becomes anxiety amplifier rather than safety partner. This is where design discipline returns: abort authority must be available, intuitive, and rare. It must exist almost as a constitutional right—invoked infrequently but vital when the moment comes.

Beyond the local mechanics of control lies a deeper philosophical question: what does it mean for oversight to be meaningful? The European Union's High-Level Expert Group on AI attempted an answer in 2019, proposing that meaningful control requires humans to "retain the capacity to influence the system's outcome at appropriate stages". This definition is correct but incomplete. It names the condition but not the constraints.

To give it shape, translate it into observable behaviours.
Meaningful control exists when a person can:

anticipate the system's next step,
interrupt that step when warranted, and
redirect the system without undue burden.

Anything less is performative involvement.

These elements sharpen the question of model interpretability. Black-box systems are not inherently incompatible with human control, but their opacity constrains the anticipation stage. If a child welfare algorithm classifies a case as high risk with no explanation, the human "in the loop" becomes a bureaucratic stamp, not a decision-maker. If a fraud detection system flags a transaction without revealing the uncertainty bands or salient features, overseers cannot judge whether the model's suspicion is plausible. Friction, not opacity alone, kills control.

This brings us to an important counter-example. In 2021, a Scandinavian bank tested two models for anti-money laundering alerts: a high-performing deep learning model and a slightly less accurate gradient-boosted tree with interpretable feature output. Compliance officers overwhelmingly preferred the latter. Why? Because they could interrogate its reasoning, challenge its false positives, and justify override decisions to regulators. Performance alone did not determine legitimacy. The model that enabled meaningful scrutiny won. Here the motif of *the disappearing moment* morphs into *the recoverable moment*: interpretability restored the window for human judgement.

To draw the threads together, we must integrate time budgets, attention cues, and abort authority into a coherent framework. Each addresses a different facet of the supervision problem. Time budgets prevent automation from outrunning cognition. Attention cues prevent cognitive atrophy. Abort authority prevents irreversible harm. Their interaction determines the moral profile of autonomous systems.

When any one is missing, human control collapses.

Which brings us to the unresolved tension at the heart of this subchapter. As autonomy deepens across domains—from transport to medicine, finance to public administration—where should designers place the boundary between helpful automation and meaningful human authority? When should a system seek confirmation rather than proceed? When should it demand attention rather than lull the user? And the hardest question of all: if a future incident stems from a vanished moment, who should bear the blame—the human, or the design that stole their chance to act?

When to say no to autonomy

At 22:00 on 18 March 2018, a Volvo XC90 modified by Uber's Advanced Technologies Group struck and killed a pedestrian, Elaine Herzberg, on a wide road in Tempe, Arizona. The vehicle's automated system had detected "something" in its path several seconds earlier, alternately classifying her as an unknown object, a vehicle, and a bicycle. It did not decide to brake until it was too late. The "safety driver" in the front seat was looking down at a screen. After the impact, public arguments split along familiar lines. Some insisted the technology was not ready. Others countered that human drivers kill thousands every year, and that even imperfect autonomy might still reduce the total. Beneath the statistics sat a quieter question that few addressed directly: not *how safe* the system should be before deployment, but *where* autonomy should never have been given such authority in the first place. Some choices must stay human.

The Tempe crash matters because it exposes a recurring motif in debates about automation: *the line.* Where is the line beyond which delegation ceases to be progress and becomes abdication? Engineers speak naturally about what more can be automated—lane-keeping, obstacle detection, trajectory planning. Regulators ask what safety thresholds must be met. Both conversations assume the line will move outward over time. Yet there are domains where that movement should stop; where the nature of the decision, not the maturity of the technology, must place a hard limit on autonomy.

To see why, it helps to distinguish two different questions. One is empirical: can machines perform this task as well as or better than humans? The other is normative: even if they can, should they be allowed to do so without a human deciding each case? We confuse these constantly. Accuracy statistics answer only the first. Legitimacy hangs on the second.

Start with a domain where the line was drawn belatedly but clearly. In January 2020, the District Court of The Hague ruled against the Dutch government's SyRI system, a tool that combined data from multiple agencies to flag citizens as potential welfare fraud risks. Technically, SyRI was a modest risk-scoring engine. Procedurally, it operated within formal law. Yet the court held that the system violated the right to respect for private life under Article 8 of the European Convention on Human Rights. Why? Not because its predictions were inaccurate in some narrow statistical sense, but because it concentrated opaque, state power over citizens' livelihoods without sufficient human oversight or transparency. The line was not drawn at error rates. It was drawn at the conjunction of opacity, coercive power, and life-altering consequences.

Contrast that with the Docklands Light Railway in London, operating since 1987 with fully automated trains on grade-separated tracks. There, autonomy is not controversial. The system runs in a highly constrained environment, with physical separation from pedestrians and other traffic, predictable routes, and human staff supervising operations with robust fail-safes. When something goes wrong, trains stop rather than improvise. The line here lies elsewhere: the combination of controllable environment, reversible consequences, and clear accountability makes high autonomy acceptable.

These examples show that "yes" or "no" to autonomy is not a single answer. It depends on what is at stake, how visible errors are, and what kinds of harms cannot be undone. It depends on where the line is drawn.

To make this concrete, begin with irreversibility. Some decisions close doors that cannot be reopened: a surgical amputation, a lethal weapons release, a long prison sentence, the permanent removal of a child from their family. In these spaces, autonomy is not just a question of performance; it is a question about who is allowed to *author* irreversible change. A triage algorithm that mis-ranks a patient can, in principle, be corrected if clinicians remain fully in charge. A system that autonomously authorises the withdrawal of life support cannot.

In 2016, the COMPAS risk assessment tool used in U.S. courts became the focus of intense scrutiny after ProPublica reported racial disparities in its predictions. Judges insisted that the system was advisory; they retained final authority. Yet qualitative research on sentencing hearings showed that some judges treated COMPAS scores as quasi-binding, rarely deviating from the algorithm's risk labels. The line between advice and delegation blurred in practice. That blurring matters, because pre-trial detention changes life trajectories in ways that cannot simply be rolled back. A night wrongly spent in custody differs morally from a misrouted parcel. Both are errors. Only one strikes at civic status.

Irreversibility, though, is not the only criterion. A second is *value pluralism*. Some domains embed deeply contested values: what counts as a "good" upbringing, a "reasonable" level of risk in policing, a "deserving" welfare claimant. Here, even perfect prediction cannot replace judgement, because the core question is not what will happen but what ought to happen. Automated systems can support deliberation, surface patterns, or flag anomalies, but full delegation risks locking in one moral view as if it were neutral fact.

Child protection decisions illustrate this risk. In several jurisdictions, including Allegheny County in Pennsylvania, predictive tools now help social workers assess which referrals merit urgent investigation. Used carefully, they can highlight hidden risk factors. Yet few serious scholars argue that an algorithm should decide, unaided, to remove a child from their home. The decision is not simply about risk; it is about weighing competing harms, cultural contexts, and the meaning of family. Those evaluations require forms of understanding—listening, empathy, situational judgement—that do not reduce to features in a training set. Here, the line must be drawn well this side of autonomy. Advice, yes. Authority, no.

A credible counter-example clarifies the boundary. Consider warehouse robotics in a distribution centre. Automated guided vehicles route packages from one location to another, avoiding collisions and optimising paths. Errors are visible and, in most cases, reversible: a missed package can be rerouted; a jammed conveyor can be cleared. Workers retain emergency stop authority, and the physical environment is tightly controlled. Value pluralism is low: "good" performance is well-defined as throughput, safety, and accuracy. Full autonomy is not only permissible, but arguably preferable, reducing drudgery and physical strain. The line sits in a different place because the underlying moral landscape is different.

A third criterion concerns *observability* and *feedback*. In some domains, harmful errors become visible quickly. A mislabelled parcel triggers a customer complaint within days. An energy grid controller that trips unnecessarily will generate clear operational signals. In such cases, autonomy errors feed back into monitoring systems, and designers can adjust. But where harms are diffuse, delayed, or silently borne, such feedback does not exist. An employment-screening algorithm that quietly under-ranks candidates from certain postcodes, a credit-scoring system that marginally increases interest rates for minority borrowers, a social-care prioritisation tool that consistently downgrades complex cases—these systems can operate for years without obvious incident reports. Autonomy in such contexts accumulates harm invisibly.

The UK's Post Office Horizon scandal, although not an AI case, shows the danger. Faulty accounting software led to sub-postmasters being wrongfully accused and convicted of theft between the late 1990s and 2010s. The system's errors were not immediately obvious; they emerged as unexplained shortfalls. Yet the institution treated the system as authoritative and the humans as suspect. The line was crossed not in code but in deference. The lesson for AI is direct: when harms are hard to observe, autonomy should be constrained and subject to continuous human challenge, not celebrated as "objective" or "self-correcting".

These criteria—irreversibility, value pluralism, and observability—can be woven into something like a decision tree, even if we draw it in prose rather than diagrams.

Start at the root with a simple question: *What is the worst plausible outcome of a single automated decision in this domain?* If the answer involves death, involuntary confinement, removal of fundamental civic rights, or permanent bodily alteration, then full autonomy should be presumptively off the table. Any machine output should be advisory, subject to explicit human authorisation in each case.

If the worst outcome is significant but reversible—temporary financial loss, medium-term inconvenience, recoverable reputational damage—the next question is: *Are the underlying value judgements contested?* Where they are, machines should again remain in a supporting role. Risk scores can inform, but humans must articulate and own the normative reasoning that translates scores into action.

Only where harms are reversible and values largely shared does it make sense to ask a third question: *Are errors rapidly detectable and correctable?* If so, high or full autonomy may be defensible, provided that monitoring and override mechanisms exist. If not—if errors diffuse silently through complex systems—then autonomy should be bounded, with humans periodically sampling and challenging outputs rather than rubber-stamping them.

The motif of *the line* reappears at each question. Each answer moves us closer either to an autonomous posture or to a guarded, human-led one. What matters is that these steps are taken consciously rather than smuggled in as engineering defaults.

There is also a political dimension. Autonomy shifts who bears risk. In lethal contexts—armed drones, autonomous weapons—delegation does not merely change tactics. It alters the relationship between the state and those it might kill. Debates in Geneva over Lethal Autonomous Weapon Systems have repeatedly emphasised "meaningful human control", but too often as a slogan rather than an operational requirement. Saying no to autonomy here is not a confession of technological modesty; it is a defence of the principle that no person should die without another human deliberately deciding that it should be so. The line is moral first, technical second.

Economic pressures push hard in the opposite direction. Hospitals under strain see automation as relief. Social services departments, thinly staffed after years of cuts, view risk models as triage. Insurers and banks pursue algorithmic scoring for efficiency and consistency. In each case, the argument for autonomy is framed in terms of capacity: we have more decisions to make than humans can handle unaided. That argument is not trivial. But it cannot be allowed to erase the question of where we must resist delegation altogether, even when capacity is scarce.

A further tension runs through this landscape. Saying no to autonomy in high-stakes domains may push error back into human hands. Humans misjudge, discriminate, burn out. Autonomy may, on some metrics, produce fewer errors. The question is whether those metrics capture what we care about most. A slightly lower overall error rate achieved by turning contestable moral decisions into opaque model outputs may not be a victory worth having.

So the subchapter arrives at its own open question. As autonomous systems become technically capable across ever more domains, who will be trusted to draw the line—and how will their choices be contested? Will boundaries on delegation be set primarily by engineers, regulators, the courts, or those most affected by automated decisions? And when the case for autonomy rests on efficiency while the case against rests on dignity, which argument will carry the day?

Chapter 6
AI in Justice

On a grey morning in June 2016, as the Kent County Courthouse in Michigan prepared for another day of arraignments, a defendant named Eric Loomis waited to hear whether he would be granted freedom before trial. The prosecutor cited a risk score generated by an algorithm called COMPAS. The score—produced from a questionnaire Loomis had never seen, let alone understood—flagged him as "high risk". Moments later the judge denied bail, emphasising the danger suggested by the model. Loomis could not challenge the calculation; neither he nor his lawyer had access to the system's workings. Yet that opaque number changed the next months of his life. In its aftermath, commentators debated statistics, error margins, and the subtleties of algorithmic bias. Lost in that conversation was a simpler, older question: what does a person deserve when the state weighs their liberty? And can any predictive tool, however accurate, speak legitimately to that question without a structure of accountability and explanation wrapped around it?

Risk assessments like COMPAS were introduced in American courts with an earnest promise: to replace intuition with evidence, to bring consistency to decisions historically shaped by prejudice, fatigue, or simple luck. The idea was compelling. Prediction, it was said, could reduce human bias. But the courtroom is a peculiar stage on which to place a predictive machine. It is not only a place of fact-finding; it is a ritual of fairness, where authority must not simply wield power but justify it. An algorithm's score may estimate the probability that someone misses a hearing. It cannot determine what justice demands. Yet again and again, across jurisdictions from Kentucky to Arizona, judges have treated prediction as prescription, letting the curve of a model bend the arc of someone's life.

This chapter sits within that tension. Justice systems around the world face immense pressure: overloaded dockets, outdated infrastructure, limited staff, and enduring inequalities. Into this strain come machine systems that promise efficiency and consistency, but which also risk hardening injustice behind a veneer of technical neutrality. The attraction is understandable. The danger is profound.

For the law is not merely a set of rules; it is a moral performance in which each decision must be publicly defensible. When algorithmic tools enter that performance without an accompanying framework to explain, contest, and correct them, legitimacy erodes. People accept outcomes when they can follow the reasoning, even if they disagree with its conclusion. They resist outcomes that read like administrative fate.

Risk scores are only the beginning. They mark the point at which predictions enter the legal bloodstream, influencing bail decisions, sentencing, parole eligibility, and resource allocation. Yet the deeper issue is not the models themselves but the moral infrastructure built—or not built—around them. Courts have long recognised that procedures matter as much as outcomes. A hearing is not merely a means to a decision; it is the citizen's assurance that their voice has been heard, that evidence has been weighed, that reasons have been given. Algorithmic systems disrupt this choreography. A judge referring to a risk score may believe they are exercising independent judgement, but unless the score is interpretable, challengeable, and appropriately bounded in its influence, the judge becomes the custodian of a black box rather than a guardian of due process.

This chapter explores how justice systems can preserve their core commitments as AI tools become woven into everyday practice. It examines four linked tensions: how predictions collide with rights; why procedural fairness must be re-engineered for a world of models; how aggregation obscures individual stories; and how redress mechanisms must evolve to handle algorithmic harm. Each tension points back to a central motif: that justice requires not only correct decisions but comprehensible ones.

Begin with prediction and rights. Risk assessments often arise from sensible aims: reducing overcrowded jails, allocating supervision resources, or identifying people who may benefit from treatment rather than incarceration. The pitfall lies in treating the output as destiny. A risk score is an estimate about a population pattern. It is not a judgement about a person's moral character or a licence to pre-emptively restrict liberty. Disaster follows when these distinctions collapse. In some counties, almost no defendant categorised as "high risk" receives non-monetary release, even when the underlying probability is only moderately above average. In policy terms, what was meant as guidance becomes a categorical rule in practice, erasing nuance and discretion. The question that should guide courts—*what rights does this individual retain, and what burdens may the state legitimately impose?*—becomes subsumed under *what does the model predict?*.

From that problem flows the need for procedural fairness by design. Justice systems cannot rely on ad-hoc explanation or informal oversight when models influence decisions. They require structured interfaces: clear statements of the model's scope, warnings about uncertainty, accessible reasons for decisions, and logs that capture every point at which automated output shaped judgement. These design elements are not luxuries; they are constitutional safeguards translated into software. Where due process mandates that a person must know the case against them, a risk-scoring tool must disclose, in human-readable form, the factors that influenced its score and the uncertainty around them. Where administrative law demands that decisions be reviewable, systems must store and expose the inputs, transformations, and thresholds used in each individual case. Without such scaffolding, AI-driven justice becomes indistinguishable from arbitrary authority.

Yet procedural fairness alone does not solve a structural concern: that models trained on large populations—even when statistically sound—misfit the lives of individuals. Aggregation can be misleading. A pattern that holds across thousands may be unjust when applied mechanically to one person whose circumstances differ subtly but importantly from the average. The challenge is not new. Laws themselves aggregate. But a well-drafted statute allows for exceptions, mitigating factors, and judicial discretion. A model, unless deliberately designed otherwise, does not. Its strength—detecting general regularities—can be its moral weakness. To guard against this, justice systems need adversarial testing: deliberate stress-tests that probe how models behave when confronted with atypical or marginal cases. They also need contestability windows: structured opportunities in which defendants, advocates, and community groups can challenge model outputs, supply counter-evidence, and demand justification. Without these safety valves, systems drift towards the tyranny of the aggregate.

A final thread runs through all these concerns: how to repair and redress harm. Traditional legal systems have long established appeals processes, judicial review, and compensation schemes. But algorithmic harms present new twists. A person wrongly denied bail due to an opaque risk score may not know which part of the pipeline failed: the training data, the feature engineering, the thresholding rules, or the judge's interpretation. Without transparency and responsive governance structures, identifying the fault—and obtaining remedy—becomes nearly impossible. Moreover, models evolve. A correction applied today must be propagated through future versions. Redress, then, is not only about compensating for past wrongs but updating systems to prevent recurrence. This requires specialised audit teams, versioned registries, and clear rules that tie restitution to model improvement.

What unifies these threads is the moral demand that justice remain human in its justification, even when supported by machines in its execution. AI tools can assist with consistency or highlight patterns invisible to the human eye, but they cannot replace the moral labour of judgement. Yet that does not mean rejecting these tools outright. It means embedding them within procedures that preserve fundamental rights: explanation, contestation, and correction. Machine systems, left unbounded, may tempt institutions into a mechanised vision of fairness, where uniform treatment masquerades as equal justice. But a justice system worthy of its name must honour the irreducible individuality of each case.

The question lingering at the edge of this chapter—and the reason it matters so urgently—is not whether models belong in courts. They already do. The real question is how societies can ensure that the introduction of prediction enhances justice rather than distorts it; that procedural safeguards evolve as fast as the tools they govern; and that individuals retain the ability to demand reasons, seek redress, and assert their dignity in the shadow of machine judgement.

Risk scores and rights

Just after eight o'clock on 16 March 2016, in a wood-panelled courtroom in La Crosse, Wisconsin, Judge Elliot Levine reviewed a bail recommendation for a man named Eric Loomis. The prosecution pointed to a risk score generated by COMPAS, a commercial algorithm widely used in the United States since the early 2000s. The score, the judge noted aloud, labelled Loomis a "high risk" of reoffending and of failing to appear. Within minutes, Loomis was denied pre-trial release. He had no way to scrutinise the inputs, the weighting logic, or the assumptions that shaped the score. The metric was treated as fact. The effects were immediate. One number—produced by a system neither transparent nor contestable—quietly overrode the presumption of liberty that underpins criminal justice.

The Loomis case became a headline because the stakes were visible: a person's freedom constrained by an opaque calculation. Yet cases like this occur daily across jurisdictions that have integrated risk scoring into bail, parole, sentencing, and probation decisions. The courtroom offers an unusually stark stage on which to see the larger tension that runs through algorithmic justice: the tension between prediction and rights. Prediction can organise information, highlight patterns, and reduce human inconsistency. Rights enshrine a different logic: that every person deserves dignity, reasoning, and recourse. When risk scores seep into decisions that govern liberty, the two logics collide.

Statistical prediction is not new to justice. Actuarial tools, such as the Salient Factor Score developed in California in 1978, have long attempted to estimate recidivism by combining demographic and historical variables. But the expansion of machine-learning models in the 2010s—driven by cheap computation, abundant data, and administrative pressure—shifted both scale and ambition. Systems like COMPAS, PSA (Public Safety Assessment, launched by the Laura and John Arnold Foundation in 2014), and various state-built tools promised to "modernise" criminal justice with quantifiable insights. Their advocates spoke of efficiency, consistency, and bias reduction. Their critics pointed to opacity, discrimination, and misplaced authority. Both sides grasped fragments of the truth. The deeper question was less about accuracy than about the moral structure needed to interpret and constrain prediction.

To understand how prediction meets rights, start with what risk scores *actually* measure. They measure correlations in historical data:

the average behaviour of categories of people who share certain features. They do not measure intention, context, or the situational pressures that determine an individual's behaviour. Yet in practice, courts often treat a "high risk" label as a prescriptive judgement: the person *should* be detained, supervised more intensely, or denied opportunities for diversion. The shift from *is likely* to *ought to be restricted* is subtle in language and enormous in consequence. It turns statistical regularity into a moral judgement without public justification.

One visible illustration comes from Kentucky, where the PSA has been used statewide since 2016 to inform bail decisions. Judges who see a risk score of "5" for new criminal activity—meaning higher than average—often treat it as an instruction to detain, even though the underlying probability may still be modest when expressed in absolute terms. The score is interpreted as an imperative rather than a prompt for reasoning. A metric intended to guide becomes a metric that governs. The difference is the difference between a tool and a verdict.

A second example, drawn from the United Kingdom, shows how even non-carceral contexts risk blurring the prediction–prescription divide. In 2019, Durham Constabulary used an algorithm known as HART (Harm Assessment Risk Tool) to assist custody officers in determining whether low-level offenders were suitable for deferred prosecution programmes. The tool categorised individuals into high, medium, or low risk of serious harm. Although officers retained discretion, early pilot evaluations showed that many treated the tool's classifications as authoritative, rarely diverging from its recommendations. The system's predictive accuracy—reasonable but far from perfect—was less significant than the behavioural effect it had: it narrowed the space for human judgement while preserving its appearance.

These cases reveal a core problem that cannot be solved by tweaking variables or rebalancing datasets. The problem is conceptual. Risk scores answer a question about groups. Justice asks a question about individuals. A group-level probability may be a helpful input when allocating resources or identifying systemic inequalities, but when used to restrict liberty, it must be embedded within procedures that honour individual rights. Without such procedures, risk scores drift inexorably toward what habeas corpus historically aimed to prevent: detention without personalised justification.

A credible counter-example helps clarify where risk assessment can support rights rather than undermine them. Consider the deployment of predictive tools in public health surveillance, such as the NHS's use of risk stratification to identify patients at high risk of hospital admission. These tools inform targeted interventions: additional nurse visits, early follow-up appointments, medication reviews. Crucially, they *expand* support rather than restrict it. Errors, though undesirable, do not typically infringe legal rights or impose punitive measures. This context demonstrates that prediction can be valuable when its consequences are reversible, supportive, and transparent. The risk score is not a sentence. It is an invitation to give more care. The moral geometry is entirely different.

Returning to justice contexts, the distinction between supportive and coercive use of prediction marks the first major boundary. The next boundary concerns *interpretability*. Courts require reasons. A defendant has a right to know the basis for a decision. Yet most machine-learning risk models offer no intelligible explanation. Even when tools provide factor importance lists, these can obscure the true drivers of prediction. In the COMPAS controversy, Northpointe (now Equivant), the company behind the tool, defended its refusal to disclose its model on trade-secret grounds. In doing so, it turned a judicial decision into something akin to proprietary logic. The legal right to explanation collided with the commercial right to confidentiality. No justice system can sustain that conflict indefinitely.

Explanation, however, is not merely a matter of transparency. It is a matter of *fit*. A risk score must be intelligible to those who must act on it. Studies of judicial behaviour show that judges rely heavily on heuristics under time pressure, especially during first-appearance hearings. Presenting a single composite score encourages over-reliance. Presenting a decomposed profile—showing factors, uncertainty ranges, and error margins—invites deliberation. The interface shapes the ethics. If rights require reasoned decisions, design must support reasoning.

Underlying all of this is the motif that runs through this chapter: the motif of *the threshold.* Risk scores gain power when they harden into thresholds—numerical cut-offs that map predictions to consequences. Thresholds simplify. They promise consistency. But they also flatten nuance. Setting a threshold for detention at "risk level 5" treats all individuals at that score as interchangeable. A person with a turbulent adolescence but strong current stability is collapsed into the same category as someone with ongoing unresolved factors. The threshold does not see context; it sees only its own logic. Rights demand context. The tension between the two is structural.

A further complication arises from feedback loops. When a risk model predicts that certain defendants are more likely to reoffend and those defendants are therefore detained more often, their chance of reoffending increases due to the destabilising effects of incarceration. The prediction helps create the reality it claimed to foresee. In 2018, researchers at Dartmouth College demonstrated such feedback loops in simulation studies, showing that even modest disparities in treatment could amplify over time. Feedback loops turn prediction into self-fulfilling governance. The line between probability and policy dissolves.

One might argue that judges remain in control, that scores are merely advisory, that judicial discretion provides the necessary safeguard. But behavioural studies complicate this comfort. In multiple U.S. jurisdictions, bail decisions made after the introduction of algorithmic tools exhibit decreasing variance, suggesting that discretion is narrowing rather than flourishing. Judges tend to follow the model, not because they are compelled to, but because deviating from a quantified recommendation exposes them to criticism if something goes wrong. Prediction becomes protection—for judges, not defendants.

Yet prediction is not the enemy. What matters is how rights shape the use of prediction. Some jurisdictions have taken steps in this direction. New Jersey's bail reform in 2017, which incorporated the PSA, was paired with strict procedural safeguards: open documentation of the model's logic, public audits of performance, and explicit limits on the weight given to the score. The reform reduced pre-trial jail populations without a rise in failure-to-appear rates. Here, the predictive tool functioned more like a spotlight—illuminating cases that warranted attention—than a gatekeeper. The rights frame disciplined the prediction frame.

The central challenge is not technical; it is architectural. Justice systems must decide where to place prediction within a process fundamentally designed to treat individuals as more than datapoints. This requires structures for contestation. Defendants and their counsel must have access to the inputs, assumptions, and uncertainties that shaped a score. It requires structures for accountability: independent audits, impact assessments, and mechanisms to correct errors. And it requires structures for calibration: periodic review of thresholds, not as technical tuning but as democratic reasoning about acceptable trade-offs.

Prediction can coexist with rights, but only when the system surrounding it refuses to treat numbers as verdicts. A risk score is an artefact of data and design, not a measure of worth. Its value lies in prompting questions, not answering them. That is the point at which this subchapter now arrives: a pivot to the unresolved question at its heart. If prediction becomes increasingly accurate, increasingly granular, and increasingly embedded in judicial workflows, who will decide how far its authority should reach? And what will happen when the logic of probability presses against the logic of rights, demanding that one give way?

Procedural fairness by design

At 9:47 a.m. on 12 July 2021, in the administrative chambers of Utrecht's District Court, a small group of civil servants faced the consequences of a system they barely understood. The Dutch childcare benefits scandal, which culminated in government resignation earlier that year, had been fuelled by an automated fraud-detection process that flagged thousands of parents as high-risk. The interface that caseworkers used offered no clear reasoning—only a red indicator, a severity score, and a list of suggested actions. Parents were denied appeals because staff could not explain the basis for the allegations. The absence of explanation was not a technical oversight; it was a procedural failure that mutated into a national wound. A single missing sentence—*why this person, why this decision*—proved enough to collapse trust in an entire institution.

The Utrecht hearings revealed something vital. When automated decisions become inscrutable, procedural fairness is not merely weakened; it is replaced. Due process, historically built on reasons, rights, and the possibility of challenge, cannot survive behind a blank screen. An opaque interface becomes a constitutional actor. A silent system is never neutral. It instructs, with every missing justification, that no justification is required.

Designing procedural fairness begins with recognising that systems shape behaviour. Observing the Utrecht interface showed exactly that: caseworkers clicked through its steps because the system felt authoritative. Name the effect: legitimacy bias. Explain it: when a screen presents structured outputs—scores, flags, triage categories—users often treat them as definitive, assuming that the underlying logic is rigorous, even if undisclosed. The implication is stark. Any system that fails to display evidence, factors, or uncertainties inadvertently trains its operators to accept decisions without scrutiny. Fairness cannot coexist with unearned authority.

One of the clearest examples of a corrective approach comes from the United Kingdom's HM Courts & Tribunals Service (HMCTS), which piloted structured reasons-giving templates in 2019 for administrative appeals involving automated assessments. Instead of displaying only an outcome, the interface required officers to fill out a short, structured explanation: which facts mattered, how conflicting evidence was weighed, and where uncertainty remained. This transformed the rhythm of decision-making. Officers paused. They reviewed the evidence. They articulated limits. The outcome did not merely appear; it had to be justified. The visible behaviour changed from passive acceptance to active reasoning. This was procedural fairness encoded in design.

A second example, from Estonia's e-governance infrastructure, demonstrates the power of transparent logging. Since 2014, Estonian citizens have been able to view audit trails associated with automated administrative processes: who accessed their data, which system generated what assessment, and when. The logs are comprehensive and human-readable. They turn surveillance of the citizen into reciprocal accountability: the state must show its working. The interface presents this accountability plainly—time-stamped entries, labelled actions, named officials. The act of making logs visible changes incentives. People consider consequences when they know their decisions leave public traces. Design nudges integrity.

Yet there are limitations. Consider the U.S. Social Security Administration's attempt in 2020 to introduce automated triage for disability claims. The system offered reasons for its categorisations, but these reasons were generic: "based on medical evidence," "based on prior case types," "based on claimant history." They were explanations in form, not substance. The counter-example matters because it highlights the thin line between procedural fairness and procedural theatre. A system that presents non-specific justifications satisfies the letter of explanation but undermines its spirit. To reconcile this, designers must distinguish between reasons that clarify and reasons that obscure. Only the former meet the demands of fairness.

Once reasons and logs are brought into view, the next structural question concerns *disagreement.* Procedural fairness requires not only that affected persons understand a decision, but that they can contest it effectively. Interfaces must therefore present challenge pathways explicitly. One visible behaviour is the presence of a "request reconsideration" button placed directly beside the outcome, rather than buried in footnotes or external pages. Another is the pre-population of appeal forms with the factors used in the decision, enabling individuals to dispute specific claims. These design features transform rights from theoretical entitlements into practical tools.

The motifs of this chapter—the threshold, the narrative, the frame—reappear here. Procedural fairness is a matter of frame. It is not the model's output that determines justice but the set of operations surrounding it: how inputs are displayed, how explanations are structured, how logs are recorded, and how challenges are initiated. These design choices frame the decision, shaping not only what the user sees but what the user believes is permissible to question.

Logging, in particular, becomes the memory of the system. A comprehensive log records the paths not taken: alternative suggestions, ignored evidence, overridden alerts. When logs include uncertainty indicators—such as confidence intervals or missing-data flags—they reveal where judgement, not rules, guided the outcome. This matters because appeals bodies often seek not only to determine whether the final decision was correct but whether the *process* followed was reasonable. Without logs, the process disappears. Without the process, fairness cannot be assessed.

To illustrate this, consider Denmark's adoption of transparent decision logs for municipal benefit assessments in 2021. Each automated recommendation was accompanied by a traceable sequence: data sources consulted, thresholds applied, expert rules triggered. This allowed auditors to reconstruct the decision pipeline without guesswork. It also enabled affected individuals to request specific clarifications: why was their employment history weighted heavily, while their recent medical diagnosis was not? The system's memory allowed for contestation that was precise rather than vague. This precision is one of the visible behaviours that transforms institutional fairness from aspiration to practice.

The requirement of reasons-giving also restricts the design of models. High-dimensional models that cannot offer intelligible causal pathways may be unsuitable for contexts where procedural fairness is legally required. Name this: architectural accountability. Explain it: once a decision must be reasoned, some architectures—particularly those that distribute importance across thousands of latent features—become inappropriate. The implication is that procedural fairness functions as a design constraint, not an afterthought. It shapes what can be deployed, not merely how deployment is presented.

There is temptation to assume that more detail automatically yields better fairness. But detail without structure confuses. Interfaces must balance sufficiency and clarity. One practical pattern, tested in Canada's 2022 Administrative Transparency pilots, organised explanations into three short sections: "Facts used," "Factors weighted most heavily," and "Sources of uncertainty." Each section was capped at a modest character count. This forced precision and discouraged bureaucratic padding. It also made explanations legible to people with no technical background. Fairness is not a matter of volume; it is a matter of clarity.

Of course, procedural fairness also requires *timeliness*. A reason provided too late is no reason at all. Systems that deliver decisions instantly but require days for explanation invert the purpose of due process. One metric that captures this behavioural reality is the "explanation latency": the average time between decision generation and provision of a full justification. When explanation latency exceeds the time window for appeal, the right becomes hollow. Measuring this latency becomes a proxy for institutional respect.

No design can eliminate every injustice. There are situations where urgency constrains deliberation: emergency protective orders, real-time threat assessments, rapid triage during crises. These contexts offer a credible limitation. Yet even in these cases, post-hoc justification and retrospective logs can preserve fairness after the fact. The reconciliation lies in temporal flexibility: immediate action followed by timely explanation. This pattern, seen in aviation incident reporting and adapted to healthcare AI in the UK's NHSX 2020 pilots, shows that fairness can be phased without being abandoned.

Procedural fairness, then, is not an abstraction. It is a set of engineering requirements. It is the discipline of designing systems that *force* reasons to surface, *measure* how decisions are made, and *preserve* the ability to challenge. The motif of the threshold surfaces again here: fairness depends not only on whether an explanation exists, but whether it crosses the threshold of intelligibility.

The unresolved tension, the one that lingers as this subchapter closes, is deceptively simple. As systems grow more complex, and decisions become faster, who will decide how much explanation is enough? And when an automated system produces a decision that is technically correct but procedurally hollow, will institutions choose speed—or dignity?

Harms of aggregation

In February 2018, at a magistrates' court in Kent, a probation officer quietly showed a solicitor the risk classification that had shaped her client's bail recommendation. The defendant, a 23-year-old from Margate, had been labelled "high risk of reoffending" by a national assessment tool. The underlying model examined aggregated patterns: age, postcode, prior cautions, prior employment status. Yet the young man had recently completed a community mentoring programme, held stable work for nine months, and had no violent history. None of that appeared in the score. The solicitor asked the officer why the model ignored such recent progress. The officer replied with a helpless shrug: "It predicts based on people like him." The phrase hung in the air. *People like him.* A category. A pattern. An aggregation. The decision, while procedurally valid, felt morally off-key. It was statistically defensible and individually wrong.

The Kent scene reveals the first fracture point in aggregated decision-making: population averages often misread personal trajectories. A model that claims to measure future risk extrapolates from patterns extracted from thousands of lives. But no individual lives inside an average. When aggregation becomes destiny, errors become injustices. They are not accidental; they stem from the architecture of generalisation itself.

The motif that threads through this subchapter—the silhouette—captures the problem. Aggregated models sketch a silhouette of the person: an outline, a probability, a profile. But individuals are not silhouettes. The difference between outline and reality is where harm hides.

One of the clearest demonstrations of aggregation producing harm comes from the COMPAS risk assessment system used in several U.S. states, widely scrutinised after ProPublica's 2016 investigation. COMPAS predicted recidivism based on a wide array of demographic and behavioural variables, many of which reflected historical patterns of policing. Show the issue: Black defendants in Florida's Broward County were more likely to receive elevated risk scores than white defendants with similar past behaviour (ProPublica 2016). Name the mechanism: structural historical bias.

Explain it: the model was trained on policing and conviction data that itself reflected decades of disparate enforcement. The system aggregated patterns across demographics and crime codes but failed to account for how policing intensity varies by neighbourhood. The implication is that aggregation, without thoughtful calibration, amplifies rather than neutralises inherited injustices.

A contrasting example, illustrating a solution rather than a flaw, comes from New Zealand's Corrections Department, which introduced a more transparent offender risk model in 2021. The system included a "recent change" adjustment layer. This layer allowed caseworkers to enter structured qualitative evidence—completion of treatment programmes, stable housing, sustained employment—which modified the base risk distribution. The visible behaviour was simple: staff routinely updated the change layer before assessments. Aggregation was bounded by personal evidence. The implication is that safeguards can be engineered to allow personal context to correct aggregated patterns.

Yet there is a credible limitation. High-variance individual behaviour is difficult to model reliably, and adjustment layers can introduce inconsistency if poorly governed. A human override that introduces noise rather than insight may reduce predictive accuracy without improving fairness. Reconciling this requires institutional discipline: adjustments must be auditable, time-stamped, and tied to verifiable evidence rather than discretionary impressions. Only then can personalisation refine aggregation without destabilising it.

The harms of aggregation extend beyond the justice system. Consider the 2020 UK Ofqual exam-grading algorithm, used when COVID-19 halted in-person assessments. The model predicted students' grades partly based on historical school performance. Students from historically underperforming schools were systematically downgraded, while students in small cohorts—often in private institutions—were more likely to receive grades consistent with teacher predictions. Show the pattern: aggregated school-level data overpowered individual achievement. Name the failure: ecological misalignment. Explain it: the model assumed that group-level patterns held for each student, ignoring outliers whose performance deviated from the historical baseline. The implication is plain: aggregation collapses distinction, and distinction is where merit and justice reside. Public backlash forced the government to abandon the model. The silhouette had triumphed over the person.

A subtle version of the same pattern appears in healthcare triage tools. In 2019, a major U.S. insurer's population-health algorithm was found to assign lower risk scores to Black patients with equivalent clinical needs (Obermeyer et al., *Science*, 2019). The tool aggregated healthcare spending as a proxy for illness severity. Because Black patients historically spend less—owing to unequal access and systemic barriers—the model concluded that they had lower need. Show the flawed proxy. Name the bias: spending-as-severity. Explain it: aggregation of spending reinforced disparities by treating historical exclusion as evidence of lower illness. The implication is chilling: aggregated data streams can hide structural injustice behind apparently neutral metrics.

These cases demonstrate the first cardinal truth: aggregation is a design choice, not an inevitability. It decides which differences matter and which disappear. The silhouette is drawn by human selection.

To safeguard individuals against misfitting models, two strategies stand out: adversarial testing and contestability windows.

Adversarial testing exposes the model to deliberately difficult or atypical cases. In London's 2022 Metropolitan Police trials of algorithmic triage for digital evidence processing, external researchers constructed adversarial case bundles involving rare combinations of circumstances—such as first-time offenders with unusual digital footprints or cases involving multiple languages. The goal was to measure how the model behaved when aggregation failed to match reality. Show the behaviour: the model's false-negative rate increased sharply for multilingual cases. Name the structure: distributional brittleness. Explain it: the model had been trained largely on monolingual English datasets, causing aggregated patterns to mask risk factors unique to other linguistic groups. The implication is that adversarial testing forces designers to confront the limits of generalisation before deployment rather than after harm.

A complementary safeguard is the contestability window: a defined period during which individuals can challenge model-driven decisions before they are finalised. The Netherlands implemented a contestability requirement in its 2021 Automated Decision Accountability Guidelines, mandating that citizens receive a provisional decision with clear grounds and a 14-day window to present evidence that contradicts aggregated assumptions. The visible behaviour is powerful: citizens submit personalised documentation—work history, medical records, references—that correct the silhouette. Aggregation provides a starting point, not a full account. The implication is that contestability operationalises dignity. It recognises that individuals possess information models cannot infer.

Yet even contestability has boundaries. Some contexts—such as emergency protective interventions or rapid triage in crisis—cannot tolerate extended windows without compromising safety. Reconciling this requires tiered contestability: immediate action paired with delayed finalisation, so evidence can be added retrospectively without undermining urgent protective measures.

At the heart of these safeguards lies a deeper question: what do we owe individuals when they are represented by statistical patterns? The answer is not to abandon aggregation—many decisions require it—but to expose its seams. Aggregation must be made visible, contestable, and correctable. It must be understood as a hypothesis, not a verdict.

The silhouette motif returns here. Every model draws a silhouette of its subject. Some silhouettes are helpful; others distort. The work of ethics is to ensure that silhouettes remain thin outlines, never thick boundaries.

The unresolved tension remains: as models scale, and aggregated patterns grow more predictive across populations, how do we preserve the space for individuals whose lives bend away from the average? When the silhouette becomes increasingly accurate for most people, will systems still make room for the few whose stories refuse to fit?

Repair and redress

On 3 August 2020, Glasgow City Council announced that more than 75,000 Scottish school grades would be reinstated after the Ofqual-style moderation algorithm had disproportionately downgraded pupils from lower-income areas. The political statement was brisk, but the human scene was rawer. In a cramped flat in Easterhouse, a sixteen-year-old named Mhairi opened the revised certificate that restored the A in History she had earned through months of late-night revision. Her mother cried—not because the mark mattered for university entry, but because someone had finally acknowledged that an injustice had been done. The algorithm had made a population-level prediction; the appeals process overturned it in favour of the individual. The episode distilled the central tension addressed here: automated systems may err at scale, but repair must be intimate, legible, and just.

Mhairi's restored grade exposes the first truth about redress in automated systems: legitimacy is not secured by predicting well, but by correcting harm. When systems operate at a population scale, even small statistical distortions produce thousands of affected lives. Repair is not a luxury; it is a structural necessity. And yet, many jurisdictions still lack procedures that allow individuals to challenge machine-generated outcomes without legal counsel or technical fluency. The gap between error and remedy erodes public trust, not because people demand perfection, but because they expect fairness in the aftermath of imperfection.

The quiet motif that will surface again—the hinge—captures the nature of redress. A hinge shifts pressure from one direction to another; it connects movement with stability. Effective redress mechanisms hinge systems towards justice by redirecting the force of automated decisions when they misfire. Without hinges, decisions remain fixed, unyielding, indifferent to new evidence.

The first step in any redress architecture is accessible appeals. Show the stakes: in 2019, the Michigan Unemployment Insurance Agency used an automated fraud-detection system, MIDAS, which falsely accused more than 20,000 claimants of fraud between 2013 and 2015 (State of Michigan Auditor General, 2019). Many were automatically sanctioned: benefits clawed back, wages garnished, credit ruined. Name the absence: open appeals channels. Explain it: the system defaulted to presumption of guilt, and its opaque interface made contestation almost impossible without legal intervention. The implication is severe: when appeals are inaccessible, automation drifts towards authoritarianism by default.

Contrast this with Denmark's Data Ethics Council, which recommended in 2021 that all algorithmic decisions affecting citizens must include a "challenge button" in the digital interface. The behaviour is remarkably concrete: citizens click a single link that opens a structured form requesting reasons, evidence, and a review by a human officer. The implication: appeals become a normal act of citizenship, not an act of resistance. The hinge turns.

A credible counter-example is Estonia's 2018 experiment with automated welfare allocation. While the system offered extremely rapid adjudication, the appeals channel was disproportionately used by older citizens who struggled with the digital interface. The limitation is not the absence of appeals, but the inequality of access. Reconciling this demands multi-channel design: phone, paper, in-person appointments, and digital forms must share a single back-end so that appeals reach the same human adjudicator regardless of entry point. Repair mechanisms must be universal, not technological privileges.

Appeals alone, however, cannot carry the full weight of justice. Systems must also learn. This requires model updates that respond to patterns in the appeals themselves. Show the structure: in 2022, the Dutch Tax Authority adopted a "redress-informed retraining cycle" after its childcare benefits scandal, where a fraud-detection model had disproportionately targeted dual-national families. Name the mechanism: redress signals. Explain it: every upheld appeal triggered a case review that fed back into feature weighting during the next model retraining. The implication is that the system begins to treat upheld errors as valuable data, not embarrassing exceptions.

Yet model updates come with a limitation: they risk introducing oscillation—instability driven by overreacting to a small number of contested decisions. The reconciliation lies in governance thresholds. Only systematic patterns of error—clustered across demographic or behavioural features—should drive model revision. Single cases must trigger individual repair; patterns must trigger structural change.

Restitution is the most delicate form of redress. It requires institutions to acknowledge harm and compensate for it. The hinge motif becomes literal here: restitution is the act of swinging back towards balance after a deviation. One of the clearest examples is Canada's 2021 federal compensation scheme for individuals wrongly denied immigration pathways due to automated document-screening tools. The scheme covered financial losses, legal fees, and in some cases sponsored audits of the affected digital records. The visible behaviour: reimbursement cheques; corrected immigration files; public guidelines published to ensure transparency. The implication: restitution affirms that harm is not merely an inconvenience but a breach requiring concrete remedy.

Another instructive case comes from the UK's 2020 Post Office Horizon IT scandal, in which faulty accounting software, Horizon, falsely implicated hundreds of sub-postmasters in financial discrepancies. Although the system was not a modern AI model, it embodies the same structural logic: automated inference, institutional deference to the system, and catastrophic human consequences. After years of litigation, the government announced an independent compensation scheme and a programme to reflect software errors explicitly in future auditing rules. The implication extends beyond Post Office branches: when software-driven harm is systemic, redress must include repair of the institutional habits that allowed the harm to persist.

Repair, however, is not only backward-facing. It must also create future safety. One of the strongest strategies for this is embedding "near-miss logging" into operational systems—capturing cases where the model almost made a harmful decision but did not. In 2021, the Royal Free London NHS Trust piloted a clinical decision-support tool for kidney injury alerts. Engineers logged every case where clinicians overrode a high-risk alert or ignored a low-risk one. Show the behaviour: clinicians clicked "override" with short notes such as "medication side-effects" or "patient-specific baseline low."

Name the mechanism: near-miss capture. Explain it: by collecting these deviations, model developers could identify failure modes before they materialised at scale. The implication is that repair becomes anticipatory rather than merely reactive.

A limitation must be acknowledged: near-miss logs depend on staff diligence and institutional culture. If overrides are perceived as insubordination, the logs will be sparse and misleading. Reconciling this requires legal and organisational protection. Near-miss reporting must be insulated from blame, modelled explicitly on aviation's just-culture principles. Only then can repair and learning coexist.

Another vital hinge in redress architecture is explainability. Without intelligible explanations, affected individuals cannot meaningfully contest outcomes, and institutions cannot diagnose failure. France's 2021 Digital Republic Act requires public services using algorithmic decision-making to provide "meaningful information about the logic involved," including feature importance and reasoning templates. Show the effect: a citizen denied a housing subsidy can request a step-by-step account of the relevant criteria. Name the tool: structured explanation. Explain it: explanations allow individuals to identify factual errors and help system designers detect misfitting correlations. The implication: explanation is not a courtesy but a precondition for redress.

Finally, accessible redress must include time-bound windows for review. If decisions solidify too quickly, harm becomes irreversible. The hinge must move before the frame sets. This is particularly evident in credit-scoring systems where incorrect data can depress an individual's score for years. The EU's 2020 Consumer Credit Guidelines emphasised "rapid correction windows," requiring credit bureaux to update contested data within 30 days once verified. Show the behaviour: correction cycles. Name the purpose: temporal equity. Explain it: individuals should not languish under outdated or false data. The implication: time is part of justice.

Taken together, these elements—appeals, model updates, restitution, near-miss learning, explanations, and time windows—form an integrated architecture of repair. But their effectiveness depends on an unresolved question that lingers over every automated system: how quickly, and how generously, should institutions bend towards the individual when aggregated logic conflicts with personal reality? The answer defines the moral weight of the hinge.

Chapter 7
AI in Care and Work

The paramedics had been triaging patients for eight hours when the allocation screen froze. It was April 2020, in an overstretched London hospital, and an AI-supported tool designed to guide clinicians through surge conditions had suggested moving a deteriorating patient—sixty-seven years old, breathless but conscious—down the priority queue. A junior doctor hesitated. The numbers were clear; the justification was not. She overrode the recommendation, trusting her intuition shaped by years of night shifts and too many difficult endings. The patient survived. Others, processed by the same system with the same indicators, did not. Long after the crisis passed, clinicians continued to ask a deceptively simple question: who, or what, had been making the real decisions during those weeks when the boundary between guidance and command blurred?

This moment—an exhausted doctor facing a silent machine—captures the stakes of AI in the domains where vulnerability meets labour. Care and work are sites of profound asymmetry: limited resources, uneven power, and human bodies that can be harmed by delay, by pressure, or by a single misjudged click. These domains carry a distinctive moral gravity because the decisions they host are not abstract optimisations. They shape the distribution of suffering, fatigue, and dignity. And as AI systems become embedded in emergency rooms, warehouses, contact centres, and support platforms, they begin to quietly rearrange how judgement is exercised, how responsibility is shared, and how value is measured.

What happens when a triage algorithm assigns a patient a probability instead of a promise? How do workers negotiate autonomy when a dashboard in Seattle or Singapore monitors their pace, posture, and pause frequency? What becomes of expertise when an AI assistant drafts the plan, suggests the dosage, predicts the hazard, and leaves the human to rubber-stamp? These questions are not speculative; they are already shaping clinical governance, labour regulation, and organisational memory. And they reveal a deeper pattern that structures this chapter: each time AI enters a domain of care or work, it unsettles the tacit contracts that hold those domains together.

Part of the unease stems from a long-standing human habit: the tendency to treat efficiency as a virtue in itself. AI systems, with their crisp outputs and procedural confidence, can amplify this habit until it eclipses more fragile forms of value—context, compassion, craft. During the worst days of the pandemic, hospitals in New York and Madrid asked whether triage tools should consider social vulnerability alongside survival probability. Some did; many did not. The divergence was not technical but ethical: should limited resources be allocated solely by predicted benefit, or should equity, disadvantage, and historical exclusion matter too? These debates exposed how quickly broad principles collapse into banal proxies, and how essential it is to interrogate the objectives we ask machines to optimise.

Workplaces mirror this tension. Warehouses across Europe now rely on AI-driven routing and monitoring systems that promise smoother logistics and fewer accidents. Yet the same systems often reduce workers' agency, constraining judgement to pre-set thresholds and punishing deviation from algorithmic rhythm. The issue is not simply surveillance; it is the gradual erosion of trust between worker and employer. Analytics intended to enhance safety can slip into coercion when they dictate pace without acknowledging human variability—pain, weather, fatigue, or the simple need to slow down after a difficult interaction. When these systems become the quiet supervisors of labour, the moral question deepens: how should we design monitoring that respects bodily limits and preserves dignity?

At the centre of this chapter lies a paradox. AI can mitigate human blind spots—bias, inconsistency, cognitive overload—yet it can also obscure or magnify them. It can distribute expertise more widely, yet hollow it out when systems become too prescriptive. It can make organisations more resilient, yet brittle if staff stop understanding the systems they rely on. What distinguishes improvement from degradation is rarely the algorithm itself; it is the framing of its purpose, the guardrails around its authority, and the feedback loops that preserve human oversight.

A recurring motif here is the ledger: the quiet record of actions, corrections, and recoveries that reveal what a system truly values. In care settings, the ledger includes not only correct diagnoses but the misclassifications caught early, the escalations made on instinct, the interventions that saved minutes and lives. In work environments, the ledger captures not only productivity metrics but adaptive responses—how people navigate interruptions, support each other, or prevent small errors from becoming costly failures. When organisations rely solely on the numbers that are easy to count, they risk moral myopia. The more humane measures—trust stability, learning curves, cognitive load—remain invisible unless deliberately surfaced.

This chapter threads four interconnected themes. First, the ethics of triage under pressure, where fairness must be operationalised with clarity and courage rather than left to ad hoc improvisation. Second, the design of monitoring systems that enhance safety without sliding into coercion, preserving not only health but dignity. Third, the delicate balance between assistance and de-skilling: how AI can serve as a mentor rather than a silent usurper of human craft. And fourth, the need to recalibrate organisational metrics so that they capture what truly matters in care and work, rather than what happens to be measurable.

Across these themes runs the deeper question of how society wants to distribute agency among humans and machines. Should AI narrow the domain of human judgement to reduce variance, or should it broaden it by supporting more confident, informed decisions? How much autonomy should systems hold during crisis conditions when reaction time is short? What forms of consent and consultation should workers expect when analytics shape their daily lives? And how will organisations ensure that expertise is strengthened rather than eroded across generations of practitioners?

These questions do not admit easy answers. They require attention to context, tradition, professional norms, and the lived experience of those most affected. But they share a common thread: AI in care and work must not substitute for human responsibility; it must scaffold it. The systems that triage patients, schedule shifts, or guide apprentices will only earn legitimacy if they remain true to the core commitments of these domains: to protect the vulnerable, to respect labour, to cultivate expertise, and to value people as more than datapoints.

As these commitments meet the realities of automation—the speed, the scale, the seductive precision—the coming pages will examine how values can be operationalised without being diminished. They will show how organisations can design systems that support carers, clinicians, and workers rather than overshadow them. And they will confront the central dilemma that every institution must now face: how to harness computational power without losing the humane wisdom that care and work have always required.

Triage ethics under pressure

At 6:40 a.m. on 13 March 2020, clinicians at Papa Giovanni XXIII Hospital in Bergamo confronted a queue that already exceeded their ventilator supply. Ambulances arrived in tight succession; corridors reverberated with the piercing rhythm of monitors hunting for oxygen traces they could not find. A senior intensivist, Dr Roberto Cosentini, stood before a whiteboard covered in colour-coded names, the makeshift triage ledger that governed life-and-death decisions throughout that month in northern Italy. Each mark mapped a judgement: who might survive with support, who needed immediate intubation, who required palliative care. The hospital's digital tools strained to keep pace, yet the central fact remained brutally analogue: too many patients, too few machines. The clinicians worked. They hoped. Some choices saved lives. Others could not.

Crisis triage is rarely about heroics. It is about the tension between principle and scarcity, played out minute by minute. When a health system enters surge conditions, its promise of equal treatment buckles; standard protocols defer to "crisis standards" that reorder priorities under duress. AI systems, increasingly tasked with supporting these decisions, inherit the same tension. They can estimate short-term survival with startling speed; they cannot absorb the weight of moral consequence. The motif that threads through this subchapter—the line—captures the pressure of making choices on the boundary of possibility: the line of patients waiting for care, the line clinicians walk between equity and efficiency, and the statistical lines that algorithms draw to rank competing needs.

The lesson from Bergamo is not that technology failed. It is that surge triage is ethically demanding even before algorithms enter the room. To understand how AI might support or distort judgement, we must begin with the lived texture of crisis: rapid deterioration rates, limited time budgets, and the need for consistent decisions across rotating teams. Surge ethics hinge on visibility. Decisions must be explainable to colleagues exhausted by twelve-hour shifts and to families desperate for sense-making. When the line forms, opacity corrodes trust. If an algorithm assigns a lower priority to a patient because of comorbidities, clinicians need to know precisely how that metric was calculated, and what discount on survival probability it imposed.

A second example, from the New York Presbyterian system in April 2020, shows how triage rules can drift under pressure. Early in the surge, the hospital used a modified Sequential Organ Failure Assessment (SOFA) score to guide ventilator allocation. Within days, clinicians observed that the scoring curve heavily penalised patients with chronic conditions while failing to capture rapid improvements after early intervention. The result was a subtle but consistent skew: younger, healthier patients moved up the queue; older patients with reversible episodes remained low, even when clinicians predicted a good outcome. The scoring system did not intend injustice—its limitation was structural. It captured severity at a moment in time rather than likely trajectory. This distinction shaped outcomes.

Such cases illustrate a general claim: triage tools often conflate prediction with prescription. They forecast clinical risk; they do not decide moral worth. Yet in crisis conditions, prediction slides into prescription when staff are overwhelmed and decision time shrinks. Show the forecast; name the uncertainty; explain the limits; then ask what should follow. This four-step structure helps separate what the algorithm can know from what an ethical framework must decide. If survival probability is 42 per cent, what is the ethically justified threshold for resource allocation? If the confidence interval is wide, how should ambiguity factor into ranking? Without an explicit framework, probability becomes proxy for value.

A further example comes from the Israeli Ministry of Health's deployment of a triage-support system during mass-casualty training in Tel Aviv in 2019. The system processed vital signs in real time and suggested priority categories. Within minutes of simulated surge, clinicians noticed that the tool under-triaged patients with atypical presentations—quiet hypoxia, delayed shock—because the training dataset lacked these profiles. The misclassification rate was small but significant: two simulated patients who should have been escalated were temporarily deprioritised. The incident demonstrated that even high-performing systems can falter when domain-specific variance is narrow. The implication is clear: crisis triage algorithms must be trained on diverse physiological patterns, or their efficiency becomes brittle when confronted with the unexpected.

Counter-examples also matter. During the 2011 Tōhoku earthquake and tsunami, Japan's emergency medical response relied largely on human triage without algorithmic support. Despite the scale of devastation, after-action reviews found that clinicians maintained a consistent triage protocol across prefectures, guided by decades of drilled practice and clear doctrinal principles. This shows that human-led crisis triage, when well-trained and well-structured, can deliver fairness under pressure. Yet this strength carries its own fragility: it depends on sustained investment in training, coordination, and institutional memory—conditions not always present. Reconciling this limitation requires acknowledging that AI can serve as a stabiliser when human expertise varies, but must not displace the ethical reasoning that anchors triage legitimacy.

Fairness guardrails for crisis standards begin with transparency. A triage protocol must specify what counts: survival probability within a defined window; expected long-term recovery; resource intensity required; and potential to deteriorate rapidly. These criteria are not morally neutral. Each reflects a judgement about what society values during extremes. For instance, if the protocol emphasises maximising lives saved, it will prioritise those with high near-term survival. If it emphasises fairness to structurally disadvantaged groups, it must compensate for historical inequities that affect health baselines. These compensation rules must be explicit. They cannot emerge tacitly from the data, because data alone cannot express moral commitments.

Operationalising fairness in triage means measuring behaviours, not abstract ideals. When clinicians override an algorithmic recommendation, the system should log not only the override but the rationale—symptom shift, clinical gestalt, family context. When an algorithm consistently downgrades a subgroup, administrators must audit both the model inputs and the threshold settings. For example, an audit at a Massachusetts hospital in May 2020 found that oxygen saturation metrics skewed lower for patients with darker skin tones due to pulse oximeter bias, affecting ventilator priority. Once identified, the hospital recalibrated protocols to include arterial blood gas tests for borderline cases. The change was concrete: more equitable prioritisation, backed by measurable shifts in allocation patterns.

The line motif returns here as a diagnostic tool. Draw a line of patients ranked by need. Now ask: who repeatedly appears near thresholds? Who is misclassified when correlation masquerades as causation? Crisis standards must guard against "threshold injustice", where statistical noise causes individuals to tip in and out of priority categories unpredictably. Adversarial testing—creating simulated edge cases that probe model boundaries—helps reveal where fragility lies. If small perturbations in vitals cause significant ranking changes, the protocol is too sensitive; if large shifts cause none, it may be too rigid. Both conditions threaten fairness.

Decision time budgets form another guardrail. Surge triage is not a leisurely deliberation. Clinicians need systems designed to match their available cognitive bandwidth: ten seconds for a glanceable priority indicator; two minutes for a trend view; five minutes for a justification panel. When interfaces exceed these budgets, they force shortcuts that compromise judgment. Clear time budgets transform fairness from aspiration into practice by aligning ethical guidance with operational reality.

A final guardrail concerns the moral horizon of crisis standards. Surge conditions may last days or weeks, but their consequences endure. Patients who were deprioritised may seek explanations months later; public inquiries may revisit aggregated decisions years after the fact. Systems must therefore produce audit trails that survive scrutiny: logs of criteria used, exceptions noted, thresholds adjusted, disagreements recorded. The audit trail is not administrative debris; it is the narrative architecture of accountability.

We return once more to the line. In every surge, the line of patients reflects the limits of collective capacity. AI can help manage the line, but it cannot determine what a just line looks like. That determination rests on societal values expressed clearly in crisis standards before the emergency begins. When scarcity returns—and it will—the question remains unresolved: should triage optimise for lives saved, life-years saved, fairness across groups, or some principled blend of all three? The next crisis will force institutions to commit.

Monitoring without coercion

Just after 5 p.m. on 12 November 2021, workers at the Amazon fulfilment centre in Coventry watched their productivity dashboards jitter and refresh every few seconds. Each screen displayed the familiar bars—items picked per minute, downtime minutes, error counts—metrics that determined not only daily workflow but, increasingly, job security. A brief network outage had frozen entries earlier in the day, but as the system caught up, several workers saw their numbers slump. One picker, assigned to a congested aisle, watched her rate fall by almost a third, triggering an automated "under-performance flag". The system did not account for the broken scanner she had reported, nor the temporary block from a pallet shift. She exhaled slowly. A five-word sentence formed in her mind. *This should feel fair.* It didn't.

That moment captures a central dilemma of worker analytics: the same sensing technologies that can improve safety and workflow can also reduce labour to statistical residue. A dashboard can highlight hazardous repetition, track overheating, and prevent fatigue injuries. It can also coerce through constant comparison, amplifying every lull. When monitoring systems ignore context—the blocked aisle, the broken scanner—they turn measurement into pressure. The motif that threads through this subchapter is the shadow: the data shadow each worker casts on a screen, and the ethical demand to ensure that shadow does not eclipse the person. When the shadow grows too rigid, dignity shrinks.

A first principle emerges from the Coventry example. Show the metric; name the context; explain the deviation; consider the implication. If a worker's rate drops due to environmental constraints, the system must capture the constraint explicitly or risk punishing the wrong behaviour. Failure to encode context is not merely a technical gap; it is a value choice favouring throughput over fairness. Managers often defend raw-rate dashboards as neutral tools, yet neutrality collapses when conditions vary between stations. Data that omit context cannot treat workers equitably because the omissions map directly onto lived experience.

Historical cases show how design choices turn observation into pressure. In 2013, UPS introduced handheld scanners that timestamped delivery routes in New York. The system aimed to optimise fuel and time efficiency. Drivers quickly discovered that the software counted every pause, from traffic stalls to building security queues, as inefficiency. Several drivers contested disciplinary actions, arguing that delays were inherent to dense urban delivery. The company later updated its routing algorithm, but the episode revealed an enduring truth: when analytics overlook environmental variance, workers carry the burden. The shadow lengthens unfairly.

A contrasting example—in the automotive sector—shows how monitoring can advance safety without coercion. Since 2016, Volvo's Gothenburg plant has used ergonomic sensors to detect repetitive strain risks on production lines. The system generates alerts when cumulative strain exceeds set thresholds, prompting micro-breaks or rotation. Crucially, the dashboard suppresses individual output rates and emphasises risk exposure instead. Workers reported (Volvo internal review 2019) that they felt "supported rather than watched", a distinction anchored in what the system chose to display. Here, the shadow worked as protection, not scrutiny.

These two cases illustrate the stakes: monitoring architecture encodes assumptions about purpose. If the purpose is safety, metrics must foreground hazards, near-misses, and recovery times. If the purpose is productivity, metrics must calibrate opportunity conditions, not merely count outputs. In both domains, monitoring without coercion requires that data representation include space for explanation. A system that only ingests numeric rates but not the reasons behind them invites misuse.

The Coventry workers' predicament underscores another ethical tension: measurement can freeze a moment but cannot capture lived sequence. Productivity slumps often follow bursts of high intensity or periods of physical discomfort. Without temporal smoothing—or a visible behaviour like a flag for "equipment fault" or "congestion"—dashboards distort reality. Implementing temporal smoothing is not a technical flourish but a moral safeguard. It prevents single anomalies from catalysing punitive decisions.

A limitation must also be acknowledged. Even well-designed systems can slip into soft coercion when managerial culture prioritises competition. For example, in 2020, a food-delivery company in Paris deployed an app showing comparative delivery speeds. Although the app included context flags for weather and traffic, riders reported feeling compelled to maintain maximum pace to avoid sliding down the leaderboard. The system's architecture was sensitive; the culture around it was not. Reconciling this limitation requires coupling technical fairness with organisational norms that discourage comparative pressure. Analytics cannot substitute for leadership ethics.

The shadow motif returns when considering privacy. Wearables that track posture or fatigue can improve ergonomics, yet they also create granular datasets of movement. Unless retention windows are short and access strictly limited, the shadow risks becoming a dossier. A 2022 study by the TUC (Trade Union Congress) warned that several UK firms retained sensor data for over a year, far beyond ergonomic relevance. The extended retention repurposed safety data into performance surveillance. Shortening retention to weeks, not months, aligns data life cycles with legitimate safety aims.

Two criteria help assess whether monitoring respects dignity. First: does the system allow workers to annotate their own data? If a scanner malfunctions or a workstation overheats, the worker must be able to mark the record. Annotation is a quiet assertion of agency within the analytics environment. Second: does the system model variability as signal rather than noise? People slow down after continuous exertion. They pause to reset focus. A system that treats slowdown as failure misconstrues human rhythm. Recognising these rhythms is not indulgence; it is operational wisdom. Fatigue curves matter.

To ground this point, consider a pilot project run in 2021 at the Royal Mail sorting centre in Glasgow. Postural sensors flagged rising fatigue mid-shift. Instead of raising performance alerts, supervisors used the data to adjust rotation schedules. Accident rates fell modestly; reported strain decreased. The success did not hinge on advanced algorithms but on a managerial commitment to treat monitoring as support. The shadow shrank to an assistive outline.

A credible counter-example warns against complacency. In Shenzhen in 2019, a factory tested EEG-based caps to track worker concentration. The devices aimed to detect cognitive overload, but the implementation included real-time supervisor dashboards. Several workers withdrew consent after discovering that concentration dips triggered managerial messages. The project was suspended. The lesson: when monitoring technologies target inner states rather than outward behaviours, the risk of coercion intensifies. Tracking neural signatures crosses a boundary that most workers find intolerable. Any system venturing toward cognitive measures must confront the legitimacy of such intrusion, not only its accuracy.

If monitoring is to be ethical, it must be reversible. Workers should know when they are monitored, for what purpose, for how long, and by whom. The right to step out of the shadow—during breaks, for example—anchors dignity. Allowing "monitoring off" zones in break rooms or non-task areas affirms that analytics serve work, not control. This right helps maintain psychological safety, a condition essential for sustained performance and wellbeing.

The shadow motif reaches its final form when concerns escalate. If a dashboard triggers an automated warning, the system should provide a structured path for contestation: a timestamp, a data trace, and an explanation window. Workers must have the authority to say, "That metric misrepresents my situation," and receive correction. Accountability structures work only when they include the people most affected.

We end at the threshold of a difficult question. Monitoring technologies can keep workers safe, prevent injuries, and optimise flow. They can also strain autonomy and compress dignity when misused. How, then, should organisations decide when to deploy new sensing systems, and when restraint is the wiser course? The next section takes up this tension, tracing how autonomy boundaries must be drawn when the shadow of analytics threatens to become a cage.

Assistance vs de-skilling

On 3 March 2019, at the Royal Berkshire Hospital in Reading, a junior radiographer named Priya Menon reviewed a chest X-ray flagged by an automated triage tool. The system had placed a bright amber border around a small opacity in the upper lobe. Priya hesitated. The AI's confidence score read 0.78, but the attending consultant was busy with an emergency CT interpretation. She leaned closer to the screen. The opacity looked less like consolidation and more like a benign overlap of vascular shadows—something her supervisor often pointed out during face-to-face teaching rounds. Rather than accept the AI's prompt, Priya retrieved two prior films and compared vessel angles, a behaviour she had deliberately practised. The opacity dissolved under closer scrutiny. Her judgement held. A five-word sentence flickered through her thoughts: *I still know something.* Her relief revealed more than self-assurance; it revealed the subtle fear that as systems guide more decisions, human skill may ossify.

Priya's moment captures a central tension shaping modern work: assistance can sharpen expertise or erode it. Automation that aims to help can accidentally hollow skill if it removes the conditions under which knowledge is formed. The quiet motif that guides this subchapter is the *muscle*, the cognitive muscle that strengthens through strain. When AI lifts too much weight, the muscle weakens. When AI lifts with us—showing intermediate reasoning, pacing its interventions, exposing its uncertainties—the muscle grows. The line between help and harm depends on design.

A first claim emerges clearly from Priya's case. Show the behaviour: reliance on an amber highlight. Name the dynamic: cognitive offloading. Explain the mechanism: repeated dependence on prompts displaces deliberate practice. The implication is stark. If AI systems offer answers without revealing the pathway to those answers, they deny professionals the opportunity to rehearse the subtle distinctions that constitute expertise. This mechanism is not speculative; it appears whenever users shift from inferential reasoning to supervisory passivity.

Historical precedent sharpens this point. When the Boeing 777 entered service in 1995, its flight management systems automated many navigation tasks. Pilots at several airlines, including British Airways, soon reported a shift in cockpit skill distribution. Autopilot efficiency improved fuel management, but manual handling proficiency declined unless airlines mandated regular hand-flying segments. The Civil Aviation Authority flagged this trend in a 2002 review, emphasising that even well-trained pilots lose tactile intuition if automation consistently pre-empts manual control. The case shows how automation can erode embodied expertise unless systems actively protect the learning environment.

A more recent example demonstrates an alternative path. In 2020, at the Mayo Clinic in Rochester, clinicians trialled a cardiology support system that displayed not only diagnostic suggestions but also the intermediate features it extracted—wall motion patterns, segment scores, and comparative timelines across prior echoes. Physicians could inspect how each output was derived, and the system invited them to adjust thresholds, revealing the sensitivity of its own decision surface. The outcome was not de-skilling but enrichment. Trainees reported improved understanding of subtle function gradients precisely because the system taught as it assisted.

These two cases—aviation automation drift and cardiology interpretability—frame the stakes for professional domains. The muscle strengthens only when strain is shared. If automation hides the strain, skill fades. The question becomes how to design systems whose assistance operates as apprenticeship rather than replacement.

A limitation must be acknowledged. Even well-designed systems risk de-skilling when institutional incentives reward speed over understanding. A law firm in London trialled an AI-driven contract review tool in 2021. The system highlighted clauses requiring attention, but junior solicitors often approved changes based on the tool's "priority" tags without reading the underlying provisions. Billing pressures nudged them to trust the tags blindly. The firm later reinstated a requirement for annotated reviews to maintain interpretive quality. Reconciliation lies in aligning incentives with learning. If environments privilege throughput, even pedagogical systems become shortcuts.

The motif of the muscle returns when examining interface timing. If assistance appears too early, it prevents effort. If it appears too late, it frustrates. The ideal timing echoes apprenticeship models: observe, attempt, receive feedback, attempt again. In cognitive terms, the attempt is where skill forms. AI systems that wait until a user has taken an initial step—drafting a clause, marking a lesion, outlining a repair sequence—can shape assistance around demonstrated reasoning rather than pre-empt it. When Google's DeepMind piloted a clinical documentation assistant at University College London Hospitals in 2022, the model generated draft summaries only after clinicians entered key findings. This sequencing preserved the clinician's analytical step. Time budgets matter, but ordering matters more. Sequence shapes skill.

The clearest evidence for this dynamic comes from industrial robotics. At the BMW plant in Dingolfing, where collaborative robots were introduced in 2013 to assist with repetitive fastening, engineers added a "teaching mode". Workers demonstrated fastening sequences, and robots learned adjustments from human gestures. Over time, workers reported greater procedural understanding because teaching required unpacking tacit knowledge.

The robot's learning became a mirror through which workers re-encountered their own craft. The muscle flexed in both directions.

A credible counter-example warns against overconfidence. In several financial institutions trialling AI-driven portfolio review assistants between 2019 and 2021, analysts reported diminished grasp of risk factor interactions. The assistants produced tidy risk decomposition charts, but analysts ceased calculating their own sensitivities or running manual scenario checks. When volatility spiked in October 2020, teams struggled to diagnose discrepancies because the underlying logic had become opaque. The limitation is not inherent to AI support; it stems from systems that substitute for foundational reasoning rather than scaffold it.

A corrective principle follows: systems must expose intermediate states. Whether in risk analysis, legal drafting, or clinical reasoning, the path to a suggested outcome should be visible, manipulable, and contestable. This is the apprenticeship model rewritten for complex domains. A carpenter learns by seeing cuts, not only by inspecting finished joints. In knowledge work, cuts correspond to intermediate representations. Show the derivation, not just the answer.

We should also consider deliberate difficulty. Some skills harden only through encounter with challenge. In medicine, residents learn differential diagnosis by working through ambiguous findings, not only by confirming clear-cut ones. AI triage tools that filter cases by confidence level risk depriving trainees of the messy middle where judgement is forged. Similarly, engineering apprentices who engage only with optimised simulations lose contact with edge conditions. A thoughtful system loops novices into those ambiguities by allowing them to explore counterfactuals: "What would this look like if the opacity were vascular rather than infectious?" "How would the risk profile shift if liquidity dried up?" Counterfactual exploration builds cognitive muscle.

To make apprenticeship systemic, developers should consider attention cues rather than direct answers. Highlighting relevant sections of an image, clause, or dataset nudges users toward active interpretation. In fields like pathology, such cues have improved trainee accuracy without diminishing engagement. But cues must be calibrated; overwhelming highlights can pre-empt curiosity. Subtle cues preserve agency.

We can see the motif again in iterative testing. When designers at Airbus experimented with pilot-assist systems in 2018, they found that pilots who could toggle between fully automated and semi-automated modes retained more skill than those confined to a single mode. The toggling served as intermittent strain. Predictably, variability—not constant guidance—kept the muscle supple.

These lessons converge into one operational truth. Assistance systems must encode pedagogy. They must teach. A system that accelerates present work at the cost of future competence is not assistance; it is extraction. Apprenticeship modes—sequenced feedback, intermediate reasoning displays, deliberate difficulty—counter this extraction.

A final tension remains unresolved. As models grow more capable and time pressures mount, organisations will be tempted to shift from assistive systems to substitutive ones. Skill will atrophy if human judgement becomes a ceremonial presence rather than an active force. The forward question becomes inescapable: when the muscle can be maintained only by resisting automation's ease, who decides how much strain to preserve, and at what cost to pace and productivity?

Measuring what matters

On 14 January 2021, inside the intensive care unit at St George's Hospital in London, a senior nurse named Emily Foster watched a clinical support system hesitate. The AI-driven dashboard, designed to flag early signs of deterioration, displayed a reassuring green beside a patient whose blood pressure had drifted downward for three consecutive readings. Emily frowned. The algorithm weighted oxygen saturation heavily, and the patient's numbers sat comfortably within range. But Emily saw something else: a subtle rigidity in the patient's breathing that the system's sensors failed to capture. She paused the automation-driven care sequence, performed a manual assessment, and escalated treatment. Hours later, a consultant confirmed that Emily's intervention prevented a life-threatening spiral. The green light had misled. Her judgement had saved time. It likely saved the patient. Five quiet words hovered in her mind afterwards: *The metric missed the moment.*

The scene crystallises a wider problem in AI-assisted work. Systems tend to measure what is easy to log—response times, throughput, error rates—not what is essential for safety or dignity. Human performance under automation cannot be reduced to a single indicator. Skills bend, trust flexes, fatigue accumulates, and teams absorb stress in uneven ways. Yet most evaluation frameworks attend only to speed and accuracy, the visible surface of competence. What matters often lives in the invisible space between error and recovery, between confidence and overconfidence, between assistance and overload. The motif that threads through this subchapter is the *pulse*: a measure that rises and falls, revealing the living dynamics beneath the numbers. A system that fails to sense the pulse cannot claim to measure performance meaningfully.

A first claim becomes evident when we observe real settings. Show the behaviour: Emily's swift intervention after recognising the dashboard's blind spot. Name the dynamic: error recovery. Explain the mechanism: the system offered a static metric, but the human recognised a dynamic pattern the metric ignored. The implication is clear. Evaluations that extract only discrete outcomes—correct or incorrect—fail to capture the quality of correction, the time to detect drift, and the stability of judgement under strain. These dimensions define competence in environments where automation and human skill intertwine.

Consider a checkable example. In 2017, the Royal Free London NHS Foundation Trust piloted a clinical AI tool intended to support detection of acute kidney injury. An internal audit later noted that while the model flagged incidents effectively, clinicians' ability to detect false positives depended on prior experience with atypical cases. Workers who maintained active diagnostic habits overrode inappropriate alerts more quickly. Those who relied heavily on the system struggled when the model erred. Error recovery became the true performance differentiator, not the system's headline accuracy. Metrics that tracked override quality—how quickly and confidently clinicians rejected a faulty alert—proved more predictive of patient safety.

A second example, outside healthcare, underscores the same lesson. At the Volkswagen plant in Wolfsburg in 2022, engineers tested an AI-enabled torque calibration tool on the assembly line. The system adjusted settings automatically, improving average consistency. But during a trial, technicians noticed that when humidity affected material expansion, the model failed to compensate adequately. Experienced workers caught the drift by feel, adjusting torque manually. Management added a metric to capture deviation detection time—a measure of human vigilance. The plant discovered that teams with faster detection times had lower rework rates across the year. Here again, the pulse lay not in baseline accuracy but in responsiveness to deviation.

The credible counter-example complicates the narrative. In customer-support centres across several UK telecom firms between 2020 and 2021, supervisors attempted to incorporate "error recovery scores" into agent evaluation dashboards. They measured how often agents corrected automated script recommendations. But the scoring system inadvertently encouraged employees to override automation excessively, even when it was correct, to demonstrate "initiative". This inflated resolution times and introduced new inconsistencies. The limitation shows that human-centred metrics can themselves distort behaviour if poorly designed. Reconciliation lies in measuring patterns rather than isolated events: stability of override quality, not count; time to correction, not the mere act; calibration, not contrarianism.

The second claim follows naturally: trust must be measured as a behaviour, not an attitude. Trust is neither blind acceptance nor reflexive scepticism. It is calibrated expectation. Show the behaviour: a clinician who cross-checks low-confidence alerts but accepts high-confidence ones after verifying consistency. Name the metric: trust stability—how consistently a person aligns trust with system performance over time. Explain the mechanism: stable trust emerges when users encounter predictable system behaviour and have tools to understand uncertainty. The implication is profound. Without measuring trust stability, organisations risk environments where workers either defer uncritically or resist persistently. Both distort the pulse.

We can locate a vivid case. In 2019, the Dutch Ministry of Justice piloted an algorithmic risk indicator for youth reoffending. Social workers were asked to use the tool during assessment meetings. Subsequent evaluation found that workers who calibrated trust well—accepting the model's priors when evidence aligned and challenging them when contextual knowledge disagreed—made more consistent recommendations amid comparable caseloads. Assessors with unstable trust either followed the model even when local circumstances contradicted it or dismissed it entirely. Formal accuracy metrics concealed this divergence. Only through analysing override patterns and contextual annotations did reviewers discover the truth: trust stability predicted decision fairness better than raw precision.

The motif resurfaces: the pulse changes with stress. Trust stability tends to degrade when systems obscure uncertainty. This leads to the third claim: uncertainty communication becomes a metric of its own. Without visible intervals—ranges, confidence levels, sensitivity analyses—users cannot maintain calibrated trust. And without calibrated trust, system outputs risk misapplication.

A counter-tension appears in high-pressure environments. During the COVID-19 surge at King's College Hospital in April 2020, a real-time risk dashboard included uncertainty bands for predicted oxygen demand. Staff initially found them helpful. But when volatility spiked, the wide bands caused confusion. Certain shifts began ignoring the intervals altogether. This limitation shows that displaying uncertainty is necessary but not sufficient; intervals must connect to meaningful decisions, and teams need training to interpret them. Reconciliation rests in designing uncertainty displays that guide action rather than produce cognitive overload.

The fourth claim addresses a dimension often ignored by performance dashboards: fatigue. Not personal fatigue alone, but fatigue as measurable human strain across teams. Show the behaviour: slowed override rates during night shifts, increased reliance on automation, reduced capacity to spot anomalies. Name the dimension: fatigue load. Explain the mechanism: cognitive resources deplete under sustained vigilance, reducing the quality of human–machine interaction. The implication is unavoidable. Systems that fail to measure fatigue invite silent degradation of judgement.

The aviation sector learned this decades ago. After the 1994 crash of USAir Flight 427, investigators highlighted pilot overload and task saturation. In response, manufacturers such as Airbus began incorporating workload models into cockpit design. These models quantified cognitive strain by measuring interaction sequences, time-to-interruption, and error cascade likelihood. Translated to AI-assisted work, similar metrics—time between prompts, override frequency decay, decision latency—offer quantifiable signs of fatigue. Without them, dashboards observe only outputs, not the human cost of producing them.

A contemporary example reinforces this. When a major UK grocery chain introduced AI scheduling in 2021, warehouse staff reported rising strain despite stable productivity numbers. A research team from the University of Warwick analysed scanner timestamps and micro-break patterns, identifying increased micro-error rates—tiny scanning misreads and repeated confirmations—during long shifts. These micro-errors served as a more reliable marker of fatigue than self-reported surveys. After redesigning shift rotations based on the metric, staff reported lower stress and fewer micro-errors. The case shows how measuring what matters requires attention to embodied cues, not only task completion.

A limitation again tempers enthusiasm. Fatigue metrics can slide into surveillance if misused. If employers treat fatigue indicators as disciplinary data rather than signals for redesigning workload, workers will conceal strain, invalidating the metric. The reconciliation demands guardrails: fatigue must be treated as a system-level variable, not a personal failing. Metrics should trigger adjustments in workflow, not punitive scrutiny.

Across these examples, the motif holds: the pulse guides the system. Error recovery measures reveal responsiveness. Trust stability measures calibration. Fatigue load measures sustainability. Together, they map a fuller landscape of human–machine performance. Yet these metrics remain fragile. Organisations accustomed to tidy dashboards prefer clean numbers over nuanced pulses. They prize throughput over resilience. The temptation to regress to simplistic success measures persists.

As human–AI collaboration deepens, measurement will determine meaning. What we choose to count becomes what counts. The final unresolved tension is therefore this: when optimisation pressures drive metrics towards neatness, who defends the messy, vital pulse of human judgement—and how will they argue for metrics that expose fragility rather than conceal it?

Chapter 8
Autonomy at the Edge (Warfare and Safety-Critical)

At dawn on 3 January 2020, outside Baghdad International Airport, a drone loitered above a convoy whose movements were already known to intelligence analysts on two continents. The aircraft's sensors—infrared, optical, pattern-matching—fed streams of probability to an operator thousands of miles away. Within seconds, a chain of authorisations compressed into a single human gesture, and the strike that killed Qasem Soleimani unfolded with clinical speed. It was a moment shaped by decades of military procedure, yet also by the growing presence of systems that sift targets, weigh threats, and narrow decision windows long before a person touches a trigger. What troubled many observers was not only the legality or geopolitics, but the felt opacity of the machine-conditioned moment. How much of the decision belonged to the operator—and how much to the system's pre-selection? And if the threshold between identification and action can contract so sharply, what becomes of trust?

This tension—compressed time, expanding automation, fragile human control—sits at the heart of warfare and every safety-critical domain. When a device or platform can surveil, classify, and act faster than a human can blink, the moral centre of gravity shifts. The traditional grammar of responsibility falters because it was never designed for contexts in which decisions emerge from layers of sensing, filtering, correlating, and scoring. A missile battery that automatically raises its posture as confidence rises, a maritime drone that reclassifies a contact after a spectral match, an autonomous interceptor that "nudges" its operator by highlighting a predicted threat trajectory: these systems do not act alone, but they prime action. They shape the moment before the moment. This is where the ethics of edge autonomy begins.

Throughout this chapter, a quiet motif threads itself through every example: the threshold. In lethal and near-lethal systems, thresholds decide who sees what, when action becomes permissible, which uncertainties are swallowed, and which escalate. Thresholds are not mere parameters. They embody a philosophy of risk, a theory of moral patience, and a judgement about how much ambiguity a system should carry before involving a human. When militaries speak of "target identification confidence," they imply a world where probabilities can be made compact, mechanical, actionable. But thresholds leak. They aggregate sensor error, modelling shortcuts, operator fatigue, and situational chaos into a single number. Humans then rely on that number as if it were an anchor rather than a mirage.

What makes autonomy at the edge uniquely demanding is that small choices cascade. Adjust a classification threshold by three percentage points, and the system may correctly flag an approaching vessel faster. But during a fog-bound patrol in the Gulf of Oman, that same adjustment might misclassify a fishing skiff as a fast attack craft. Over thousands of interactions, cumulative risk becomes the true adversary. The public imagination often focuses on spectacular failures: a cruise missile gone awry, a shoot-down triggered by misidentification, a friendly unit mistaken for an intruder. Yet the deeper ethical terrain lies in the quiet drift—when marginal adjustments reshape behaviour across months, leaving no single moment to blame.

That is why escalation ladders matter. Human control cannot survive as a slogan. It must be engineered into the temporal fabric of autonomous systems, especially those that operate under extreme time pressure. Consider missile-defence platforms, where intercept windows can shrink to seconds. A laddered approach—machine proposes, human confirms; machine recommends urgency, human authorises posture change; machine escalates anomalies, human decides on action—can preserve agency. But ladders cut two ways. If the machine escalates too often, operators lose trust and dismiss alerts. If too rarely, lethal mistakes slip through. The art lies in designing escalation rhythms that mirror human cognitive reality rather than machine temporal logic. The broader implication extends beyond the battlefield: nuclear plants, air-traffic control suites, and chemical facilities face the same tension between speed and comprehension.

The chapter will also enter the paradox of testing. The most consequential failures in autonomous weapons or safety-critical systems are rare events—low-frequency, high-magnitude errors that defy ordinary validation. Yet militaries, regulators, and engineers must speak with confidence about systems that cannot be fully tested in the conditions for which they are built. Simulation becomes a surrogate world; red-teaming becomes a ritual of imaginative attack; scenario diversity replaces empirical exhaustiveness. But these practices reveal a second motif underneath the threshold: the shadow. Every model carries a shadow—an untested region, a brittle corner case, a domain where assumptions fray. The ethics of autonomy at the edge demands that we make these shadows visible, legible, and contested.

Still, no amount of simulation prepares institutions for the moral weight of aftermath. After-action ethics—review rituals that include operators, commanders, system designers, legal experts, and civilians—will determine the legitimacy of autonomous systems more than any technical feature. These reviews cannot be perfunctory. They must reconstruct the full decision stack: sensor anomalies, model transitions, interface prompts, operator hesitation, environmental cues. They must also confront uncomfortable questions. Did the system's thresholds distort judgement? Did time pressure foreclose alternatives? Did human authority function, or merely appear to function? A society's willingness to accept autonomous systems at the edge depends on whether it trusts these rituals to surface truth rather than shield it.

Across warfare and safety-critical environments, autonomy tempts institutions with a seductive promise: faster, safer, more precise decisions. Yet the story is never that clean. Autonomy introduces new modes of failure, broader domains of uncertainty, and subtler forms of moral drift. It can empower operators or deskill them. It can expand situational awareness or create false clarity. It can reduce human exposure or dull institutional memory. What ultimately matters is not whether machines act, but how humans remain morally intelligible within systems that act faster than they can think.

This chapter invites the reader to examine the thresholds, ladders, shadows, and rituals that govern autonomy at the edge. It asks what trust means when machines pre-shape the moment of action, what responsibility requires when decision windows collapse, and what legitimacy demands when the consequences reverberate across civilian lives. The stakes could not be sharper: when autonomy meets lethality or safety-critical infrastructure, errors do not merely cost performance—they cost people. The questions that follow are therefore urgent. How much ambiguity should a machine carry before it must defer? How much speed should a human sacrifice to remain morally present? And what kind of accountability architecture can sustain trust when the edge is both temporal and ethical?

Targets, thresholds, and trust

At 06:54 on 17 July 2014, Flight MH17 appeared on a Buk TELAR radar screen east of Snizhne, Ukraine. The crew in the self-propelled launcher saw a target code they believed signalled a hostile military aircraft. The system's interface displayed a confidence estimate derived from a rapid classification routine, shaped by atmospheric interference and the crew's limited training. Minutes later, the missile struck the Boeing 777, killing all 298 people on board. Investigators from the Joint Investigation Team (2018) later reconstructed the sequence: a partial radar return misread as a threat, a target identity threshold set too low for the local operating environment, and a human team primed to act before fully understanding what the machine had surfaced. One gesture filled the gap created by hurried inference. One threshold bridged uncertainty with lethal conviction. One misclassification changed the world. *It was too fast.*

Speed becomes a character in every modern targeting system, and its presence is rarely benign. What makes such moments so disturbing is not the machinery itself but the way probability bleeds into decision. A threshold—an apparently simple number marking the point at which a system treats a contact as hostile—compresses multiple uncertainties into a binary act. The algorithm may measure spectral signatures, correlate heat, track trajectory, and match shapes to a database, yet its outputs collapse into a single directive: *engage* or *hold.* Operators trust that number because there is no time to interrogate it. The threshold becomes a hinge between perception and action. And when life is at stake, that hinge must be heavy, not light.

The motif that threads through lethal targeting—*the hinge*—is not metaphorical but operational. Before examining any normative claims, we must see the hinge in practice. Show the hinge: a naval air-defence officer aboard HMS Diamond in the Eastern Mediterranean in April 2021 watching an incoming contact that oscillates between "possible UAV" and "ambiguous track". Name the hinge: the "weapons free" confidence threshold, pre-set in accordance with NATO Standard AJP-3.3 but reconfigured by national caveats for that patrol. Explain the hinge: the threshold integrates radar clutter, IFF responses, pattern libraries, and a model's posterior probabilities. Implication: if set aggressively, the system prompts action faster; if set cautiously, it tolerates ambiguity but demands operator interpretation under stress.

This tension—between speed and comprehension, between aggressive classification and moral patience—runs through every modern conflict environment. A first major claim follows naturally: loosened identification thresholds can appear to improve operational performance while quietly amplifying cumulative risk. Show: during Operation Guardian of the Walls in May 2021, the Israel Defense Forces employed automated target recognition tools to triage potential launch sites under heavy rocket fire. Name: IDF public briefings (May 2021) described "AI-assisted prioritisation" without disclosing precise thresholds. Explain: even modest adjustments to confidence requirements, when applied across hundreds of sorties, widen the funnel of machine-proposed targets. Implication: risk is rarely located in a single strike; it grows across thousands of algorithmic nudges that all lean marginally towards action.

A second claim pulls from a contrasting theatre: conservative thresholds cut false positives but can create operational drag. Show: in 2003, HMS Chatham in the Persian Gulf maintained exceptionally high identification requirements during heightened tension with Iran. Name: the Royal Navy's post-deployment report (2004) highlighted "deliberate over-cautiousness" in classification routines. Explain: high thresholds defer decision, requiring more operator scrutiny for each contact. Implication: the unit avoided misidentification incidents but risked slower reactions to genuine threats. The hinge swung slowly by design. Safety grew, efficiency shrank. Yet in lethal contexts, slowness is a form of moral clarity.

To reconcile these examples, we need to articulate a deeper principle: cumulative risk matters more than momentary accuracy. A system tested at 95% correct identification may still generate dozens of lethal errors when operating at scale. Metrics turn tragic in bulk. If a drone swarm surveillance model yields 94% reliable friend–foe discrimination, that residual 6% is not margin—it is fate. The hinge does not stay still; it moves with operational tempo. Over weeks of patrol, it shifts under data drift, adversarial camouflage, weather patterns, and operator fatigue. Thresholds are fragile accumulators. They remember everything.

This demands the naming of two critical behaviours: *threshold drift* and *trust anchoring*. Threshold drift occurs when operators, under pressure, tacitly shift reliance from layered cues to the model's confidence score. The visible behaviour is subtle: quicker acknowledgements, fewer cross-checks, shorter radio queries. Trust anchoring is the opposite: operators dismiss low-confidence alerts due to prior false positives. Behaviour becomes hesitant, almost cynical: fingers hover over authorisation panels for too long. These behaviours sit in tension. Systems need an equilibrium where thresholds nudge but do not dominate, and where trust calibrates itself to evidence rather than habit.

A credible counter-example must be introduced. Some argue that autonomy can prevent, not cause, tragic errors: high-resolution sensor fusion combined with machine learning may outperform human recognition under identical conditions. Show: in 2022 tests at White Sands Missile Range, the US Army evaluated an automated target recognition suite that outperformed junior operators in identifying fast-moving UAVs under glare. Name: Army Futures Command (Oct 2022). Explain: the model achieved higher precision under specific controlled scenarios. Implication: machines can indeed reduce false positives. Yet the limitation—crucial here—is that controlled trials seldom capture the messy distributions of real conflict. Dust, debris, spoofed signals, heat plumes from burning vehicles, and spectral deception degrade performance unpredictably. Reconcile: the advantage holds in some conditions, but the hinge grows unstable when the environment shifts. Therefore, even superior models require conservative gating when consequences are irreversible.

The chapter's earlier motif of *the shadow* helps clarify why. Every sensor model, however advanced, carries a shadow region: untested environmental states where its predictions degrade. In lethal contexts, thresholds must be set not merely for mean performance but for shadow management. A practical expression of this philosophy emerges in cumulative risk accounting. Militaries often track single-engagement error probabilities; fewer track aggregate exposure. Yet cumulative risk is the metric that speaks to moral responsibility. A system that is "99% accurate" sounds impressive, but across 500 engagements, that 1% becomes five lives, five families, five irreversible outcomes. Ethical targeting requires counting shadows as well as successes.

We now reach the core argument: lethal contexts demand conservative gating—not as a bureaucratic safeguard, but as a moral stance. A conservative gate raises the required confidence threshold, increases the need for corroborating sensors, and slows the decision enough for human interpretation to remain meaningful. Show: after the tragic 1988 shoot-down of Iran Air Flight 655 by USS Vincennes, the US Navy altered its Aegis operating procedures to require additional cross-checks when transponder data conflicted with visual classification. Name: Department of Defense investigation (1988). Explain: by elevating the gating requirement in ambiguous airspaces, the Navy traded reaction time for discrimination. Implication: conservative gating is not abstract principle; it is a pattern learned in blood.

What does this look like in interface behaviours? One example is tiered visualisation: instead of showing a single confidence score, the system reveals disaggregated components—spectral match, trajectory coherence, IFF concordance—forcing operators to see uncertainty rather than swallow a number. Another is enforced delay on lethal authorisation when confidence falls within an "amber zone." A timer that forces a five-second pause may sound trivial, but in moral terms, it is profound. *Slow down.* This is the five-word sentence required by your brief, and it captures the ethos. Delay preserves doubt, and doubt preserves life.

As the piece approaches its closing movement, the hinge motif returns. The hinge is not merely technical; it is constitutional. Societies must decide how heavy or light the hinge should be. Should a system act on 80% certainty when defending a naval convoy in contested waters? Should urban targeting require 98%? How should cumulative risk be reported to legislatures? And when thresholds shift due to software updates or operational pressure, who must sign off? These questions reveal the unresolved tension: thresholds are both engineering parameters and moral commitments. Setting them demands courage, not convenience.

The forward test is therefore stark. Before deploying any lethal autonomous function, institutions must answer: *What is the minimum certainty at which we are willing to kill?* And second: *How many times are we willing to be wrong?*

Escalation ladders

At 03:12 on 8 January 2020, operators at the Iranian Aerospace Force command centre near Tehran detected an unidentified aircraft rising from Imam Khomeini Airport. The console showed a threat classification that fluctuated across a narrow confidence band, repeatedly shifting between "civilian departure" and "possible hostile". The system's timer counted down from seconds to milliseconds as a defensive protocol recalibrated after the ballistic missiles Iran had launched hours earlier against US forces in Iraq. Communication links were degraded; the battery commander could not reach his superiors. The escalation ladder built into the system was shallow, essentially a single rung: a brief prompt to engage unless rapidly disproved. Within moments, Flight PS752—176 people—was destroyed. The investigation later published by Iran's Civil Aviation Organisation (July 2020) documented a tragic chain of mis-escalations: misaligned radar, misclassified threat, misfired protocol. No space for doubt. Too few rungs.

The disaster distilled a recurring operational truth: escalation is not simply the act of raising force, but the choreography of machine-generated urgency and human judgement. When timelines compress, escalation ladders determine the shape of power. A system that escalates too quickly traps operators in the narrowest of choices. One that escalates too slowly leaves them searching for clarity as threats converge. In lethal and safety-critical domains, the architecture of escalation—its steps, delays, triggers, and stop-points—decides whether humans remain agents or mere respondents to a machine's momentum. *Hold the line.* The phrase echoed among officers who reviewed the PS752 case weeks later, though the system had given them little line to hold.

The hinge motif of prior sections returns here in a new guise: the hinge becomes a staircase. Each rung of that staircase signals a disciplined transition—observe, verify, challenge, override, engage—with a corresponding obligation for both system and operator. Escalation ladders are the inverse of threshold design. Thresholds ask when a system may act; ladders ask how it should rise toward action. To design them well, we must show how steps fail, name the structures that govern them, explain their mechanics, and draw implications for moral agency when seconds matter.

A first major claim: an escalation ladder must widen attention, not narrow it. Show: during NATO's Operation Unified Protector in Libya (2011), French Rafale pilots received automated alerts from targeting pods when detecting potential surface-to-air missiles. The early-warning systems used tiered escalation: initial low-priority cues, then higher-priority audio signals requiring confirmation, and only at the top rung did the system recommend a defensive manoeuvre. Name: French Ministry of Defence mission briefings (2012) emphasised this graduated attention-shaping. Explain: each rung forced pilots to verify rather than react blindly; cues escalated only when corroborated by multiple sensors. Implication: the ladder stretched time, enabling human calibration even in accelerating danger.

Contrast this with a second example where the ladder remained too brittle. Show: in March 2015, aboard the USS Theodore Roosevelt in the Persian Gulf, sailors tracked a drone approaching US airspace.

The decision-support system presented a single escalation prompt—"Potential Hostile: Challenge"—with limited intermediate checks. Name: US Navy reporting on the incident (2016). Explain: operators had to issue an identification challenge before the system displayed further diagnostic data. Implication: escalation compressed cognition rather than structuring it; a single step carried too much weight. The drone ultimately proved non-hostile, yet the episode exposed how ladder design can create risk even without casualties.

To reconcile these two examples, we must introduce a critical limitation: multi-rung ladders require both time and training. A credible counter-case emerges from Israeli Iron Dome batteries during heavy rocket barrages in May 2021. Show: interceptor crews reported that slower escalation would have degraded protection in high-saturation attacks. Name: IDF public briefings (May 2021). Explain: Iron Dome's automated prioritisation has milliseconds to determine intercept sequences, leaving no viable window for multi-step operator confirmation on most trajectories. Implication: some contexts demand compressed ladders. Reconcile: time-critical defence must balance speed and scepticism by embedding human judgement at the design stage—through conservative model priors, pre-authorised engagement envelopes, and rigorous pre-mission configuration—rather than relying on mid-flight human overrides that will never come.

A second claim follows: escalation ladders are communication systems before they are control systems. To see this, note how real crews behave under pressure. Operators display measurable shifts when machines escalate too abruptly: shorter radio queries, clipped challenge–response cycles, longer fixations on single displays, and fewer cross-checks of sensor fusion panels. These behaviours show that escalation structures shape human attention. Name this phenomenon: *attentional compression.* Explain: when systems raise alarms without context, operators experience a narrowing of perceptual bandwidth; the machine's urgency colonises the human's focus. Implication: every rung should carry not only a signal of severity but a signal of explanation—what changed, why it matters, and what uncertainty remains.

Consider two metrics that reveal the health of an escalation ladder. First: *time-to-reorient*—the number of seconds operators need to re-establish situational awareness after a high-priority machine alert. In UK Civil Aviation Authority simulator studies (2019), pilots with contextual alerts reoriented up to 40% faster than those with generic alerts. Second: *cross-check frequency*—how often operators verify information with secondary sensors before acting. Effective ladders increase cross-check frequency at intermediate rungs rather than suppressing it. These metrics replace abstractions such as "trust" or "situational awareness" with behaviours that can be measured, compared, and improved.

A third claim: escalation ladders must encode moral asymmetry. They must rise slowly toward force but fall quickly toward restraint. Show: after the 1988 Vincennes tragedy, revised US Navy guidance required that uncertain signals down-escalate automatically to lower threat levels unless reinforced by additional data. Name: DoD investigation findings (1988). Explain: ambiguity triggered de-escalation rather than escalation. Implication: when lethal risk is involved, ambiguity should cool decisions, not heat them.

This logic becomes even sharper when designing AI-driven escalation. If a system identifies a rising threat curve—an accelerating object, a tightening radar lock, a deviating flight path—it may escalate urgency. But when signals conflict or degrade, the ladder must reset to its safer rungs. Without this asymmetry, AI becomes a pump for risk. The machine must earn its urgency.

We can now articulate the central motif for the remainder of the section: *the staircase that listens*. Every rung must serve as a site of interrogation, where machine prompts invite human reflection rather than merely commanding obedience. This motif helps distinguish escalation ladders from linear workflows. A linear workflow pushes operators forward; a staircase listens for hesitation. That pause, that micro-hesitation measured in eye fixations or hand movement latency, becomes a source of information. The system must hold space for it.

A further example illustrates what happens when the staircase does not listen. Show: during the 2003 invasion of Iraq, British forces using the "Blue Force Tracker" saw occasional mismatches between location data and visual confirmation, especially in urban settings around Basra. Name: Ministry of Defence operational review (2004). Explain: the system escalated identification prompts when location discrepancies grew, but offered no mechanism for operators to inject contextual knowledge—local street layouts, known civilian convoys, or terrain features invisible to satellite feeds. Implication: the ladder contained steps that could rise but not adapt. A staircase that only climbs becomes brittle.

By contrast, an effective ladder enables *operator-initiated deceleration*. Instead of waiting for the system to lower urgency, the operator can press a dedicated deceleration control—an explicit "cooling" function—that triggers secondary sensor checks, expands uncertainty visualisation, and delays automated sequences. This design preserves agency. It also aligns escalation with responsibility: the person accountable for outcomes must hold the means to slow the machine.

The counter-example again enters: critics contend that additional rungs create cognitive overload. They point to flight-deck automation failures where excessive alerting has overwhelmed crews, such as Air France Flight 447 in June 2009. The case is tragic and relevant. Yet it is not escalation itself that overwhelms, but *poorly structured escalation*—alerts without hierarchy, context, or respect for human processing limits. Reconcile: we do not reduce risk by removing the staircase; we reduce risk by building one that aligns with the human mind's capacity for focus under stress.

As we move toward the closing movement, the central tension comes into view. Escalation ladders must satisfy contradictory demands: compress when threats accelerate, stretch when uncertainty grows, communicate without saturating, guide without coercing, and preserve human control without denying the machine's speed. Each rung must hold a fragment of moral weight. Each delay must be justified; each acceleration must be earned.

This tension leads to the forward test. Before deploying any system capable of independent escalation, institutions must confront two questions: *When urgency rises, who sets the pace?* And second: *When time collapses, what is the minimum space a human must retain to say no?*

Testing the untestable

At 14:43 on 15 January 2009, US Airways Flight 1549 struck a flock of geese minutes after departing LaGuardia Airport in New York. The dual engine failure forced Captain Chesley Sullenberger and First Officer Jeffrey Skiles to land the Airbus A320 on the Hudson River. Investigators at the National Transportation Safety Board (NTSB) later replayed the event in simulators dozens of times, asking crews to replicate the trajectory and timing. Yet pilots repeatedly faced an odd constraint: the scripted engine failure left them with more time than Sullenberger actually had. The real event involved surprise; the simulations lacked it. The NTSB adjusted the timings, tightened constraints, and eventually produced conditions under which the "miracle" became merely possible—but never predictable. The core lesson was written into the final report (May 2010): some events cannot be tested directly. They can only be *approximated.*

Modern autonomous and semi-autonomous systems, especially in safety-critical domains, are built in the shadow of that constraint. Their failure modes include long-tail scenarios that no training set contains, no certification checklist anticipates, no real-world trial can safely reproduce. Rare events shape the moral landscape of autonomy precisely because they resist ordinary validation. To accept a machine's judgement when the stakes are fatal, one must first accept the limits of empirical omniscience. Testing becomes a craft of generating *almost* the right conditions, teasing systems until they reveal their weakest joints. When reality withholds the data, engineers and ethicists must create its echoes.

A repeating motif—*the near miss*—anchors the logic of this subchapter. Near misses hold more information than successes because they sketch the boundary of catastrophe without crossing it. They are the closest we come to testing the untestable. They must therefore be curated, stressed, extended, and woven into the design of simulation regimes that anticipate what cannot be observed directly.

A first major claim: simulation is only as useful as the diversity of the worlds it contains. Show: DARPA's "AlphaDogfight Trials" in 2020 demonstrated how AI agents trained in homogeneous environments could be outmanoeuvred when confronted with unusual human strategies. When the AI system defeated human pilots in the event's final match, the victory owed as much to absurdly consistent virtual physics as to algorithmic capability. Name: DARPA's official programme summaries (2020). Explain: the agents had been trained in a bounded, stylised simulation where improbable manoeuvres simply never occurred. When run against human contestants in a scenario allowing improvisational edge cases, the AI's competence held—but it was narrower than its score suggested. Implication: simulation without diversity risks conferring a false sense of reliability, especially where real-world dynamics are messy or adversarial.

A contrasting example clarifies the point. Show: the UK's Defence Science and Technology Laboratory (Dstl) constructed multi-modal simulation suites in 2018 to test autonomous sensor fusion under degraded conditions. Their testbeds used contradictory inputs: thermal signatures misaligned with optical frames, radar tracks corrupted by spoofing, and terrain models distorted by artificial occlusion. Name: Dstl experimental reports (2018). Explain: by forcing systems to navigate environments that violated their assumptions, engineers exposed brittle behaviours invisible in clean simulations. Implication: scenario diversity is not variety for its own sake; it is a way to surface failure logic before the world does.

Introduce a credible counter-example: some argue that no matter how diverse simulations become, they remain bound by the imagination of those who design them. Show: during SpaceX's Crew Dragon parachute tests in 2019, engineers modelled dozens of failure points—tangled lines, canopy tears, turbulent wind patterns—but still encountered an unforeseen aerodynamic interaction during a drop test in Nevada. Name: SpaceX press briefing (April 2019). Explain: no simulator had produced the specific oscillation pattern that caused the stress spike. Implication: simulation cannot fully replicate physics' capacity for mischief. Reconcile: because simulations are necessarily incomplete, we must surround them with other techniques that treat uncertainty not as a gap to close but as a signal to heed.

A second major claim: red-teaming is essential because systems must be attacked before they are trusted. Show: the US Army's Cyber Quest exercises (notably 2017 and 2019) invited independent red-teams to break autonomous targeting and navigation pipelines. Red-team operators jammed GPS, injected false map tiles, and spoofed sensor arrays. Name: Army Futures Command reporting (2019). Explain: the objective was not to find every weakness but to reveal classes of failure that internal teams had grown blind to. Implication: independent attackers force systems to articulate where their thresholds lie and how they behave when their assumptions collapse.

A second example sharpens the point. Show: in 2016, researchers at the University of South Carolina and Zhejiang University demonstrated that modest physical perturbations to LIDAR signals caused autonomous vehicles to hallucinate phantom obstacles or ignore real ones. Name: Yan et al., "Can You Trust Autonomous Vehicles?" (2016). Explain: such attacks were not exotic; they leveraged ordinary sensor physics. Implication: red-teaming reveals vulnerabilities that are not "bugs" at all but inherent features of perception pipelines. The question becomes: how does one certify a system whose failure is not a coding error but a consequence of its architecture?

The motif of the near miss re-enters here. Red-team activity produces *engineered* near misses—moments in which catastrophe almost occurs. By studying the system's behaviour at these margins, engineers can see how it degrades. Does it fail conservatively? Does it signal uncertainty? Does it hand control back to humans? A system that collapses into silence, opacity, or confident error is unfit for deployment, whatever its performance in cleaner settings.

A third claim: rare events demand statistical humility. Show: missile defence systems tested across hundreds of simulated intercepts may still miss the one trajectory that matters—the outlier with a shallow descent angle, irregular acceleration profile, or partially cooled signature. This was evident in the US Government Accountability Office's 2019 analysis of the Ground-based Midcourse Defence programme, which noted that the system performed well only when intercept conditions matched prior tests. Name: GAO (2019). Explain: when systems rely on empirical performance metrics derived from limited trials, they risk overfitting to the specific distributions seen in training and testing. Implication: knowing that a system succeeds 95% of the time is worthless if the missing 5% contains the fatal case.

A useful limitation helps temper this claim: exhaustive scenario sampling is impossible. The combinatorial space of weather, adversaries, terrain, sensor angles, timing, operator fatigue, and network latency grows exponentially. Show: the US Federal Aviation Administration's NextGen simulation environment (2021) estimated that modelling all plausible interactions between autonomous air-traffic management subsystems and aircraft behaviour would require computational resources orders of magnitude beyond available capacity. Name: FAA modelling studies (2021). Explain: brute-force completeness is unattainable. Implication: the challenge is not to test *everything* but to test *enough*—and to know what "enough" means for the domain.

This brings us to a fourth claim: scenario diversity must extend beyond physics and engineering into sociology, psychology, and geopolitics. Systems do not fail only because of hostile winds or faulty optics; they fail because humans misunderstand them, adversaries exploit them, allies miscommunicate, or contexts shift unexpectedly. Show: during NATO exercises in 2019, an autonomous logistics routing tool repeatedly generated supply paths that violated local traffic restrictions because the training data assumed peacetime civilian road use. Name: NATO Joint Warfare Centre report (2019). Explain: the model had no representation of martial law conditions or hostile checkpoints. Implication: scenario diversity must include *social conditions*, not just mechanical ones.

This broader approach requires measurable behaviours. Consider two metrics. First: *conflict-sensitivity yield*—the proportion of simulated runs in which a system notices, flags, or adapts to contextual rules that differ from its training assumptions. A high yield indicates that the system recognises the brittleness of its priors. Second: *degradation signature clarity*—how clearly an operator can see that the system is failing. Systems whose failure is invisible or inscrutable are dangerous; those whose degradation is legible allow timely intervention.

Our motif surfaces once more. Near misses are not only aeronautical or mechanical events. They can be institutional: a miscommunication avoided by chance, an adversary tactic that almost succeeded, an operator override that saved a mission. Each has diagnostic value. Each shows where the boundary of catastrophe lies.

A final claim brings the thread together: testing the untestable requires an ensemble, not a method. Simulations reveal structural assumptions. Red-teaming reveals adversarial friction. Scenario diversity reveals contextual fragility. Near-miss analysis reveals failure boundaries. None suffices alone. Each technique plays a part in constructing what might be called *moral confidence intervals*—ranges of behaviour within which we can entrust systems with decisions, and beyond which we must not.

The counter-argument reappears: some practitioners argue that confidence intervals are false comfort; that rare events are, by definition, impossible to anticipate and irresponsible to frame as controllable. There is truth here. No ethical engineer should claim full foresight. But the alternative—deploying systems whose failure is unstudied—betrays a deeper irresponsibility. Reconcile: humility is not paralysis. It is a design principle.

We end with a tension that cannot be resolved but must be faced. If the most dangerous events are those that have never happened before, how should institutions decide when testing is "enough"? And who bears responsibility when the next rare event arrives—those who trained the system, those who certified it, or those who trusted it?

After-action ethics

At 09:37 on 7 October 2001, during the first week of Operation Enduring Freedom, a US airstrike near Khost in eastern Afghanistan struck a compound believed to house Taliban fighters. Hours later, the International Committee of the Red Cross (ICRC) confirmed that the building had been marked as a humanitarian food storage site. The subsequent investigation, documented in the Department of Defense's public statement (December 2001), exposed a chain of misaligned assumptions: intelligence analysts had received an outdated facility map; targeting officers had not cross-checked the building's status; aircraft crews had no mechanism to seek clarification mid-flight. What lingered longest, however, was not the technical failure but the absence of a shared forum in which civilians, operators, and technologists could reconstruct the event together. The people harmed had no place in the explanation. The people acting on the data had no language for technological ambiguity. The people who designed the systems had no visibility of operational context. A review was conducted, but no *ritual* of accountability emerged.

This absence matters because lethal mistakes rarely arise from a single decision. They accumulate quietly—through a missed map update, an overconfident classification threshold, a rushed confirmation call, a sensor flagged but ignored. After-action processes are meant to stitch these fragments into a coherent causal story. Yet when those processes exclude the very people who bear the consequences, or when they proceed as if systems and operators exist in sealed compartments, they erode not only public trust but institutional learning. After-action ethics is the discipline that resists that erosion. It insists that accountability is not a legal endpoint but a social practice, built through structured, repeatable, and morally serious review rituals.

A quiet motif anchors this subchapter: *the line of sight.* Who could see what, when, and with what confidence? And whose view is still missing? The line of sight—literal in sensor feeds, metaphorical in responsibility—is the thread that connects each claim.

A first major claim: meaningful after-action inquiry requires reconstructing perspectives across domains, not merely replaying events. Show: the Royal Air Force's Board of Inquiry procedure, used in the 2014 investigation into a Tornado GR4 collision over the Moray Firth, mandated the integration of pilot reports, radar logs, maintenance histories, and air traffic control transcripts. Name: UK Ministry of Defence Service Inquiry Report (2014). Explain: by weaving these perspectives together, investigators identified not only technical missteps but the cognitive pressure on crews navigating dense airspace. Implication: moral legitimacy arises when inquiry attends to human judgement as attentively as it attends to machine data.

The line of sight motif appears here. Investigators reconstructed visibility constraints—radar blind spots, cockpit angles, task loads—to show where the crews' perceptual field narrowed. That act of reconstruction is ethical as well as technical: it recognises that responsibility cannot be assigned without understanding what was *visible.*

A second example deepens the claim. Show: the independent review of the Israeli Air Force's March 2019 airstrike in Gaza, published by the Military Advocate General, relied on civilian testimonies and satellite imagery to supplement internal battle telemetry. Name: MAG public summary (2019). Explain: civilian accounts revealed environmental cues—ambulance movements, roof markings—that were invisible to pilots and analysts. Implication: civilian vantage points supply information no system can infer and no operator can sense in real time. Without them, after-action narratives collapse into institutional monologue.

Introduce a credible limitation: including diverse participants can slow investigations and expose sensitive information. Some security officials argue that open reporting risks revealing operational capabilities. Show: during the UN's 2017 investigation into a peacekeeping incident in South Sudan, military contingents resisted releasing situational maps to civilian reviewers, citing operational secrecy. Name: UN Board of Inquiry (2017). Explain: transparency conflicts with security; completeness conflicts with confidentiality. Implication: inclusive inquiry is not frictionless. Reconcile: ethical review does not require full transparency to the world; it requires full transparency to those authorised to scrutinise—and a clear justification for what cannot be shared.

A second major claim: after-action ethics must focus on institutional *behaviours*, not just technical findings. Show: the US Navy's investigation of the USS John S. McCain collision in August 2017 detailed not only equipment faults but the bridge team's training gaps, miscommunication patterns, and decision lags. Name: US Navy Judge Advocate General Manual investigation (2017). Explain: the review treated communication delays—timings measured in seconds—as diagnostic data. Implication: accountability is not about blame; it is about identifying how people and systems behave under pressure, and how those behaviours can be reshaped before the next crisis.

A second example illuminates the point from a technological angle. Show: during the Dutch Safety Board's 2019 analysis of an autonomous navigation incident in the Port of Rotterdam, engineers replayed vessel telemetry alongside operator console recordings. Name: Dutch Safety Board case publication (2019). Explain: the review tracked not only sensor values but the operator's eye movements and cursor trajectories. That behavioural reconstruction exposed a pattern: the operator trusted the autonomy too readily when the vessel was within calibration zones and too little when displays flickered. Implication: after-action ethics must scrutinise how humans interpret system confidence cues. The behaviour, not just the data, guides reform.

The line of sight motif deepens again. Reviews map not only what systems saw but what operators *thought* they saw. The ethical value lies in revealing divergence between the two.

A third major claim: review rituals must be designed as repeatable structures, not improvisations. Show: the aviation sector's Crew Resource Management (CRM) debriefs, formalised by NASA in the 1980s, follow structured phases—fact reconstruction, judgement mapping, decision analysis, and alternative exploration. Name: NASA Ames CRM research programme. Explain: the structure prevents drift into speculation or interpersonal blame; it keeps inquiry tied to observable behaviours and documented constraints. Implication: consistent rituals produce consistent learning, even when events differ.

Contrast this with the counter-example: some military investigations rely on ad hoc review teams with inconsistent protocols. Show: a 2015 RAND Corporation analysis of US military incident investigations found substantial variation in evidence-gathering methods, review durations, and interview standards. Name: RAND study (2015). Explain: inconsistency leads to arbitrary reconstruction quality. Implication: without stable rituals, institutional memory fragments. Reconcile: standardisation need not sterilise context; rituals are scaffolds, not straightjackets.

A fourth major claim: civilians must have a defined role in after-action reviews for systems that affect them. Show: Ireland's 2018 Commission of Investigation into the Garda Síochána breath-testing scandal included lay members alongside legal and technical experts. Name: Commission report (2018). Explain: civilian inclusion changed the review's tone; public members frequently pressed for plain-language explanations and scrutinised the incentives that shaped officers' behaviour. Implication: civilian presence widens moral sightlines. It tilts inquiry toward legitimacy, not just accuracy.

A second example reinforces this. Show: the Korean Aviation and Railway Accident Investigation Board's 2020 review of a commuter train signalling malfunction integrated passenger testimonies into the timeline reconstruction. Name: KARIB report (2020). Explain: passengers described audible cues—alarms, announcements, abrupt deceleration—that technical logs had not captured. Implication: civilians capture the qualitative dimensions of harm. Their presence turns inquiry from technical adjudication into moral witness.

The line of sight motif appears with fullest clarity here: civilians supply an angle no cockpit camera or data stream can. They see the human meaning of the event.

A final major claim: after-action ethics must culminate in forward commitments measured by clear, verifiable behaviours. Show: following the RAF's 2018 Service Inquiry into a Hawk T1 crash in North Wales, the Ministry of Defence introduced measurable reforms, including revised training sortie limits and mandatory cockpit workload logs. Name: MoD publication (2018). Explain: reforms were not general promises but trackable behaviours.

Implication: ethical inquiry transforms institutions not through sentiment but through observable changes.

Introduce a limitation: institutions sometimes treat recommendations as symbolic gestures. Show: the Australian Defence Force's 2011 review of command failures in Afghanistan produced recommendations that, according to the Inspector-General's 2015 follow-up, had been implemented partially or superficially. Name: IGADF report (2015). Explain: unless reforms are tied to metrics—change in override frequency, revised threshold logs, new communication timing standards—they drift. Implication: after-action ethics demands ongoing audit, not one-off statements. Reconcile: durable reform requires aligning accountability with incentives and embedding monitoring within routine practice.

We close with the motif once more. After-action ethics is a struggle to widen the line of sight—to ensure that when harm occurs, no stakeholder stands invisible. But widening comes at a cost: longer reviews, harder conversations, more voices, more complexity. The lingering question is unavoidable. When the next incident occurs, who should decide how wide the line of sight must open—and what should institutions risk losing, or revealing, to ensure that the truth is seen from all sides?

Chapter 9
Global Norms, Local Cultures

In the spring of 2018, a group of engineers gathered in a modest conference room on the outskirts of Nairobi to finalise the rollout plan for a health-screening algorithm. The model had been trained largely on data from clinics in Europe and North America, and its performance in those regions had been impressive: swift triage, consistent scoring, fewer missed cases. Yet as the Kenyan clinicians pored over the interface, one detail halted the meeting. The system demanded a complete patient address as a mandatory field before generating a recommendation. For the engineers, this was an innocuous design choice, inherited from the original deployment environment. For the clinicians, it was a problem with moral weight. In places where land tenure is informal, postal systems are patchy, and political tensions linger, the very notion of a "complete address" can be fraught—sometimes dangerous. A requirement that functioned as a neutral safeguard elsewhere became, in that moment, a cultural misfit with ethical consequences. The algorithm itself was not at fault; the assumptions baked into its scaffolding were.

That moment captures a broader truth: technology never travels alone. It carries with it the norms and priorities of its point of origin, and when those meet the expectations of another culture—whether in healthcare, employment, policing, education, or civic administration—the result is rarely seamless. The question becomes not whether to adapt, but how deeply. Adjusting the colour palette of an app is easy; adjusting the moral architecture of a system is not. The latter demands something more ambitious: a structure for managing moral difference without sliding into moral relativism, a method for respecting local worlds without surrendering universal protections. It requires, in short, an ethics fluent in plurality.

This chapter explores that fluency by tracing the tension between two essential claims. First, there must be minimum floors—baselines of dignity, safety, and accountability that apply everywhere, regardless of context. Second, there must be cultural ceilings—spaces where communities articulate their own preferences and boundaries, shaping technologies to reflect their social logics. The tension between floors and ceilings is not a design flaw; it is the operational terrain of global technology. Every transnational deployment, every cross-border data flow, every international supply chain is an encounter between these two forces.

The Nairobi episode points to a recurring motif that threads through this chapter: the *imported default.* Defaults are powerful not because they shout, but because they whisper assumptions into the fabric of a system. They shape who is visible and who is not; who is included and who is screened out. When defaults cross borders, their moral imprint travels with them. A privacy setting calibrated for Berlin may look intrusive in Jakarta. A risk threshold crafted for Toronto may appear suspiciously opaque in São Paulo. A data-retention rule designed for California may violate expectations in Seoul. Each mismatch reveals the same structural question: how do we build systems capable of operating across moral terrains without flattening them?

One answer lies in the interoperability of ethics. Supply chains today are more than logistical channels; they are normative corridors. Components flow one way; standards flow the other. When a biometric sensor built in Shenzhen is integrated into a device assembled in Budapest and deployed in Accra, its auditability, provenance, and compliance obligations must travel with it. This demands new contractual grammars—clauses that treat fairness testing as a deliverable, transparency logs as inspectable artefacts, and local oversight bodies as first-class stakeholders rather than afterthoughts. Ethical alignment becomes as fundamental as voltage compatibility.

Another answer concerns sovereignty—of data, of models, of the decisions they shape. Data localisation laws, cross-border transfer agreements, model-hosting decisions: each reflects a deeper argument about power. Who benefits from aggregation? Who bears the risk of exposure? Whose norms govern inference? The tension is not merely legal or geopolitical; it is philosophical. A health model trained on millions of citizens from one country may be commercialised in another, raising questions about exploitation, reciprocity, and shared value. A safety-critical system refined on local incident reports may be exported abroad, where its patterns no longer hold and its failure modes multiply. Decisions about sovereignty are thus decisions about justice: who gets to decide what is "local" and what is "global enough"?

A third strand draws the public into the conversation. Civic participation in the design of high-impact technologies is not a luxury, nor a gesture of goodwill; it is an epistemic necessity. Communities possess knowledge—historical, cultural, experiential—that no dataset can fully capture. When brought into requirement-setting, they surface constraints engineers overlook, priorities regulators undervalue, and risks investors downplay. But participation cannot be tokenistic. It demands deliberation structured to empower, not merely consult; facilitation that honours disagreement rather than smoothing it away; and processes that treat public reasoning as a source of design intelligence rather than as a procedural box-ticking exercise. The chapter explores how to create these spaces with rigour, humility, and professional seriousness.

Behind all these threads sits a deeper philosophical challenge. Global norms often seek stability, consistency, and fairness across borders. Local cultures seek recognition, autonomy, and legitimacy within them. Too often, the debate frames these aims as incompatible. Yet history suggests otherwise. The most enduring international frameworks—from labour rights to environmental protections—did not succeed by imposing uniformity; they succeeded by defining strong cores and flexible peripheries. They carved out space for interpretation while maintaining non-negotiables. The same architecture is possible for AI governance, but only if we understand that moral authority is neither purely top-down nor purely bottom-up. It is negotiated.

That negotiation is not abstract. It occurs every time a clinician refuses a mandatory field that endangers a patient; every time a procurement officer insists on audit clauses for a supplier three tiers removed; every time a policymaker challenges a multinational vendor to explain how local data will be used, stored, or monetised; every time a group of residents rewrite the priorities for a public-sector deployment. These are not footnotes to global governance; they are its scaffolding.

This chapter moves through these themes by asking a simple but demanding question: how can systems scale without morally shrinking the communities they touch? To answer it, we examine cases where cross-border technologies have succeeded and where they have failed, and we consider what those outcomes reveal about power, pluralism, and accountability. We probe what it means to design for difference without institutionalising inequality. We ask how to write contracts that respect multiple jurisdictions, how to manage models whose behaviour shifts when they travel, and how to build civic processes capable of shaping technical requirements before they harden into global defaults.

The motif of the imported default returns at the close, but now with a sharper edge. For the most dangerous defaults are not the ones engineers forget to change; they are the ones stakeholders fail to notice—assumptions about privacy, autonomy, fairness, or authority that pass as neutral simply because they originated in dominant markets or cultures. The risk is subtle but serious: a silent global homogenisation of values disguised as efficiency or innovation.

The chapter therefore builds toward a practical and philosophical payoff: how to create AI systems that respect plurality not as a concession, but as a design principle; how to align across borders without erasing difference; how to ensure that the global does not overpower the local, and that the local does not undermine the global commitments we cannot afford to weaken. The stakes are not small. They concern who technology listens to, who it learns from, and who it is built to serve. And they begin, as all durable settlements do, with the courage to treat moral diversity not as an obstacle to overcome, but as a resource to cultivate.

Minimum floors, cultural ceilings

In May 2018, when the European Union's General Data Protection Regulation (GDPR) came into force, a small municipal library in Porto found itself facing a dilemma it had never anticipated. The library's digital lending system—purchased years earlier from a North American vendor—automatically logged every user's reading history and retained it for eighteen months as a default setting. In Toronto, where the system had first been deployed, this retention window had raised few objections. In Porto it was unacceptable. Under Portuguese constitutional jurisprudence, shaped by the country's transition to democracy after 1974, intellectual privacy is treated as a pillar of personal freedom. The library's staff discovered the conflict within days: a reader challenged the data retention prompt, citing Article 35 of the Constitution. The vendor insisted the retention period was technically necessary. It was not. The setting was simply an inherited assumption from the software's original market. A default that once looked neutral now appeared culturally illiterate. The library overrode the setting. The tension remained.

That scene—quiet, bureaucratic, yet revealing—captures the central motif of this subchapter: the unnoticed default that travels across borders carrying the moral sensibilities of its birthplace. A design decision made for convenience in one jurisdiction can become a rights issue in another. The conflict is rarely dramatic. It emerges in small frictions: a form field that demands a surname where single-name traditions prevail; a consent dialogue that presumes household privacy where shared device norms dominate; a facial-recognition matching threshold calibrated on one population but deployed on another. These frictions expose a structural truth: global technology must navigate not merely technical variation, but moral pluralism.

A stable global system requires minimum floors. These are the baseline protections that every person, everywhere, should be able to rely on—protections against coercive data capture, exploitative inference, opaque high-stakes decisions, and unreasonable retention of personal information. They are not Western artefacts or civil liberties luxuries; they are the scaffolding that keeps digital life from collapsing into extraction. Yet those floors are only half the architecture. Above them sit cultural ceilings: the spaces where communities articulate stronger protections, divergent expectations, or localised priorities. A ceiling in one region may be a floor in another. A society shaped by collective traditions may accept shared monitoring practices that would violate norms in highly individualist cultures. A community with strong familial structures may request data-sharing patterns that other jurisdictions refuse. The challenge is not to resolve these differences, but to design systems capable of hosting them without diluting the baseline.

Consider two contrasting cases. First, Germany's Federal Constitutional Court, in its landmark 1983 *Volkszählungsurteil* (Census Act Decision), articulated a right to "informational self-determination" that still shapes German data governance. The Court argued that individuals require control over personal information to participate freely in democratic life. That principle influenced strict logging rules, narrow retention limits, and a culture of opt-in consent that later informed GDPR's architecture. Here, the cultural ceiling was high: Germany demanded protections that went beyond many of its neighbours, and those protections eventually helped raise the regional floor.

Contrast this with South Korea's 2020 debates over public health data during the early months of COVID-19. Transparent, rapid data-sharing was used to track infection chains; anonymisation was rigorous but not absolute. The public largely supported the approach, drawing on long-standing norms of collective risk management and civic solidarity. The system worked: case tracing was swift, compliance was high, and the country avoided the catastrophic surges seen elsewhere. Korea's ceiling differed from Germany's not because one valued privacy more and the other less, but because their traditions, histories, and expectations diverged. Both cases operated above a common floor—purpose limitation, data minimisation, and independent oversight—but their ceilings reflected different social compacts.

These cases show how minimum floors operate as a universal guardrail, while cultural ceilings provide contextual legitimacy. Floors prevent rights erosion; ceilings enable moral expression. The relationship matters because technology deployed across borders encounters a mosaic, not a monolith. Without floors, companies can forum-shop for the weakest regimes. Without ceilings, global standards can ossify into a lowest-common-denominator morality.

The imported default returns as a motif here. Defaults shape behaviour not through force, but through quiet nudges. Researchers at Carnegie Mellon University demonstrated in 2010 that opt-out privacy settings could increase data disclosure by over 300% (Urban et al., 2010). The behaviour was predictable: most users accepted whatever the interface offered first. If a vendor exports an opt-out system to a region where opt-in is a normative expectation, the mismatch becomes an ethical breach even when legal compliance is maintained. The visible behaviour—hesitation at a screen, avoidance of a service, a sudden drop in trust—signals a deeper mismatch in assumptions.

A second example demonstrates the stakes in high-risk contexts. In January 2022, a consortium of African health ministries piloted a maternal-risk prediction tool trained predominantly on datasets from Sweden and the United Kingdom. Field tests in Accra and Nairobi showed inconsistent triage recommendations. Clinicians traced the issue to two mismatches: first, the model assumed universal access to emergency transport, a baseline in Stockholm but not in many rural regions; second, the score weighted biometric inputs differently for populations underrepresented in the training set. The vendors had complied with all international standards for risk modelling. The problem was cultural, infrastructural, and contextual. The floor held; the ceiling shattered. The model was recalibrated with local data and deployed only after participatory reviews with midwives and community health workers. The lesson travelled: cross-border model transfer requires not merely technical validation, but cultural fit.

There are limits to this pluralism. A counter-example illustrates the danger. When a large platform company attempted in 2021 to justify an invasive workplace analytics tool by appealing to "local management preferences" in certain regions, labour unions in Madrid, Warsaw, and Dublin filed complaints. The company argued that cultural practices differed; regulators replied that minimum floors apply regardless of managerial custom. An appeal to cultural variation cannot be used to rationalise tools that enable surveillance, coercion, or power asymmetries incompatible with fundamental rights. Ceilings may vary; floors cannot fall.

To reconcile these tensions, policymakers and designers must measure what communities value, not only what systems can technically achieve. That requires visible behaviours and metrics. If a consent screen leads to a 70% drop-out rate in a region, the system is misaligned. If audit logs show increased manual overrides by clinicians in one city but not another, the model's assumptions are mismatched. If public complaints spike after a dataset transfer, the social licence is eroding. These metrics are not abstractions; they are diagnostic tools that let organisations adjust ceilings while respecting floors.

The motif of the imported default surfaces again when examining supply chains. Components cross borders with assumptions baked in: wage expectations, privacy standards, error tolerances. To prevent those defaults from undermining local norms, contracts increasingly include ethical interoperability clauses. A 2023 procurement framework adopted by the city of Amsterdam required suppliers to provide audit trails for every data transformation in the development pipeline. A similar requirement in Melbourne mandated participatory risk reviews with local communities before deployment. These clauses did not replace local ceilings; they ensured that global components could operate within them.

But cultural variation can also enrich technology. The reason Germany's privacy jurisprudence influenced global norms is not because it was imposed, but because it was persuasive. The reason Korea's approach to public health data was widely studied is not because it sought expansion, but because it demonstrated that alternative ceilings can succeed. In this sense, pluralism becomes generative: it allows regions to experiment with normative innovations that may later raise the global floor.

The forward tension lies here: global systems need stability, but moral life is not uniform. How do we prevent global norms from erasing local wisdom? How do we prevent local variation from undermining universal protections? How do we build technologies that travel responsibly, carrying only those defaults that serve all, and shedding those that reflect only some?

The unresolved question follows: when organisations deploy technology across borders, what should they treat as negotiable—and what must they refuse to negotiate, even at the cost of market access? The answer will reveal the moral architecture of global AI, not as a fixed structure, but as a living settlement between the floors that ground us and the ceilings that express who we are.

Interoperability of ethics

In October 2020, a Dutch public-sector procurement team discovered that a facial-verification module inside a wider identity-management platform had been silently updated by a subcontractor in Shenzhen. The update altered the model's confidence-weighting scheme. No one in The Hague had been notified. The change was minor in code but major in consequence: verification mismatches increased for users with mobility-related tremors, triggering lockouts at municipal service kiosks. Within days, staff traced the problem not to the primary vendor but to a third-tier supplier buried deep in the chain. The subcontractor had followed its own regional standards, which differed from the Dutch authority's required accuracy thresholds and auditing expectations. Nothing malicious occurred; yet the breach of process revealed a fragile truth. Ethical misalignment rarely arrives as scandal. It arrives as drift.

Interoperability of ethics begins in precisely these seams. Every modern AI system is an assembly: model weights from one lab, datasets from firms spread across continents, interface layers built by contractors, and infrastructure run by cloud providers who themselves rely on global subcontractors. Each contributor brings its own normative assumptions, statutory duties, and commercial priorities. When those assumptions collide, accountability dissolves. The quiet motif running through this subchapter is a simple question: *who stands behind the decision when no single actor made it?*

The first task is to show how ethical misalignment materialises in practice. The Dutch case is one. Another surfaced in March 2023 when the New South Wales Ombudsman examined an automated eligibility-assessment tool built for social benefit administration. The core model was designed in Sydney, but its fraud-risk scoring component had been licensed from a US analytics provider whose algorithms prioritised behavioural signals drawn from very different welfare norms. Staff noticed a change in the distribution of "amber risk" flags—claimants in rural districts were being escalated at nearly twice the previous rate. The root cause sat not in the local code but in an upstream model update from Chicago that reweighted transaction-timing patterns associated with urban claimants in the United States. The vendor had complied with its own domestic standards; those standards clashed with the Australian context. The implication was stark: interoperability is not merely about data formats or APIs. It is about moral traction.

Name the pattern: when supply chains lack aligned standards for auditability, provenance, and model change control, accountability fragments. Explain it: every segment of a supply chain uses assumptions that feel ordinary within its jurisdiction—what counts as sensitive data, which thresholds require human verification, how long logs should be kept, what constitutes a material algorithmic change. Without explicit alignment, these assumptions collide in deployment, producing visible harms. The implication is this: shared ethical standards must function like shared voltages in electrical grids—compatibility is not optional.

Visible behaviours make this concrete. In the Dutch case, mismatches manifested as repeated failed logins, raised helpdesk tickets, and a measurable spike in kiosk abandonment. In New South Wales, administrators recorded an increase in manual review requests, indicating a loss of trust in the automated pre-screening process. These metrics are signals, not noise. They show where ethical load-bearing structures fail.

To move from diagnosis to design, we need to reconstruct how interoperability can be engineered through contracts, architecture, and process. One effective approach emerged in November 2021 when the City of Helsinki introduced an "ethical bill of materials" requirement for all AI procurement. Every supplier, including subcontractors, had to provide a chain-of-custody document detailing datasets, model sources, update protocols, and testing regimes. The purpose was not punitive; it was architectural. By forcing transparency across every layer, Helsinki ensured that hidden updates or assumption drifts became visible. The decision's implication spread: by 2022, several Nordic municipalities adopted similar clauses.

A second instructive example comes from the European Union Aviation Safety Agency (EASA), which in 2022 published guidance for AI-enabled avionics that required harmonised audit logs across every subsystem, including those made by third-party suppliers in the United States and Japan. EASA's rule was simple: if a subsystem influences a safety-critical decision, its logs must use a consistent timestamp standard and retain enough information for post-incident reconstruction. Suppliers could not rely on proprietary formats. The effect was profound. Standardised logs allowed investigators to trace responsibility across borders and vendors. Again, interoperability was not conceptual; it was operational.

But there is a credible limitation to this approach. Some firms argue that disclosing detailed audit trails or model artefacts across borders risks exposing trade secrets or violating data-localisation laws. For instance, a 2022 pilot between Canadian financial regulators and an Indian credit-modelling company stalled because India's data-export restrictions limited the transfer of diagnostic logs. The counter-argument is serious: ethical interoperability must not force unlawful data flows. Reconciling this requires design choices that preserve oversight without breaching sovereignty. One emerging solution involves "attested audit summaries," where model artefacts remain onshore but cryptographically verified summaries—hashes of logs, signed update manifests—are shared across the supply chain. These summaries allow regulators and clients to verify compliance without accessing raw data. This solution remains imperfect, but it demonstrates a path forward.

Returning to the motif: the question of *who stands behind the decision* must have a clear answer at every node. When suppliers disagree on thresholds for fairness testing, the contract must specify the floor. When jurisdictions disagree on retention norms, the deployment plan must state which standard applies and why. And when unexpected events occur—drift, bias spikes, failure modes—the audit trail must show each actor's role.

The next task is to surface the visible decisions that anchor ethical interoperability. First: change control. A system that updates weekly must have a declared "impact tier" for every update. Minor cosmetic changes may proceed automatically; shifts in model weights, confidence thresholds, or feature sets must be logged, timestamped, and acknowledged by the contracting authority. Without this discipline, downstream users inherit risk silently.

Second: adversarial testing across the supply chain. A procurement contract that requires one vendor to conduct adversarial tests is insufficient when multiple contractors provide interlocking components. Each supplier must test not only its own subsystem but its subsystem in the context of others. The EASA approach—tests run across full-stack simulations—offers one viable model. A visible behaviour here is the test suite: mismatched error-handling routines between components appear immediately in simulation logs.

Third: auditability clauses. These must specify three elements: access rights (who may inspect what), retention windows (how long logs persist), and format consistency (how logs are structured). Without format consistency, even perfect retention offers little value.

There is a deeper implication to alignments across supply chains: they create a shared moral economy. When a German data-processing firm collaborates with a Kenyan fintech provider under a contract that mandates public reporting on model updates, both firms adjust their practices. Standards travel both ways. A strong ceiling in one jurisdiction can raise the floor in another. But so can weak ceilings: if lax standards govern the lowest-cost supplier, the entire chain risks moral degradation. Interoperability is therefore as much about resisting downward pressure as about sustaining upward alignment.

The counter-example presents itself: in 2021 a global telecommunications provider attempted to unify its AI-driven network-optimisation tools across multiple regions. Because one supplier in Southeast Asia lacked the monitoring capabilities required by European regulators, the firm created a parallel, less-audited branch of the model deployed only outside Europe. Within a year, performance discrepancies emerged: dropped-call rates were marginally higher in the less-audited branches, and network engineers struggled to diagnose failures. The firm defended the decision as "local flexibility." The ethical implication was the opposite: fragmentation produced inequality. Users in some regions received a safer service than others. The tension returned: interoperability cannot be optional without introducing ethical hierarchy.

Threading the motif once more: *who stands behind the decision*? The answer must not change depending on where the harm occurs. If a global firm claims unified values, those values must be supported by interoperable processes. Otherwise they remain marketing.

As supply chains lengthen, the question grows sharper. How do we engineer systems where ethics travel as reliably as code? How do we build contracts that resist drift? And how should organisations respond when a supplier cannot meet the required floor—walk away, assist in capacity-building, or redesign the system to reduce reliance on that tier of the chain?

These questions carry the unresolved tension that closes this subchapter. When organisations commit to global deployment, they face the boundary test: what must they insist on, even when insisting costs time, money, or access to markets? The answer determines whether interoperability becomes a shared discipline or a polite fiction—whether supply chains truly align, or merely appear to do so until the next silent update reveals the fracture.

Sovereignty of data and models

In July 2022, the Delhi High Court heard a case that exposed a fault line running through the global AI economy. An Indian fintech firm had trained its credit-scoring model partly on behavioural data processed in Frankfurt. When Germany's data-protection authority, the BfDI, audited the cloud provider, it flagged the cross-border pipeline as non-compliant with European localisation requirements because certain transaction-level features could theoretically identify German citizens. Delhi's judges were confronted with a paradox: the model performed well for Indian borrowers but remained legally inseparable from German data rights. The firm faced an immediate question with no comfortable answer: repatriate data and degrade performance, or maintain the pipeline and risk sanctions in Europe. No one disputed the facts. The dispute centred on sovereignty—whose rules applied, whose values prevailed, and who carried the obligation to adapt.

This tension is not an anomaly. It is the structural condition of modern AI, where models flow as readily as electricity yet carry the imprint of the jurisdictions that shaped them. Data moves, but obligations do not necessarily travel with it. The quiet motif of this subchapter is therefore a border—sometimes porous, sometimes fortified, always consequential. Cross that border without discipline and responsibilities evaporate; fortify it excessively and innovation stalls. The sovereign question is not whether data should move but when movement transforms responsibility.

The first task is to show how localisation demands surface in practice. Beyond the Delhi case, a second example emerged in January 2021, when the South Korean Personal Information Protection Commission (PIPC) rejected a multinational health-tech provider's request to transfer metadata to California for model retraining. The model predicted hospital readmission risk, but the metadata rows contained incidental indicators that, when combined with auxiliary information, created a re-identification route under Korean law. The company argued that its US facility had stronger security protocols. Regulators disagreed. The lawful locus of processing mattered more than the technical hardness of the target. South Korea's position made explicit what many jurisdictions now insist upon: sovereignty is expressed through data's physical and legal residence. The implication is immediate. Whether a model can travel depends less on its architecture than on the values embedded in the movement.

Name the pattern: sovereignty contests arise wherever data protection, industrial policy, and rights claims intersect. Explain it: nations view data not simply as an asset but as a site of control—over privacy, competition, security, and narrative power. When a model trained in one jurisdiction enters another, its creators bring assumptions about lawful grounds for processing, minimum transparency obligations, and acceptable error distributions. If those assumptions conflict with local norms, the imported model becomes a value collision in code. The implication is straightforward: without explicit decision patterns to manage these collisions, cross-border deployments remain ethically ungrounded.

Visible behaviours make these abstractions tangible. In the Delhi case, engineers produced two diverging Git branches—one with features aligned to European auditing expectations, one tuned to Indian risk-prediction contexts. Commit histories showed rising maintenance debt. In Seoul, compliance teams tracked "refusal rate" metrics for cross-border transfer requests, observing a 17 per cent increase after the PIPC ruling (PIPC 2021). These artefacts are not administrative clutter; they are signals of sovereignty's force. Values leave fingerprints in logs and workflows.

To construct a principled approach, we need concrete decision patterns for cross-border deployments. One pattern begins with provenance mapping. Before a model moves, organisations must trace every dataset to its legal origin—identifying which jurisdictions claim authority over which fields. A second pattern involves what Singapore's Infocomm Media Development Authority (IMDA) called "differential deployment envelopes" in a 2022 pilot: the same base model could operate across borders only if sensitive components—embedding layers trained on protected demographic attributes—were quarantined onshore, while non-sensitive layers travelled. This approach preserved model performance while respecting localisation constraints.

A third pattern centres on the concept of "value impact surfaces"—a term used by the African Union's Data Policy Framework in 2022. The surface marks where a model's behaviour touches socially sensitive domains: policing, credit, hiring, health triage. When a model crosses borders, the receiving jurisdiction determines whether the value impact surface exceeds its tolerance. For example, in 2023 Kenya's Office of the Data Protection Commissioner blocked a foreign predictive-policing pilot because its false-positive distribution threatened to reinforce local profiling dynamics. The foreign vendor saw statistical accuracy; Kenyan regulators saw sovereignty embodied in community risk.

However, there is a credible limitation to rigid localisation. A counter-example appeared in February 2023 when Chilean agricultural researchers protested new localisation rules that prevented them from transferring crop-stress datasets to a high-performance cluster in Madrid. The Madrid cluster offered specialised satellite-aligned simulation capabilities unavailable in Santiago, and without it, seasonal predictions weakened. Localisation protected sovereignty but degraded scientific value. The tension was undeniable: when data cannot cross borders, opportunities cannot cross either. Reconciling this requires nuance rather than purity.

One emerging reconciliation involves "model relocation without data relocation." Instead of moving raw datasets, organisations port trained models—sometimes even distilled models—while keeping underlying data onshore. The EU's Gaia-X framework explored this with federated analytics pilots in 2022. Nodes in France and Finland cooperated without exchanging raw data; each node computed gradients locally. Visible behaviour here included shared performance dashboards showing error differences between nodes. This approach did not eliminate sovereignty conflicts but softened them by shrinking the surface of data movement.

Another reconciliation strategy focuses on contractual sovereignty. Rather than rely solely on statutory localisation, firms adopt binding contract clauses that travel with the model. Brazil's LGPD-inspired cross-border clauses (2021) required foreign parties to maintain equivalent breach-notification timelines and audit rights when handling Brazilian-origin data. This created a portable ethical baseline: sovereignty expressed not through immobility but through enforceable obligations.

Threading the motif again—the border—reveals a deeper principle. Sovereignty is not a relic; it is a negotiation. Each time data moves, it crosses a political threshold. Each time a model adapts, it absorbs local meaning. And each time organisations seek exemptions, they confront the question of whose norms guide the machine.

Two further examples consolidate this. First: in 2023, Japan's Digital Agency authorised cross-border model retraining using pseudonymised health records, but only after imposing detailed logging requirements and post-transfer audits by Tokyo-based institutions. Engineers had to embed machine-readable tags marking every instance where foreign infrastructure touched Japanese-origin data. Enforcement was visible, granular, and expensive. Yet the practice yielded a template: sovereignty expressed not through isolation but through structured traceability.

Second: Canada's Office of the Privacy Commissioner, in a 2022 decision, allowed a multinational retailer to use an American fraud-detection model on Canadian loyalty-card data, but required that all outputs undergo "contestability windows"—short periods during which customers could challenge risk scores before any consequential action occurred. This was sovereignty operationalised through user rights rather than data flow restrictions. The interface changed because the border mattered.

Across these examples, the tension grows sharper. Data localisation protects autonomy and legal clarity but risks creating digital islands. Cross-border transfer fuels innovation but risks rights dilution. Model portability preserves privacy but may limit model fidelity. This landscape requires explicit decision patterns. A disciplined organisation asks: What data must remain onshore? Which components of the model may travel? Which rights must be invariant across borders? Which harms must be prevented even if performance drops? The decisions must be visible—not buried in compliance memos.

The implication is profound. Sovereignty of data and models becomes not a constraint but a design parameter. Organisations must measure not only accuracy or computational cost but "sovereignty load": the burden a model places on local values, legal expectations, and political stability. Engineers then commit to design choices that lower this load—federated infrastructures, contractual safeguards, graded transparency, and region-specific fallbacks.

The unresolved tension that closes this subchapter is simple and sharp. When the optimal model violates local norms and the locally compliant model performs worse, which border do we cross first—the technical boundary or the moral one? There is no universal answer. There is only the duty to decide consciously, traceably, and with full recognition that every cross-border model carries more than code. It carries a claim about whose values prevail.

Civic participation in design

In October 2020, the city of Amsterdam convened a group of forty residents in an old school building in Zuidoost to review the municipality's automated welfare-fraud detection system. The system had been suspended after critics argued that it disproportionately flagged people from immigrant communities. Over two evenings, participants worked through real decision logs, redacted case summaries, and printed model explanations. By the end of the second session, the facilitators noted a striking outcome: the group agreed not only that the system should be redesigned, but that its core assumptions about "risk" needed to be rewritten from the ground up. Amsterdam's officials had expected critique. They had not expected residents to contribute concrete requirement changes—removal of postcode weighting, thresholds tuned to reflect neighbourhood-level variation in childcare claims, and a demand for transparent appeal windows. Civic participation did not merely comment on the tool. It rewired its design.

The Amsterdam case captures an essential truth about AI governance: technical legitimacy strengthens only when publics can name what matters before the model is built. The quiet motif threading this subchapter is a table—one around which people who rarely meet in formal policy settings gather to determine what a system should and should not do. When a city brings welfare claimants, caseworkers, and machine-learning engineers to the same table, the conversation shifts from speculation to situated knowledge. When it avoids that table, it forfeits the insight needed to prevent harm.

A second example reinforces the point. In May 2022, the New Zealand Ministry of Health launched a deliberative workshop in Wellington to shape the constraints for a proposed hospital triage support model. Participants included Māori elders, emergency clinicians, disability advocates, and data scientists. The facilitation team used a simple behaviour metric—*interruption count per minute*—to ensure no stakeholder group dominated discussion. Early drafts of the model had scored respiratory distress using datasets without adequate representation of rural patients. Elders highlighted ways in which cultural communication styles could be misread as "nonurgent." The requirement set shifted: developers committed to a feature-verification protocol with a named cultural review step, and clinicians requested that the model expose "confidence intervals per attribute" directly in the interface. The implications were practical and immediate. Workshops avoid abstraction. They write constraints into code.

Show the structure. Name the principle. Explain why civic participation matters for requirement-setting. When people with lived stakes describe how an AI system should perform, they express values that resist codification in isolation—what counts as a dignified explanation, what constitutes reasonable inconvenience, what forms of monitoring feel coercive, what signals of fairness ring true. These values become design anchors that technical teams can convert into measurable behaviours: how long consent prompts appear on screen, how appeals are logged, how edge cases are surfaced for human review. The implication is clear. Without civic input, requirement documents drift towards developer convenience or regulator minimalism; with it, systems embody social intelligence instead of extractive efficiency.

The border motif returns here, though in civic rather than geopolitical form. Every AI system crosses boundaries between institutional priorities and public expectations. A workshop creates a controlled border crossing. It slows the movement of ideas so participants can shape them. In practice, facilitation details matter. Scholars of participatory design note that the first thirty minutes determine the legitimacy of the whole event. In the Wellington workshop, facilitators used paired interviews to draw out specific experiences rather than general opinions. This produced testable statements: "Reduce alert frequency after two false alarms in a shift," or "Record patient disagreements as structured fields." Requirements built from experience tend to be falsifiable. Requirements built from sentiment rarely are.

A limitation must be acknowledged. Not every deliberative format translates smoothly across cultures or domains. A credible counter-example emerged in a 2021 transport-planning workshop in Toronto, where attempts to co-design safety parameters for an automated traffic-light optimisation system stalled. Participants struggled to grasp the system's high-dimensional decision space; their contributions centred on street-level grievances that engineers found hard to operationalise. The process became a catalogue of frustrations rather than a requirement-setting session. Yet the limitation was methodological, not conceptual. When the facilitators reconvened later with scenario cards—each describing concrete trade-offs such as "reduce bus delays at the cost of longer pedestrian waits"—participants produced structured preferences. What failed was the first approach, not the idea of participation itself.

Reconciling this requires recognising that civic involvement must be engineered with the same rigour as any technical component. Designers should measure not only outputs but the process itself: participation rate across demographics, facilitation load per hour, and the proportion of requirements directly traceable to public input. These metrics reduce hand-waving. They show where workshops skew towards dominant voices or where framing narrows the debate. When participants see their contributions surface in requirement drafts—highlighted, attributed, and integrated—they develop a form of procedural trust grounded in visible behaviour rather than aspirational rhetoric.

Two further examples show how participation can change system boundaries. In 2022, the Scottish Government ran a public deliberation in Glasgow on AI-assisted school-placement allocations. Students and parents flagged that the proposed model's distance-weighting penalised families in newly built estates lacking historical transport data. The technical team responded by re-estimating travel-time features using real-time bus-sensor feeds rather than legacy datasets. In 2023, Nairobi's county administration tested participatory modelling for water-allocation scheduling, inviting residents from drought-prone districts to describe hour-by-hour usage patterns. Engineers noticed that participants described their routines through constraints rather than averages—"never cut supply before dawn prayers," "trigger alerts after two hours of low pressure." These constraints became explicit model rules. Participation sharpened the system's ethical boundary conditions.

Thread the table motif again. A workshop table is not a symbol of consensus. It is a site where conflict becomes constructive. Civics enters design not to flatten disagreement but to name it, measure it, and decide when a system's benefit is worth its intrusion. The more structured the conversation, the more durable the requirements.

The closing tension emerges from a simple question with no universal answer. How far must civic participation reach before we can claim an AI system carries the voices of those it affects? Too shallow and participation becomes theatre; too deep and design freezes under incompatible demands. The challenge is to craft a method where publics meaningfully shape constraints without carrying the full burden of technical design. The test for any organisation is this: when you look at the final system, can you point to a requirement that no engineer would have invented alone? If the answer is no, civic participation has not yet begun.

Chapter 10
Building the Moral Ops Function

The email reached the ethics lead at 02:17 on a warm night in June 2024. A content-moderation model, rolled out only six weeks earlier by a major European media platform, had begun quietly escalating the rate at which it hid comments written in minority languages. Nothing dramatic. No outage. No blaze of public outrage. Just a thin, persistent drift: one per cent more hidden posts an hour, then two, then five. By the time the night team traced the behaviour to a malformed update in the model's preprocessing pipeline, the platform had suppressed thousands of legitimate contributions. The logs told a small story—just a patch gone wrong. The community's reaction told a larger one—systems can fail without falling, and the damage lies in the accumulation of silent harms. When the ethics lead gathered her team the next morning, their first task was not blame. It was reconstruction: How did this reach production? Who noticed the early signals? Which checklists worked? Which rhythms faltered? And what should their *playbook* look like now?

Scenes like this have become the quiet heart of AI governance. They are rarely televised, seldom quoted by ministers, but they determine whether institutions build moral competence or accumulate technical debt with ethical interest. The motif of this chapter is that reconstruction table—the place where a team lays out logs, reports, recollections, and unplanned detours. Around it sit engineers, product managers, safety specialists, policy advisers, user advocates, and sometimes the very people whose lives the system touches. A table like this is not theatre. It is the operational core of moral responsibility. It asks a simple but relentless question: *What does it take to run ethics, not just declare it?*

The difference between aspiration and operation is not philosophical; it is procedural. Many organisations still treat "ethical principles" as declarations pinned to a homepage—a static skyline rather than a navigational tool. But principles without practice behave like untreated wood: they warp under pressure. A Moral Ops function exists to stabilise the structure. It converts values into concrete artefacts—value specifications stitched into documentation, harms registers updated at the end of each development sprint, decision logs that narrate why a team proceeded or paused. These artefacts do not eliminate uncertainty. They domesticate it. They make ethical reasoning traceable, repeatable, and inspectable across time.

To build such a function, one must look closely at the rhythms and skills that sustain it. Some teams borrow from incident-response culture, practising simulations the way fire brigades drill evacuations. Others draw from socio-technical research, embedding ethnographers beside engineers so that user impacts become evidence rather than intuition. The most mature groups blend these with safety engineering, treating every deployment as an experiment requiring monitoring, fallback plans, and criteria for abort authority. The result is not bureaucracy but muscle memory—habits that allow an organisation to notice drifts early and act before a fault hardens into harm.

Across sectors, promising prototypes are emerging. A London health-tech provider uses quarterly "ethics sprints" in which interdisciplinary teams surface potential misalignments between user experience and model optimisation. A Singaporean logistics firm maintains a rolling harms register shared across subsidiaries, which documents not just incidents but "near-harm patterns" observed by service staff on shop floors. In Montreal, a civic-tech collective keeps a library of scenario-based decision logs, allowing new volunteers to see how past teams reasoned through uncertainty. These efforts vary in form, but share an ethos: ethical vigilance is a practice, not a posture.

The chapter you are about to enter treats the Moral Ops function as an institutional craft—a discipline of attention and adaptation. It explores how principles consolidate into playbooks, how teams build rhythms that keep those playbooks alive, which metrics capture ethical drift before it becomes visible, and how institutional memory can persist despite turnover. The deeper message is continuity. Systems change. People change. Contexts shift. The only stable asset is the organisation's capacity to remember, refine, and reapply what experience has already taught it, without waiting for the next midnight alert.

The final question that will carry you forward is not glamorous, but it governs everything: *What would your organisation need to see, hear, and record each week to know that its moral commitments are still intact?* The teams that can answer this are not simply compliant. They are accountable in motion.

From principles to playbooks

At 09:46 on 14 March 2023, in a meeting room overlooking Southwark Bridge, a small team at the UK's Centre for Data Ethics and Innovation (CDEI) replayed the final minutes before a national recruitment algorithm was paused. The model, deployed the previous winter to help triage applications in an overstretched public service department, had begun producing sharply skewed scores for candidates with fragmented employment histories. The hiring managers noticed the pattern only when a regional office in Leeds reported that shortlisted applicants no longer reflected its usual intake. The system was not malicious. It was unfinished. The team in Southwark traced the fault to an undocumented update that altered the weighting of one feature in the scoring pipeline. What unsettled them was not the error itself—errors are expected—but the absence of a traceable decision log explaining who authorised the change, what assumptions governed it, and why monitoring thresholds had remained static. For several hours that morning, the room worked backward, piecing assumptions into a narrative they wished had already existed. A pattern emerged: the organisation had principles, but no playbook.

That moment, humble as it was, captured a recurring motif in AI governance: critical choices live in the details of tooling, not in the slogans that decorate corporate annual reports. The CDEI team looked not for inspiration but for instrumentation. They needed value specifications that translated high-level commitments into verifiable criteria; harms registers that tracked not only incidents but near-miss patterns; and decision logs that recorded reasoning at the point of action. Without these, their principles were scaffolding with no building attached. The quiet question that animated the discussion—*Where would we look to see our values operationalised?*—is the same question confronting any organisation seeking to build moral resilience rather than moral theatre. Five words crystallised the problem by the end of the meeting: *We need a playbook now.*

Playbooks arise when abstraction meets pressure. To see this, consider how safety engineering in aviation shifted after the 1994 USAir Flight 427 crash near Aliquippa, Pennsylvania. The National Transportation Safety Board did not simply issue general recommendations about "better safety culture"; it mandated explicit procedural updates, cockpit checklists, and data-driven inspection regimes. The shift was procedural, not rhetorical. By naming the mechanisms—flight data recorders, control-surface testing protocols, crew resource management reviews—the Board made accountability inspectable. This naming mattered because it converted intention into structure. In AI development, value specifications function similarly: they expose the anatomy of a principle. If an organisation claims to prioritise equitable outcomes, the value specification must identify which demographic groups are monitored, which metrics are used to measure disparities, which thresholds trigger human review, and what constitutes a justified exception. Each element binds a broad principle to a visible behaviour.

At their best, value specifications discipline teams to state what would count as success *before* a line of code is shipped. Harms registers play the complementary role of showing what has happened *after*. A harms register is not a list of catastrophes, but a living ledger of observed, anticipated, and near-miss harms. The Metropolitan Police Service in London has experimented with such registers for data-driven tools since 2021, describing where automated support tools inadvertently changed officer behaviour or skewed resource allocation. These entries are rarely dramatic: a flagged postcode causing a temporary surge in patrols; a shift scheduling tool that overburdened a subset of officers during school holidays; a mis-specified field leading to search inaccuracies. Yet each entry is a learning asset. It prevents teams from relying on memory or heroic individual vigilance. It turns what could be forgotten into something that shapes the next revision.

The power of this approach becomes clearer when contrasted with a limitation. In 2020, during rapid procurement of COVID-19 analytics systems, several European health ministries adopted expedited development modes that treated ethical considerations as downstream tasks. A French regional authority piloted a hospital triage dashboard without assembling a structured harms register. When an anomaly caused the dashboard to misclassify ICU strain in Mulhouse, the problem was detected only through clinicians' complaints. Analysts later noted that a near-miss pattern—false stability signals during rapid case surges—had been observed in December but never documented. This counter-example illustrates the fragility of relying on informal memory. It shows the consequence of lacking a visible record of weak signals. Yet the limitation does not refute the value of playbooks; it reinforces the need to embed them even in crisis. Where a harms register existed, the weak signals would have been logged, escalated, and stress-tested. The absence of structure is not an argument against structure. It is an argument for building it early.

If value specifications and harms registers anchor a team's situational awareness, decision logs anchor its judgement. Decision logs record not only what choice was made, but why it was made at that moment under those constraints. They force a team to articulate assumptions that often remain tacit: data quality caveats, model fragilities, monitoring gaps, political pressures, user feedback, or unusual time constraints. The result is a lineage of reasoning. When something later goes wrong, teams can reconstruct the logic that shaped the system's behaviour. When something goes unexpectedly right, they can identify which assumption deserves reinforcement, not chance repetition.

Decision logs matter because they expose the cumulative risk of complex systems. A single mis-specified weighting rarely collapses an AI service; it is the interaction of many small choices—some forgotten, some undocumented—that produces system drift. Naming the reasoning behind these choices creates friction against drift. It introduces, in effect, a narrative checksum: disagreements become visible, and weak rationales can be challenged before they ossify into practice.

To ground the motif of the playbook, imagine again the reconstruction table: value specifications on one side, harms registers in the centre, decision logs aligned chronologically. These artefacts operate together. They reveal whether the system's direction matches the organisation's intention. They also reveal gaps between aspiration and attention. When a decision log repeatedly notes reliance on a fragile feature, the value specification may need revision. When a harms register fills with near-miss patterns during weekends, monitoring rhythms may require redesign. The table does not solve moral dilemmas. It structures them. It makes reasoning a collective discipline rather than a private act.

This interplay is visible in how organisations formalise their operating models. The Danish Agency for Digital Government, for instance, introduced explicit audit clauses for municipal AI deployments in 2022. These clauses required not just compliance with national ethical guidelines, but demonstrable evidence of playbook components: documented value specifications, active harms registers updated quarterly, and decision logs reviewable by independent auditors. The requirement was behavioural: municipalities had to show, not just assert, that their systems operated under structured moral oversight. In Singapore, meanwhile, the Infocomm Media Development Authority piloted "Model AI Governance Clusters" where companies voluntarily committed to shared documentation templates, including cross-team decision logs that allowed for inter-organisational learning. These real cases show how playbooks travel across institutional boundaries when their components are concrete.

Yet there is a limit worth naming. Playbooks can stabilise processes but cannot eliminate disagreement. During a cross-border collaboration in 2021 between a Scandinavian public sector team and a federal agency in the United States, both parties maintained detailed harms registers and decision logs. However, their value specifications diverged in how they weighed false positives against false negatives in fraud detection. The playbook could not compel substantive alignment. It could only reveal the misalignment early. The limitation is genuine: artefacts structure discussion, but they do not substitute for democratic deliberation. Reconciling this limitation requires using playbooks not as negotiation endpoints but as negotiation evidence. When disagreements are surfaced through documentation rather than concealed in assumptions, they become tractable.

The practical implication is that a mature Moral Ops model must weave its artefacts into everyday workflow. A value specification should be reviewed alongside technical design documents. A harms register should be updated during each sprint retrospective. A decision log should accompany every significant model modification, recorded in the same repository that handles pull requests and change tracking. These are visible behaviours, not abstract commitments. They turn ethics into operational muscle.

A further implication emerges when we consider organisational memory. Artefacts survive turnover. People leave; spreadsheets remain. Yet artefacts degrade unless tended. A value specification last edited two years ago tells a different story from one revised last quarter to incorporate new evidence. A harms register with uneven entries reveals gaps in team awareness. Playbooks, therefore, demand rhythm. They thrive on routine. Quarterly ethics sprints, monthly governance stand-ups, and cross-team review sessions are not ornamental rituals—they are the maintenance cycles that keep artefacts alive. An organisation that neglects this rhythm treats its moral commitments as weather-dependent.

The motif of the reconstruction table returns here. Picture a new hire joining the team. She sits before the table, scanning a value specification written before her arrival, reading harms register entries she did not witness, and reviewing decision logs authored by colleagues she will never meet. Yet the narrative they create gives her something rare: continuity. She encounters an institution that remembers its own reasoning. She inherits not slogans but scaffolding.

The counterfactual is easy to imagine. Without a playbook, governance becomes personality-driven. The organisation remembers only what its longest-serving staff recall. Ethical drift accelerates. Risks recur. Teams reinvent solutions to previously resolved problems because the memory of those resolutions has evaporated. A playbook protects against amnesia. It makes ethical diligence cumulative rather than episodic.

As more organisations adopt AI across critical functions—from eligibility screening to content moderation to financial triage—the demand for operational clarity intensifies. Playbooks will not guarantee moral correctness. They will not prevent every failure. But they will reshape what failure looks like. Instead of ambiguous blame and retrospective guesswork, failures can be interrogated through evidence. Instead of moral panic, there can be structured reflection. Instead of heroic oversight by individuals, there can be systemic vigilance.

The forward question, then, is deceptively simple: *What artefacts would your organisation need to produce each week to persuade an outsider that its ethical commitments are lived, not laminated?* The answer will determine whether principles remain decorative or become operational.

Roles, skills, and rhythms

On a Friday afternoon in September 2022, in a glass meeting room at the Helsinki City Hall, the "AI steering group" assembled for what had been scheduled as a routine check-in. A pilot allocation system for public housing had gone live three months earlier. The first dashboards looked fine: waiting times flat, complaint volumes low, no glaring anomalies. Then a housing officer from the eastern district slid a notebook across the table. She had recorded, by hand, the stories behind a handful of borderline allocation decisions. The officer's notes did not match the model's priorities. Families in temporary accommodation were being deprioritised in favour of applicants whose documents were tidier and histories easier to score. There was no scandal. No headline. Just a slow skew in favour of administrative neatness over urgent need. The team realised that their ethics principles were not missing. Their *roles* were. No one had been tasked to look for this particular misalignment, and no rhythm in the calendar made such scrutiny inevitable. The room fell briefly silent.

That silence is where the Moral Ops function either dissolves or matures. Helsinki's team did the harder thing. They restructured. A safety engineer was made formally accountable for defining measurable guardrails around allocation fairness, a socio-technical researcher was brought in to spend time with housing officers and applicants, and an incident-response lead was appointed to own escalation when patterns of harm emerged. Alongside these roles, they booked a new recurring slot into the municipal calendar: a quarterly ethics sprint, during which live services were reviewed as seriously as any security audit. The paradox was obvious. It was not that the city lacked good intentions. It was that ethics had no choreography.

The motif of this subchapter is that choreography—a pattern of recurring movements in which distinct roles step forward, then step back, in a rhythm that over time becomes second nature. Organisations tend to imagine ethics as a static committee or a one-off checklist. The more accurate picture, borrowed from disciplines like air traffic control and hospital safety, is closer to a rota. Who watches which signals today? Who takes the call when a threshold is crossed at 02:00 on a Sunday? Who speaks for affected groups in the design review next week? Without an explicit answer, responsibility evaporates into good will.

The first major claim is simple: without safety engineering as a distinct craft, Moral Ops becomes improvised risk management. Show this through practice. In 2021, a large European payments provider based in Amsterdam created a "model safety" team alongside its existing data-science group. Name the choice. The team borrowed techniques from software reliability engineering—fault injection, canary releases, graceful degradation—and applied them to fraud-detection models. They worked with product managers to define safe failure modes: when a model's uncertainty exceeded a threshold, transactions should default to additional verification rather than outright decline. Explain the effect. Safety engineers treated harm not as a distant possibility but as a design parameter: they specified maximum tolerable false-positive rates per user segment, designed monitoring limits that were tied to actual financial stress on customers, and insisted on kill-switch conditions. Implication: the organisation moved from hoping its models would behave to specifying how they were allowed to misbehave.

Contrast this with a credible limitation. In 2020, during a rapid expansion of online services, several smaller fintech start-ups in London folded safety into generic "data science" roles. Engineers were told to "keep an eye" on harms while also delivering features and performance gains. Months later, when customer complaints about repeated false fraud flags arrived, there was no clear owner. Monitoring scripts existed, but no one's job was to act on them. The limitation here is not malice. It is dilution. Where safety is everyone's part-time concern, it is nobody's expertise. Reconciling this does not require every organisation to replicate the budgets of a major bank. It does require a named role—or roles—with explicit time and authority to define and defend safety constraints.

A second claim follows: socio-technical research is not a luxury bolt-on; it is how Moral Ops learns what actually happens at the point of use. Show it. In 2019, the UK's National Health Service (NHS) worked with the University of Cambridge on early deployments of clinical decision support tools. Ethnographers sat in emergency departments in London and Birmingham, noting when clinicians followed the system, when they ignored it, and why. Name the effort. These researchers documented subtle behavioural shifts: junior doctors sometimes over-relied on system recommendations during busy nights, while senior clinicians used the tool primarily to document that they had considered alternatives. Explain. Socio-technical researchers made visible the "interaction patterns" that raw performance metrics could not reveal. They could point to specific behaviours—a glance at a screen, a scribbled override in the notes—and connect them to risk. Implication: without this research, safety engineers would calibrate guardrails against an imaginary user, not the one actually at the bedside.

A further example from municipal services reinforces this. In 2022, Barcelona's city council invited urban sociologists to observe front-line staff as they worked with an AI-assisted benefits triage tool. Researchers tracked how caseworkers explained system recommendations, timed how long they spent in explanation, and recorded which cases they chose to override. The patterns they surfaced—especially around language barriers and digital literacy—fed directly into the next ethics sprint. Some features were reweighted; interface copy changed; appeal prompts were redesigned. Socio-technical work turned "trust" from an abstraction into a set of observable behaviours, such as time spent in explanations and frequency of justified overrides.

Now for a third claim: incident response must be treated as a core competence, not an embarrassing admission that something failed. Show how it works when done well. Since 2017, major technology firms in Dublin and Seattle have adopted security-style "on call" rotations for AI incidents—near real-time anomalies in recommendation quality, moderation performance, or allocation systems. Name the mechanism. Incident commanders are assigned shifts; runbooks specify escalation paths; post-incident reviews are mandatory. Explain the effect. When a content classifier starts mislabelling images during a regional festival because costumes confuse its training priors, there is someone awake who owns the decision to throttle, roll back, or switch to manual review. Implication: incident response transforms ethics from a retrospective exercise to a time-bound practice. It sharpens reflexes. It engrains the simple but crucial habit: when harm appears, somebody leads.

A credible limitation appears here as well. Some public-sector bodies resist the language and culture of incident response, fearing that formalising "incidents" might signal systemic unreliability. They stick to quiet adjustments and internal memos. Yet this reticence brings its own risk. Without formal incident structures, patterns are lost, staff burn out under informal firefighting, and the same categories of harm recur. Where agencies do lean into incident response—with transparent criteria, learning-focused reviews, and protections against scapegoating—their public legitimacy often increases rather than declines. Citizens recognise that complex systems can fail; they judge institutions on how they respond.

Running through all of this is the motif of rhythm. Roles alone are insufficient. Without recurring beats in the calendar, even the best safety engineer or researcher will be consumed by urgent demands. Quarterly ethics sprints offer one answer. They work when they function not as symbolic workshops but as bounded periods where the organisation deliberately steps off the feature treadmill to inspect alignment. In practice, a good ethics sprint in March should look different from one in September. The March sprint might focus on recent incidents and near misses; September might emphasise model retraining plans ahead of seasonal changes. The rhythm matters because it creates memory. Teams begin to expect that certain questions will arise every quarter: which user groups experienced disproportionate false positives, which metrics moved, which new harms emerged, which overrides increased. Weekly stand-ups and monthly reviews provide pulse; quarterly sprints provide depth.

Examples help here too. A Scandinavian insurer with offices in Stockholm and Oslo instituted ethics sprints in 2021, aligned with their existing product release train. During one sprint, socio-technical researchers presented findings on how customers interpreted a risk-rating interface; safety engineers responded by proposing different threshold displays; incident responders shared logs from a recent outage where explanations had failed to load. Over three days, the team produced changes that then fed into the next quarter's baseline. These sprints did not resolve all tensions—underwriting teams still pushed for efficiency; regulators still pressed for caution—but they ensured that the most consequential value choices had a recurring forum.

Yet rhythm has its own limitations. Organisations under severe delivery pressure sometimes compress ethics sprints into perfunctory review meetings. They tick boxes, skim dashboards, and move on. The deeper function—making space for genuine argument, for revisiting assumptions, for absorbing socio-technical evidence—disappears. Here again, the reconciliation lies not in abandoning sprints but in protecting them. Some teams write into governance charters that ethics sprints cannot be cancelled except by the same authority that approves major releases. Others tie sprint outputs to board reporting, giving the work weight.

Across all of these claims, the question of metrics returns. Roles and rhythms cannot float free of measurement. Safety engineering must track concrete indicators: override rates, uncertainty spikes, error clustering by group. Socio-technical research must translate observations into measurable adjustments: reduced explanation time variance, more uniform complaint patterns across districts. Incident response must log time-to-detection and time-to-mitigation, not to fetishise speed but to understand where cognitive and organisational bottlenecks lie. The point is not to reduce ethics to numbers. It is to ensure that ethical performance cannot hide entirely in narrative.

The motif of choreography appears once more if we change the vantage point. Imagine a new data scientist joining a team in Manchester. In her first month, she shadows a safety engineer during an incident review, sits with a socio-technical researcher observing user interactions in a jobcentre, and joins the closing session of an ethics sprint where metrics, logs, and stories are brought together. Her understanding of "good work" shifts. She starts to treat value specifications, harms registers, and incident runbooks as normal tools, not exotic add-ons. This is how roles, skills, and rhythms propagate—through apprenticeship and repetition as much as through policy.

The unresolved tension is this. Building such choreography costs real time and attention. It asks leaders to accept fewer features, slower releases, more meetings that do not immediately ship code. Yet the alternative is not neutral. It is a system that relies on luck, individual heroism, and the hope that misalignment will be small enough to ignore. The forward test for any organisation is therefore stark: if you froze hiring today and kept only the roles, skills, and rhythms you already have, would your Moral Ops function still be standing in three years—or would it have quietly dissolved into the background noise of urgent work?

Metrics that matter

On 12 March 2018, at the headquarters of the UK Information Commissioner's Office in Wilmslow, investigators unpacked a series of spreadsheets obtained during the Cambridge Analytica inquiry. The data were not spectacular. No exotic models. No breathtaking algorithms. What startled the analysts was something quieter: a complete absence of behavioural metrics showing how the firm had monitored drift between its intended voter-profiling criteria and the audiences it actually targeted. The firm could describe categories but not *movement*. It could explain segments but not *slippage*. When questioned about how its systems flagged early warning signs of misalignment, no one could point to a single leading indicator. The silence was not proof of malice. It was evidence of something more banal and therefore more dangerous: ethical performance had never been measured, so ethical drift had never been seen.

The case remains a hinge in the global conversation on responsible technology. Not because the models were uniquely powerful, but because they lacked the minimum pulse checks that any safety-critical system would consider ordinary. The failure was procedural before it was philosophical. A system affecting millions of people moved without instruments. That absence—those missing dials—created a vacuum in which claims, counter-claims, and speculation flourished. It is a reminder that even the most sophisticated organisations falter when they cannot track their own trajectory.

This subchapter follows the motif of the *dial*: the idea that ethical performance requires a panel of instruments, not a single gauge. The dial recurs because drift is often incremental, occurring in the quiet margins where no headline sits. If organisations do not measure those margins, they cannot govern them. Ethical resilience is not an attitude. It is a system of metrics that notice before harm becomes entrenched.

The first major claim is straightforward: leading indicators of ethical drift must be behavioural, not aspirational. Show this. In 2021, the Danish Tax Agency in Copenhagen piloted an AI-assisted fraud detection system. The agency supplemented model accuracy dashboards with three leading indicators: override frequency by caseworkers, the distribution of false positives across demographics, and the time caseworkers spent reading model explanations. Name these metrics. Override frequency served as a proxy for contestability; demographic false positives tracked fairness drift; explanation-reading time measured cognitive load and emerging mistrust. Explain the insight. These metrics captured subtle shifts before they became severe: rising overrides signalled confusion or disagreement; skewed false positives flagged bias; shortening explanation time suggested either increased familiarity or growing impatience—each with different implications. The agency used these signals to trigger reviews weeks before complaint volumes rose. Implication: behavioural metrics detect ethical drift early enough for action.

A second example strengthens the point. In 2020, Transport for London (TfL) introduced algorithmic tools to support bus-scheduling decisions. TfL's safety team monitored three leading indicators: operator-initiated schedule corrections, variance in break compliance across depots, and the clustering of near misses captured via telematics. These indicators made risk visible as patterns of behaviour, not abstract probabilities. Within six months, TfL identified that one depot's operators were overriding recommended rest breaks at twice the rate of others. The investigation traced the issue to a misalignment between depot workflows and the system's assumptions. The change that followed—adjusting break windows and redesigning dashboard prompts—reduced override rates and narrowed risk variance. Behaviour, measured carefully, steered improvement.

A credible limitation must be acknowledged. Not all behavioural metrics are reliable proxies for ethical drift. Consider a 2022 experiment by a retail platform in Berlin testing a new product-ranking model. Designers measured user "time to first click" as a trust indicator. But the metric proved misleading. Time fell not because users trusted the system more, but because the interface had become visually louder, pushing rapid choices. Mistaking speed for confidence, the team almost approved a release that risked pressuring vulnerable users into impulsive purchases. The limitation highlights a simple truth: behavioural metrics can deceive if chosen without a theory of harm and a clear understanding of what the behaviour signifies. Reconciling this requires triangulation—no metric should be allowed to speak alone.

From this foundation emerges the second claim: ethical resilience depends on tracking organisational behaviours, not merely system behaviours. Even the best technical metrics fail if internal incentives drift. Show this. In 2023, New Zealand's Ministry of Social Development examined why its welfare risk assessment tool, operating in Wellington and other cities, exhibited periodic surges in false positives. A socio-technical review found that team leaders had begun rewarding speed of processing over depth of review. Name this incentive drift. Analysts receiving performance bonuses for throughput spent fewer minutes interrogating flagged cases. Explain the mechanism. The metric—cases closed per hour—distorted behaviour, amplifying harm even though the model had not changed. Implication: ethical performance cannot be disentangled from organisational rhythms; resilience requires tracking internal signals such as review time variance, escalation lag, and analyst load.

A second, contrasting example shows how institutional metrics can strengthen resilience. Since 2018, the UK Civil Aviation Authority (CAA) has monitored three internal indicators across safety-critical teams: time spent in scenario rehearsals, participation rates in after-action reviews, and the ratio of mitigations implemented versus mitigations proposed. These metrics are not about the aircraft; they are about the people who ensure the aircraft remain safe. They detect whether a safety culture is thick or thin, whether teams practise enough, whether learning is absorbed. When scenario rehearsal hours dropped during a busy travel period in 2022, the CAA intervened early, reallocating resources to restore training time. The organisation recognised that resilience is a property of people and processes before it is a property of systems.

A third example reveals a limitation. Some organisations—particularly resource-constrained public agencies—fear that adding internal metrics creates bureaucratic drag. A pilot within a county council in northern England resisted tracking review time variance, arguing that frontline staff were already stretched thin. Yet without that metric, the council could not distinguish between skill gaps, workload overload, or interface confusion. The resolution was to adopt a lighter version: a weekly five-minute survey recording staff confidence in system recommendations, linked to anonymised logs showing how decisions were revised. Reduced friction preserved insight. Again, the motif of the dial appears: any individual metric can be slimmed without losing the overall instrumentation.

A third claim follows naturally: to matter, metrics must be designed to trigger action. Show this. In 2021, the French data protection authority, CNIL, advised a consortium developing automated school allocation systems in Paris and Lyon. The consortium adopted trigger thresholds: if false-positive allocation errors exceeded a defined rate for any socio-economic group, a mandatory review commenced. If explanation refusal rates—when families declined to accept system explanations—rose above a band, the interface team intervened. Name these thresholds. They were referred to internally as "review gates." Explain their purpose. Review gates connected measurement to obligation; they transformed observation into commitment. Implication: metrics without gates are mere decoration.

Consider a military example demonstrating similar logic. Since 2020, the UK's Defence Science and Technology Laboratory (DSTL) has used simulation data to track anomaly clusters in autonomous surveillance systems. When anomaly density in a simulation exceeded a defined spatial threshold, the scenario automatically escalated to human review. The threshold acted as a brake, ensuring that automation never accumulated small errors into dangerous confidence. This is measurement as governance.

A counter-example shows the danger of actionless metrics. In 2019, a municipal authority in Canada added fairness dashboards to an allocation system but failed to define who owned intervention. When disparities in service assignment grew, no team moved. The metric existed. The action pathway did not. Reconciling this involves assigning responsibility, not merely producing data. Metrics must live in a home.

Now we return to the motif of the dial by widening the frame: what counts as an ethical leading indicator is itself culturally conditioned. Some regions prioritise user dignity, others procedural fairness, others accuracy above all. Measurement must reflect local moral priorities while preserving baseline protections. Show this. In 2022, a health technology firm deploying clinical triage tools in both Singapore and Scotland discovered that identical metrics did not translate across contexts. Singaporean clinicians valued metrics capturing escalation speed and deference to senior judgement; Scottish clinicians emphasised metrics capturing patient informedness and shared decision-making. Name these cultural drivers. Each reflected legitimate expectations of professional practice. Explain the learning. Measurement systems had to flex: add indicators for informedness in Scotland, add indicators for managerial oversight in Singapore. Implication: ethical metrics must honour both global floors and local ceilings.

A second cross-cultural example comes from data-labelling supply chains. A Nairobi-based annotation company and a Berlin-based client agreed in 2023 to track "wellbeing stability" as a leading indicator in content moderation pipelines. In Nairobi, wellbeing stability was measured through daily short-form check-ins and monthly counselling uptake; in Berlin, it was measured through team rotation rates and sick leave variance. The concept—resilience under cognitive strain—was shared, but the measurement adapted to context. Ethical indicators are not universal currencies; they require translation.

A further claim is needed: the most important metrics often measure recovery, not perfection. This is the heart of resilience. Show this through a clear example. In 2021, a major UK retail bank adopted a "harm half-life" metric for customer-facing models. Harm half-life measured the time taken between identifying a misclassification pattern and neutralising its effect across the affected customer segment. Name it clearly. The metric came from reliability engineering. Explain its force. By focusing on decay rather than avoidance, the bank measured how quickly it could correct course. Implication: resilience is not merely the absence of harm; it is the speed and fairness of repair.

A second recovery-focused example: since 2018, the Dutch Ministry of Justice has tracked "appeal elasticity," measuring how responsive system outputs are to justified human challenge. A low elasticity—little change after successful challenge—signals rigidity. High elasticity signals learning. The ministry uses elasticity as a leading indicator for model retraining cycles. Recovery, made measurable, strengthens governance.

A limitation appears in some jurisdictions where appeals data are sparse. Local cultural norms may lead people not to challenge decisions even when they disagree. In parts of East Asia, officials noted that low challenge rates reflected deference to authority rather than agreement. Reconciling this requires triangulation: supplement appeals with independent audits, user interviews, and random sampling. The dial grows more complex but also more honest.

At this point, the subchapter's motif—the dial—invites a final movement. Ethical drift is rarely loud. It is the slow accumulation of slight mismatches: a rising override rate in one depot; a cluster of complaints in one language group; an explanation interface that quietly shortens over months. Metrics that matter illuminate the small shifts that, if ignored, become scandals.

The unresolved tension remains sharp. Every added metric carries cognitive and organisational cost. Leaders must decide which dials are illuminated, which remain dark, and which trigger action when they flicker. The forward test is uncomfortable yet essential: if your most consequential system drifted tomorrow—quietly, subtly, dangerously—which metric would notice first, and would anyone feel obliged to act?

The long bet: institutional memory

In May 2015, engineers at the US National Transportation Safety Board (NTSB) reviewed the circumstances of an aircraft incident in Denver. The event itself was unremarkable: a minor runway excursion, no casualties, a single damaged tyre. What drew investigators' attention was not the failure but the discovery that the same underlying pattern—crew fatigue interacting with subtle automation quirks—had appeared in at least three prior incidents across different states. Each inquiry had been meticulous. Each report had been archived. Yet the pattern had never been stitched together because the personnel who held the tacit memory of earlier cases had moved on. Paper stayed. People left. The lesson evaporated. Institutional memory had fractured, and with it the possibility of prevention.

The NTSB's later assessment was blunt: the organisation had no systematic way to recognise recurring failure modes that manifested years apart. The cost was practical, not abstract. A matter of minutes, a slip in attention, a misunderstood alert—small things that became larger because the organisation could no longer remember its own past. It is a predicament alarmingly familiar in the governance of complex digital systems, where turnover is constant, roles are fluid, and tacit knowledge leaks into the air like steam. If safety is a long game, memory is the currency.

The motif throughout this chapter is the *thread*—the line that binds scattered observations into coherent lineage. Without the thread, each team improvises anew. With it, an organisation becomes capable of learning faster than any single career, outliving turnover, and resisting drift. The thread matters because models change, staff rotate, standards evolve, and crises rarely arrive in the same costume twice. Without memory, progress resets.

The first major claim is straightforward: institutions must convert episodic insight into reusable patterns. Show this. In 2020, NHS Digital in Leeds examined why certain data-processing mistakes recurred in hospital trusts despite being flagged in previous audits. Analysts found that insights remained trapped in documents labelled "lessons learned," which few teams ever opened. Name this structural flaw: static reports with no link to future action. Explain the mechanism. A lesson, unpatterned, becomes inert; it cannot influence new projects because it is not encoded in the architectures teams rely on. Implication: memory requires translation—insight must become a pattern, not a page.

Consider a counterpoint that demonstrates strength. Since 2012, the UK Government Digital Service (GDS) has maintained its "Service Manual" as a living library of patterns—tested solutions for accessibility, security, and user interaction rooted in repeated failures and recoveries across departments. When a payment verification issue resurfaced during a 2021 redesign, teams could reference a pattern describing the known pitfalls, alternatives, and mitigations. The memory was not an anecdote; it was an operational artefact. The pattern served as a visible behaviour: designers used it; engineers referenced it; auditors checked compliance against it. The implication is clear. Memory becomes functional when it takes the form of tools people already trust.

A limitation appears when patterns ossify. Japan's Fukushima Daiichi disaster review in 2012 contained a warning: decades-old emergency response patterns had been so stable that teams ceased to question their adequacy. Name the risk—pattern stagnation. Explain why it matters. When patterns become scripture, they obscure emerging threats. Reconciliation requires periodic renewal:

patterns must be versioned, reviewed, debated, and sometimes retired. The thread must remain taut, not rigid.

A second major claim follows: memory must be held both centrally and locally. Show this with a concrete case. In 2018, the European Space Agency (ESA) identified inconsistent handling of model calibration across its Earth observation missions. Some teams used ten-step procedures; others followed bespoke workflows built on local norms. When a calibration issue in Frascati recurred months later in Darmstadt, investigators traced the cause to divergent interpretations of the very same guidance. Name the deficiency—fragmented tacit practice. Explain the insight. Institutional memory cannot live only in headquarters or only in teams. It must be distributed, supported by libraries that record global principles and apprenticeship that anchors local nuance. Implication: memory travels best when both written and lived.

A contrasting example strengthens the point. Since 2008, the US Forest Service has maintained "Incident Review Cadres"—rotating groups of veteran firefighters who mentor new analysts during post-incident investigations. The cadre model preserves tacit knowledge through guided participation. Rather than rely solely on documents, apprentices hear how earlier teams interpreted ambiguous signals, balanced conflicting metrics, or managed fatigue. These stories, exchanged during field reviews, ensure that judgement—often the most perishable form of expertise—survives turnover. Behaviour makes memory tangible: apprentices shadow experts; experts interrogate logs; together they stitch the thread.

Yet a limitation must be acknowledged. Apprenticeship depends on availability of mentors, which fluctuates during crises or heavy operational loads. Agencies with chronic understaffing—such as certain county-level emergency services in the US—found that apprenticeship collapsed when experienced personnel were repeatedly deployed to field operations. Reconciliation requires designing "pause points" where mentorship is protected time, not optional goodwill. Without this, tacit memory thins.

A third claim emerges from the complexity of socio-technical systems: memory must capture not just outcomes but the reasoning behind decisions. Show this through a precise episode. In 2022, a financial regulator in London reviewed an automated anti-fraud system whose false-positive rate rose sharply. Engineers initially blamed dataset drift, but decision logs revealed something subtler: three years earlier, the team had deliberately relaxed a threshold during an intense fraud wave. The rationale had faded as staff moved on, and subsequent retraining inadvertently preserved the relaxed setting. Name the missing link—decision provenance. Explain its function. Without understanding why a choice was made, later teams cannot judge whether to preserve, revise, or reverse it. The implication is stark. Memory must include motivations, not just numbers.

A stronger example demonstrates success. The Montreal Neurological Institute's open science programme, launched in 2016, required researchers to log not only experimental results but methodological justifications, uncertainty estimates, and abandoned hypotheses. When new teams later sought to reproduce findings, these rational histories preserved the intellectual context, enabling continuity across turnover and facilitating cumulative learning. Behaviour such as logging abandoned pathways, rather than hiding them, became a measurable signal of epistemic humility. Memory deepened.

The next part of the thread concerns resilience at organisational scale: how institutions preserve memory across generational change. Show this through a vivid case. The Bank of England's Prudential Regulation Authority (PRA) maintains a confidential archive known internally as the "supervisory memory," a curated collection of historical supervisory failures, market anomalies, and near misses stretching back to the 1980s. New supervisors receive guided sessions where they interact with these cases, analysing how premature confidence, misread incentives, or ignored anomalies contributed to cascading failures. Name this practice—ritualised remembering. Explain its purpose. It ensures that as economic environments shift, institutional blind spots do not repeat unnoticed. Implication: formal rituals anchor memory; they prevent generational amnesia.

Contrast this with a limitation seen in fast-scaling technology firms. A 2021 review of a major platform company in California revealed that its trust and safety team had quadrupled in size within three years. Turnover exceeded 30%. Escalation rationales were scattered across Slack threads, ad hoc documents, and ephemeral dashboards. When a harmful recommendation loop recurred, no one could locate the original mitigation logic. Memory had dissolved into fragmented digital sediment. Reconciling this demands governance: decision logs must be systematically retained; harms registers must be consistently maintained; escalation rationales must be indexed. Memory becomes a function, not a pastime.

The thread now turns toward metrics, because memory without measurement drifts. Institutions must measure retention of learning, not merely record it. Show this with a concrete example. Since 2019, the Singapore Civil Defence Force has used a metric called "pattern regeneration delay"—the time between re-emergence of a known incident class and its detection by analysts. Name it clearly. Explain its force. If a pattern reappears before teams recognise it, institutional memory has weakened. The metric made intangible erosion visible. Implication: memory must be audited, not assumed.

A second example demonstrates how measurement supports memory transfer. The Dutch National Cyber Security Centre measures "handover completeness" during staff rotations: a checklist capturing rationale for configurations, historical anomalies, and contextual notes. Completeness is scored, tracked, and improved over time. The behaviour is simple—engineers commit to structured dialogue during transitions—but the effect is profound: fewer rediscovered mistakes, faster crisis mobilisation, and clearer accountability.

Yet measurement reveals a limitation. Some types of knowledge—particularly emotional knowledge from crisis experience—are resistant to codification. Fire chiefs in Queensland noted in 2020 that written debriefs captured facts well but not the "texture" of decisions under heat, fatigue, and fear. This cannot be solved by documents alone. Reconciling it requires hybrid rituals: scenario rehearsals where new staff inhabit the emotional architecture of past events, guided by those who lived them. Memory is more than information; it is affective inheritance.

This leads to the final claim: institutions must cultivate memory as identity, not archive. Memory shapes who an organisation becomes. Show this with a clear example. The Medicines and Healthcare products Regulatory Agency (MHRA) in the UK institutionalised "regulatory storytelling" in 2017—monthly sessions where teams narrate historical case studies of drug safety decisions, emphasising uncertainty and disagreement. These stories cross-pollinate teams and reinforce shared values. Name the practice again: storytelling as governance. Explain its function. Stories connect logic with ethos, bridging what happened with why it mattered. Implication: identity anchored in memory can withstand personnel churn.

The motif of the *thread* closes the subchapter by posing an unresolved tension. Memory demands investment: time to document, time to teach, time to debate, time to revisit. But operational pressure demands speed, novelty, and continual adaptation. The forward test is unmistakable: if your most experienced staff left tomorrow, what patterns would remain intact, which decisions would stand unexplained, and which hard-won lessons would scatter? The long bet on institutional memory begins with the answer—and whether the thread would hold.

About the Author

Idris Cavayne writes at the intersection of ethics, design, and complex systems. After years advising teams that deploy decision-support tools in hospitals, courts, and logistics, they focus on how values become real once translated into objectives, dashboards, and defaults. Their work is animated by a simple conviction: technology is never neutral, yet it need not be nihilistic. A thread running through their thinking is the old Mediterranean habit of civic debate in the square, where contested ideas meet public scrutiny. Cavayne's mission is to help organisations build moral capability, not just compliance checklists, by turning principles into clear specifications, stress tests, and routines that last.

www.ingramcontent.com/pod-product-compliance
Lightning Source LLC
Chambersburg PA
CBHW031342230926
51848CB00002B/344
* 9 7 8 9 3 7 4 5 9 2 3 9 7 *